The Special Education Handbook

Third Edition

The

Special Education Handbook

Third
Edition

Michael Farrell

with a foreword by

Maria Landy

David Fulton Publishers
London

David Fulton Publishers Ltd
The Chiswick Centre, 414 Chiswick High Road, London W4 5TF

www.fultonpublishers.co.uk

First published in Great Britain by David Fulton Publishers 1997
Second Edition 2000
Third Edition 2003

Note: The right of Michael Farrell to be identified as the author of this work has been asserted by him in accordance with the Copyright, Designs and Patents Act 1988.

British Library Cataloguing in Publication Data
A catalogue record for this book is available from the British Library.

ISBN 1-85346-974-2

Typeset by FiSH Books, London
Printed and bound in Scotland by Scotprint, Haddington

Contents

Acknowledgements

I am most grateful to the following people who read parts of the book and made valuable comments and suggestions:

Alan Dyson, Department of Education, University of Newcastle upon Tyne; Maria Evans, Head of Audit, Monitoring and Learning Support Services, Surrey Local Education Authority; Dr Ann Hackney, Westminster College, Oxford; Geof Sewell, Special Educational Needs Coordinator, Bishopsgarth School, Cleveland; Martin Sharpe, Special Educational Needs Policy Division, Department for Education and Skills (DfES); and Christopher Stevens, Subject Professional Officer for Special Educational Needs, School Curriculum and Assessment Authority.

Helpful advice on coverage of topics was kindly given by Professor Peter Mittler, then Dean and Director of the School of Education, University of Manchester; and Joan Boucher, President of the National Association of Special Educational Needs 1996–7.

The following people generously read the A–Z text and made helpful comments: Professor Mel Ainscow, Professor of Special Education, and his colleagues at the School of Education, University of Manchester; Pat Locke, Head teacher, Christchurch Church of England Infant School, New Malden; Maria Landy, Education Consultant and Past President of the National Association for Special Educational Needs 1995–6; Clive Webster, Principal Education Psychologist; and John Dewhurst, Education Inspector, London Borough of Hillingdon.

Cedric Dowe, Robert Green and Martin Sharpe of the Special Educational Needs Policy Division, DfES kindly read the section on legislation and made many invaluable comments. Arabella Wood, Library and Information Resource Centre, DfES, was most helpful in providing information and documents. The various drafts and final version were word processed with great efficiency by Sue Foster to whom I am indebted. My daughter Anne gave valuable help in contacting organisations and in indexing.

Second Edition

I am grateful to the following people for advice and information in connection with the second edition of the Handbook:

Heather Fry, Award Scheme Development and Accreditation Network; Caroline Geraghty, Marketing Coordinator, RSA Examining Board; Nicki Little, Midland Examining Group; C. J. Mitchell, Deputy Secretary General, The Associated Examining Board; Mel Pierce, City and Guilds of London Institute; and Brian Rogers, Welsh Joint Education Committee.

I also acknowledge the advice received from Mike Bubb, Architects and Building Branch, Department for Education and Skills.

Third Edition

I am grateful to the representatives of many of the organisations mentioned in the text for their help in updating details relating to their particular organisations.

While I am most grateful to the above-named colleagues who have assisted with this and previous editions, their assistance does not imply that their views are the same as those given in the text. The views expressed in this Handbook are my own; as, of course, are any of the book's shortcomings.

Michael Farrell
September 2002

Foreword

The *Special Education Handbook* will be very useful for a wide range of readers. There are few aspects of education as complicated as those associated with special educational needs (SEN), the legislation alone surrounding SEN being a quagmire. This book provides a helpful, practical guide for anyone wishing to understand more about the many complex and wide-ranging issues related to SEN. That is why it will be so valuable. It has a common-sense approach as its main aim, and it succeeds.

The book provides an A–Z guide to issues related to SEN with down-to-earth explanations and many useful references and contacts. Michael Farrell has also succeeded in clarifying and simplifying the most difficult area of legislation. The whole book is written in accessible language that is both informative and – best of all – simple.

Anything that saves time in our busy lives is worthwhile and this book will certainly be helpful in saving that precious commodity! As a source of reference I am sure that the *Special Education Handbook* will be consulted again and again. I warmly commend it and hope it will go from strength to strength.

Maria Landy
Past President of the National Association
for Special Educational Needs (NASEN)

About the Author

Dr Michael Farrell trained as a teacher and as a psychologist at the Institute of Psychiatry and has worked as a head teacher, a lecturer at the Institute of Education, London, and as a local authority education inspector for special education. He has managed national projects both for City University and for the Department for Education.

Michael Farrell presently works as a special education consultant in Britain and abroad. This has included policy development and training with local education authorities, work with voluntary organisations and universities, support to schools in the independent and maintained sectors and advice to the State Bureau of Foreign Experts, China, and the Ministry of Education, Seychelles. He has lectured widely in the United Kingdom and abroad.

The author of many articles on education and psychology, Michael Farrell has edited 30 educational books. Among his other publications are:

The Blackwell Handbook of Education (Blackwell 1996) with T. Kerry and C. Kerry
Key Issues for Primary Schools (Routledge 1999)
Key Issues for Secondary Schools (Routledge 2001)
Standards and Special Education (Continuum 2001)
Understanding Special Educational Needs: A Guide for Student Teachers (Routledge 2002)
Special Educational Needs: An Introduction (Paul Chapman/Sage 2003).

Preface

It is a great pleasure to write the preface to the third edition of the *Special Education Handbook*. The generous reviews that earlier editions received and the numerous kind letters sent to me by SEN coordinators, parents, school governors, inspectors, local counsellors, students and others indicate that the book is meeting a real need. A growing readership in other English-speaking parts of the world and the publication of the Japanese translation in 2001 are just two indicators of the keen interest the book has attracted abroad.

The first edition, which appeared in 1997, and was updated in 1998, was revised in 2000. This third edition has been extensively revised and updated to keep up with current developments, yet without becoming unwieldy. At the same time, the underlying structure of the book that so many readers reported they found helpful has been kept, and this is explained in the introduction and is reflected in the thematic index.

Suggestions

I have tried to cover areas and topics in this Handbook that potential readers would find most helpful. I would be pleased to hear from any readers with suggestions for amendments and additions so that future editions will continue to be as informative as possible. Please write to me care of the publishers.

Michael Farrell
September 2002

Introduction

Readers of this Handbook

This Handbook is intended to be helpful for:

- teachers and teaching assistants in mainstream and special schools and elsewhere;
- students and newly qualified teachers;
- senior managers and school governors;
- parents and carers;
- professionals in the social services and the health service;
- voluntary workers;
- anyone wishing to gain an overview of special education.

The Handbook concentrates on special education in the United Kingdom (particularly England) and has proved useful not only for those in the UK but also for those in other countries who wish to understand the UK situation better.

The underlying structure of the Handbook

Special education embraces a wide and complex area of knowledge and skills. Underpinning the approach and choice of entries in this Handbook are several broad areas or themes. These areas, and the layout of the *Special Education Handbook,* are similar to those in the *Blackwell Handbook of Education* (Farrell, Kerry and Kerry 1994). While the entries have an A–Z format there is an underlying structure that is reflected in the Classified List/Thematic Index. Many readers have said that a few minutes spent familiarising themselves with the classified index helps in negotiating the book effectively. There are six broad areas – some of which are subdivided – as follows:

1. Basic terms, ideas and values

    (a) special education issues/terms
    (b) disciplines associated with special education
    (c) age phases and special education.

2. Venues relating to special education and school organisation.

3. Roles, duties and responsibilities, procedures and rules

    (a) roles in, or relating to, schools and other areas
    (b) duties and responsibilities, procedures and rules.

4. Individual differences among learners with special educational needs.

5. Curriculum, assessment and resources

   (a) curriculum
   (b) assessment
   (c) resources.

6. Pedagogy

   (a) teaching and learning
   (b) therapy/treatment/support
   (c) teacher training in special education.

The rationale for the Handbook's underlying structure

The rationale for the structure underlying this Handbook is reflected in each broad heading:

1. Basic terms, ideas and values. Becoming familiar with the basic terms, ideas and values of special education, their significance and their interrelationships, is essential to understanding special education itself. Special education involves concepts associated with various disciplines – psychology and sociology, for example – and it is important to be aware of such concepts in understanding special education. The age phases of special education also have different implications.

2. Venues relating to special education, and school organisation. The range and variety of venues relating to special education provision is indicated along with aspects of school organisation, particularly important when seeking to meet special educational needs (SEN).

3. Roles, duties and responsibilities, procedures and rules. The implicit or explicit agreements between those working in special education underlie these entries. The variety of people contributing to effective provision is reflected. Procedures and rules are included because they can be confusing, particularly for those new to special education.

4. Individual differences among learners with special educational needs. If children with SEN are not to be seen as an amorphous mass, individual differences among them and the implications of these differences are important. However, to avoid making the Handbook too long, these entries cover the educational implications of broad topics such as 'emotional and behavioural difficulties' and 'hearing impairment', rather than extensive lists of particular conditions which can be found in many reference books, including medical dictionaries. Where particular conditions are included this is generally because of the frequency with which the condition occurs (e.g. epilepsy), or the particular attention which a condition has attracted in recent years (e.g. dyslexia).

5. Curriculum, assessment and resources. The curriculum offered to pupils with SEN should reflect the content and structure of that offered to all pupils as far as this is possible. Certain aspects of the curriculum play a particularly significant role for some pupils with SEN and these are focused upon. The

National Curriculum and other curriculum perspectives are outlined. Intimately related to the curriculum are kinds of assessment by which teachers and others try to determine attainment or progress. Entries on specific psychometric and other tests are not given, as the most recent information on such tests can be easily obtained from organisations marketing them. Resources include such topics as journals and other publications, as well as various items of equipment.

6. Pedagogy. Central to education is the way in which its content is learned by the pupil and taught by the teacher. In special education, approaches grouped broadly as therapies also make a major contribution. Teacher education clearly contributes to this area.

These entries, in A–Z order, form the main part of the Handbook. There are three appendices relating to special education in the United Kingdom and particularly England.

● Appendix 1: 'Legislation and Related Reports and Consultation Documents' selectively covers, in chronological order, reports and Education Acts from the 'Warnock Report' to the present day.
● Appendix 2: 'Regulations' outlines in chronological order regulations from 1981 to the present.
● Appendix 3: 'Guidance' sets out a selection of Circulars and Circular Letters as well as the Special Educational Needs Codes of Practice, chronologically from 1981 to the present.

A Classified List/Thematic Index of A–Z Entries guides the reader through the Handbook reflecting the six main areas outlined above.

Uses of the Handbook

The Handbook can be used for flexible but systematic reading, using the classified list of entries. Any systematic reading would most profitably begin with the entries grouped under 'Basic terms, ideas and values'. However, the order in which subsequent sections are consulted will be according to your own preferences and previous experience. Cross-referencing helps you to move across broad areas in the course of reading as desired. As well as using the Handbook for systematic reading, it can equally be used as a handy reference book. Further reading is suggested and relevant addresses are given, as appropriate, at the end of an entry.

A–Z Entries

Access

Enabling access for pupils with special educational needs usually refers to access to learning and the curriculum. For example, enabling access to a broad and balanced curriculum might, among other factors, involve a school in looking at the accessibility of each subject or curriculum area, reviewing teaching strategies and assessment procedures, reviewing working partnerships with parents and professionals and developing advocacy. In one sense, a reverse side to the coin of access is barriers to learning and participation. To the extent that barriers and hindrances refer to an interaction of personal and environmental factors suppressing performance, they may be reduced or removed.

(See also *Disability*)

Reference

Ashdown, B. and Bovair, K. (ed. Carpenter, B.) (2001) *Enabling Access: Effective Teaching and Learning for Pupils with Learning Difficulties.* London: David Fulton Publishers.

Accreditation of achievement

For students with special educational needs (SEN) taking General Certificate of Secondary Education (GCSE) examinations, special arrangements may be made.

General National Vocational Qualifications (GNVQs) are broad based vocational qualifications designed mainly for students aged 16 to 19. They are intended to provide young people with the knowledge, skills and attitudes valued by industry. Nationally recognised, they are accepted as a route to Vocational Certificates in Education (VCE), higher education or further training for employment. They give young people the opportunity for vocational study at various levels. GNVQs are available at two levels: foundation and intermediate. VCEs are an advanced level qualification. Parity is very broadly that:

- foundation level is equivalent to four GCSE examination passes at grades D to G;
- intermediate level is equivalent to four GCSEs at grades A to C;
- A VCE six unit award is equivalent to two Advanced level examination passes.

Foundation GNVQ is made up of six vocational units, three of which can come from different vocational areas. Intermediate GNVQ comprises six vocational units from one vocational area. An Advanced VCE is made up of six vocational units from one vocational area. An Advanced VCE award is made up of 12 vocational units from one vocational area and, in some subjects, an Advanced Subsidiary VCE is available comprising three units from one vocational area. Unit certification is also available.

National Vocational Qualifications (NVQs) are designed to recognise the learner's performance in the workplace and outside. Competency based, they give standards against which learners can be assessed primarily in the workplace. Learners are assessed on work skills and the knowledge that underpins those skills to achieve a qualification which is nationally recognised by employers and which provides evidence that the learner can carry out the job to a nationally set standard. NVQs are accredited by the Qualifications and Curriculum Authority (QCA) which provides quality assurance on NVQs but does not act as an awarding body. NVQs are awarded at five levels and each level is made up of a series of units. Each unit constitutes a precise specification of competence and can be individually assessed and certified. The five levels are as follows:

- Level 1 indicates competence in the performance of a wide range of workplace activities, most of which may be routine or predictable.
- Level 2 indicates competence in a significant range of varied workplace activities, performed with a variety of complexity and indicates a degree of individual autonomy. Collaboration with others may often be a requirement.
- Level 3 indicates competence in a broad range of varied workplace activities most of which are varied and non-routine. Considerable individual responsibility and autonomy is required and control and guidance of others is often expected.
- Level 4 indicates competence in a broad range of complex, technical or professional workplace activities. A substantial degree of personal responsibility and autonomy is required, and responsibility for others and the allocation of resources is often expected.
- Level 5 indicates the application of a significant range of fundamental principles and complex techniques across a wide variety of contexts. Substantial personal autonomy; and accountability for analysis and diagnostics, design planning, execution and evaluation is required. Significant responsibility for the work of others and for the allocation of substantial resources is often expected.

NVQs accredit competence against specified criteria. All of these criteria must be met by all candidates. However, candidates may use mechanical, electronic and other aids in order to demonstrate competence so long as these aids are generally commercially available and can be feasibly used on employers' premises.

Certain programmes are especially relevant to some learners with SEN. An example is ASDAN (Award Scheme Development and Accreditation Network) who have developed a number of programmes. The Transition Challenge (14–16 years) and Towards Independence (post-16) programmes provide an opportunity to develop and accredit personal, independent and learning skills. They are designed for students with severe, complex, profound and multiple learning difficulties. 'Workright' was designed in collaboration with Skill: National Bureau for Students with Disabilities. Written in units, elements and criteria relevant to work skills, the award is appropriate also for learners working towards Level 1 (GNVQ) with particular reference to Key Skills. The Bronze award promotes the development of interpersonal skills and is particularly suited to those with moderate learning difficulties. In addition to these awards, ASDAN is approved by the Qualifications and Curriculum Authority, the Awdurdod Cymwysterau Cwricwlwm ac Asesu Cymru (the curriculum and assessment authority for Wales) and the Northern Ireland Council for the Curriculum, Examination and Assessment. Specifically, ASDAN is approved to accredit life skills at entry levels 1 to 3, Key Skills at levels 1 to 4, and career planning at levels 1 and 2.

The National Skills Profile, offered by OCR, is an accreditation framework intended to meet the needs of learners working at Entry Level, those with learning difficulties and those for whom existing qualifications frameworks are inappropriate. The award, designed to provide positive recognition of achievement, is suitable for young people as well as adults. The scheme consists of six essential skill areas and 13 vocational areas. The essential skills areas are: Communication Skills; Number Skills; Information and Technology Skills; Practical Work Skills; and Learning Skills. These essential skill areas are available at three grades (broadly in line with the three levels of Entry Level). They have been designed to underpin, and to aid progression to, the QCA Key Skills. Each essential skill area consists of 15 modules – five modules at each of the three grades. The 13 vocational areas are: Care, Catering, Farm Animal Care, Floristry, Hairdressing, Horticulture, Leisure and Tourism, Manufacturing, Media, Motor Vehicles, Office Practice, Performing Arts, and Retail. These areas are available only at third grade and have been designed to underpin, and aid progression to, NVQs and GNVQs at Foundation Level/ Level 1. Each vocational skill area consists of five modules. National Skills Profile has been designed to be flexible. Candidates may mix and match modules in any combination that is appropriate for their individual needs.

The Welsh Joint Education Committee (WJEC) offers Entry Level Certificates to enable students to access national qualifications at Entry Level. Its target group includes students who have not reached level 3 of the National Curriculum by the end of Key Stage 3. These Entry Level Certificates are offered in 30 subject areas including English, mathematics, science and business studies. The courses, initially intended for Years 10 and 11 are based on six teaching terms. Each course is assessed through a combination of school-based continuous assessment and externally marked or moderated end of course examinations. WJEC has also devised a series of life skills and work skills awards to underpin Key Skills, personal and social education, and work experience at Entry Level. These awards have a unit structure allowing a flexible approach. Also available is a series of vocational awards in ten occupational areas to underpin NVQ Level 1.

Accreditation may relate to a course based on an externally prescribed syllabus, assessed by formal tests either at the end of the course unit and/or in succession at the end of modules or sub-units. Alternatively, accreditation may be carried out by an outside agency after a scheme of work or unit has been designed within a school (or group of schools) written according to the agency's specifications, validated by the agency and moderated externally.

Further reading

Joint Council of National Awarding Bodies (annually) *Assessment in General National Vocational Qualifications: Provision for Candidates with Special Assessment Needs.* London: JCNAB.

Addresses

ASDAN Central Office
Wainbrook House
Hudds Vale Road
St George
Bristol BS5 7HY

Tel: 01179 411126
Fax: 01179 351112
e-mail: info@asdan.co.uk
www.asdan.co.uk

ASDAN has devised and operates a range of awards relating to personal and social development. The ASDAN award schemes aim to offer activity based curricula for those of all abilities from 14 to 25+ together with a framework for assessment which facilitates the development, demonstration and accreditation of key skills within a variety of contexts.

OCR
Cambridge Office
1 Hills Road
Cambridge CB1 2EU

Tel: 01223 553998
Fax: 01223 552627
e-mail: helpdesk@ocr.org.uk
www.ocr.org.uk

OCR
Coventry Office
Westwood Way
Coventry CV4 8HS

Tel: 024 7647 0033
Fax: 024 7646 8080

OCR offers a range of Entry Level Certificate courses (formerly Certificate of Achievement courses) which aim to offer positive learning experiences for low achievers. The courses cover English, mathematics, information and communications technology, science, design technology, physical education, modern foreign languages, religious education, geography, art and design, child development, citizenship studies and history. It also offers Entry Level Certificate in a range of vocational areas. OCR provides vocational qualifications, offering over 500 qualifications including a wide range of NVQs through over 8,000 recognised centres.

Welsh Joint Education Committee
245 Western Avenue
Cardiff CF5 2YX

Tel: 029 2026 5000
Fax: 029 2057 5994
e-mail: info@wjec.co.uk
ww.wjec.co.uk

The WJEC offers accreditation to students with a wide range of learning difficulties. The Certificate of Education (CoE), which has been run successfully for 15 years, has now been adapted to ensure its readiness as an Entry Level qualification. In its new form the Certificate of Educational Achievement (CoEA) is offering 30 different syllabuses. In addition to the CoEA, the WJEC have developed a further initiative – the First Skills Awards (Diploma/Certificate), designed to underpin Key Skills provision at Entry Level (14–19+), with a strong vocational bias.

Achievement

The report of a survey (Ofsted 1996) of primary and secondary schools in 33 local educational authorities indicated the following:

Standards achieved by pupils with special educational needs (SEN) are satisfactory. Standards tend to be higher in the nursery stage and at Key Stages 1 and 2 than at Key Stages 3 and 4. The quality of the joint planning of work between the class teacher and the support teacher/assistant most strongly influences the effectiveness of in-class support. Insufficient support by senior management for SEN coordinators in secondary schools and insufficient time for primary SENCOs affected the provision made across the school. Many schools are unable to identify the exact level of resourcing available for SEN and are therefore unable to monitor the use of resources accurately. Insufficient attention is being paid to the development of teachers' skills. Less than half the LEAs surveyed gave suitable support for their learning support and advisory staff. Between schools and within LEAs there is a wide variation in the number of pupils identified as having SEN, caused by differences in identification procedures. However, since the introduction of the Code of Practice, schools have become more consistent in identifying children with SEN. Most LEAs have policies and guidance on SEN in place and provide appropriate information. Many are carrying out reviews in the light of the Code of Practice.

Reference

Ofsted (1996) *Promoting High Achievement for Pupils with Special Educational Needs in Mainstream Schools.* London: HMSO.

Address

Office for Standards in Education (OFSTED) Tel: 020 7421 6800
Alexandra House Fax: 020 7421 6707
33 Kingsway e-mail: geninfo@ofsted.gov.uk
London WC2B 6SE www.ofsted.gov.uk

Ofsted Publications Centre Tel: 020 7510 0180

Acronyms

Acronyms are now so numerous that it is often helpful to specify the full version before the acronym is used. Some of the most commonly use acronyms in special education are listed below.

ADD	Attention Deficit Disorder
ADHD	Attention Deficit Hyperactivity Disorder
AEP	Association of Educational Psychologists
AFASIC	Association for all Speech Impaired Children
ASDAN	Award Scheme Development and Accreditation Network
BAAT	British Association of Art Therapists
BAC	British Association of Counselling
BATOD	British Association of Teachers of the Deaf
BDA	British Dyslexia Association
BECTa	British Educational Technology and Communications agency
BPS	British Psychological Society
BSL	British Sign Language
CAIT	Citizen Advocacy Information and Training
CAL	Computer assisted learning
CB	Challenging behaviour

CBA	Curriculum-based assessment
CSIE	Centre for Studies on Inclusive Education
CSW	Certificate in Social Work
CTLD	Community Team for People with Learning Difficulties
DfES	Department for Education and Skills
DRA	Differential reinforcement of alternative behaviour
DRI	Differential reinforcement of incompatible behaviour
EBD	Emotional and behavioural difficulties
EP	Educational Psychologist
ESW	Educational Social Worker
EWO	Educational Welfare Officer
FE	Further education
HA	Health Agency
HAS	Health Advisory Service
HE	Higher education
HI	Hearing impairment
ICT	Information and communications technology
IE	Instrumental enrichment
IEP	Individual Education Plan
INSET	In-service education and training
IQ	Intelligence quotient
JCPD	Joint Council for Pupils with Disabilities
LEA	Local Education Authority
LSC	Learning and Skills Council
LST	Learning Support Team
MLD	Moderate Learning Difficulties
MLE	Mediated Learning Experiences
MOVE	Movement Opportunities in Education
NASEN	National Association for Special Educational Needs
NC	National Curriculum
NFER	National Foundation for Educational Research
NRA	National Record of Achievement
PH	Partially hearing
PMLD	Profound and Multiple Learning Difficulties
PRU	Pupil Referral Unit
PS	Partially sighted
PTR	Pupil–teacher ratio
QCA	Qualifications and Curriculum Authority
RADAR	Royal Association for Disability and Rehabilitation
RNIB	Royal National Institute for the Blind
SEE	Signed (Exact) English

SEMERC	Special Education Microelectronic Resource Centres
SEN	Special educational needs
SENCO	Special educational needs coordinator
SENNAC	Special Educational Needs National Advisory Council
SI	Sensory Impairment
SIB	Self-injurious behaviour
SLD	Severe Learning Difficulties
SpLD	Specific Learning Difficulties
SSD	Social Services Department
SSE	Signs Supporting English
TA	Teaching assistant
TEACCH	Treatment and education of autistic and related communication handicapped children
VI	Visually impaired

Adaptive behaviour

Adaptive behaviour refers to skills in social and personal competence. These include motor skills (fine and gross); social interaction and communication; personal living skills (such as eating, toileting, dressing, personal self-care) and community living skills (for example money, time, orientation). The limitations of using tests of intelligence as the main criteria from which to make decisions about suitable provision and other decisions about a person with special educational needs has been recognsised. At the same time, interest in adaptive bahaviour, particularly in relation to people with learning difficulties has increased. One way of assessing adaptive behaviour is through norm-referenced assessment scales. An example is the Scales of Independent Behaviour (Bruininks *et al.* 1996) which assesses adaptive behaviour and 'malaptive behaviour'.

Reference

Bruininks, R. B., Woodcock, R. W., Weatherman, R. F. and Hill, B. K. (1996) *Scales of Independent Behaviour – Revised (SIB-R)*. Windsor: NFER-Nelson.

Addresses

(Test suppliers)

NFER-Nelson
The Chiswick Centre
414 Chiswick High Road
London W4 5TF

Tel: 020 8996 8444
Fax: 020 8996 5358
e-mail: edu&hsc@nfer-nelson.co.uk
www.nfer-nelson.co.uk

The Psychological Corporation
Foots Cray High Street
Sidcup
Kent DA14 5HP

Tel: 020 8308 5750
Fax: 020 8308 5702
e-mail: tpc@harcourt.com
www.hbtpc.com

Adaptive equipment

Adaptive equipment helps those having physical disabilities with normal positioning and movement. Examples are tricycles with trunk support and a low centre of gravity. A walking trainer supports the weight of a person and helps maintain the appropriate posture and balance to enable him to be taught to take reciprocal steps. Trays attached to walking trainers can enable communication while mobility is allowed. Equipment may combine a lifting action for transfer of positions and walking support allowing the person's weight to be borne by the trunk and forearms. Standing support equipment including mobile versions allows those who cannot bear their full weight to be held upright through supporting straps. Special chairs allow a functional sitting position suitable for toilet use, eating and writing. Chair frames allow activities such as self-feeding while other adjustable chairs with tables and trays allow a range of activities.

Padded 'supine' boards can be positioned at any angle from horizontal to vertical and give adjustable weight bearing and support for the head, trunk, pelvis, knees and feet.

Other specialised chairs include bath, shower and toileting chairs (giving head and trunk support while using the toilet). Where people require specialised communication aids, advances in technology are providing new opportunities.

(See also *Information and Communications Technology*)

Address

Disability Equipment Register   Tel: 01454 318818
4 Chatterton Road   Fax: 01454 883870
Yate   e-mail: disabreg@dial.pipex.com
Bristol BS17 4BJ   www.dspace.dial.pipex.com/disabreg/

Recycles equipment for those with disabilities.

Advisory teacher

An advisory teacher provides advice and support to schools and is usually employed by a local educational authority. If a particular school does not require a full-time teacher to teach pupils with special educational needs, an advisory teacher may teach these pupils for an agreed number of sessions.

(See also *Support services (LEA)*)

Advocacy

Advocacy aims to secure rights and facilities for a person with disabilities and others appropriate to her or his needs. A nominated person speaks and acts on behalf of the represented person who is unable to plead effectively for themselves. The advocate may be a professional or a volunteer who is independent of existing or potential service providers and can represent the disabled person's case.

Self-advocacy involves local self-help groups of people with disabilities to advocate their rights.

Lay (citizen) advocacy provides one-to-one assistance by advocates who have been selected, trained, coordinated and supported. Lay advocates usually work on a voluntary basis. Such advocacy may be: expressive (expressing the person's concerns and preferences) or instrumental (ensuring that appropriate services are provided). It may involve giving emotional and practical support.

Legal advocacy is provided by lawyers and other appropriately trained people. It aims, among other things, to help clients exercise their rights or defend them. It may require casework, careful checking of legislation and regulations and representing a client in front of an administrative tribunal or a court.

Related to self-advocacy for pupils with SEN are efforts by teachers to encourage self-awareness and self-assessment in pupils. Examples include pupils making choices, reflecting on their own performance, reflecting on the performance of their peers and buiding up Records of Achievement.

Such approaches come within the framework of the National Curriculum. For example in design and technology Key Stage 1, pupils should be taught to 'talk about their ideas, saying what they like and dislike' (3a) and 'identify what they could have done differently or how they could improve their work in the future' (3b). Also the *Special Educational Needs Code of Practice* (DfES 2001) emphasises involving the child in decision making (e.g. 3.18–3.20).

Reference
Department for Education and Skills (2001) *Special Educational Needs Code of Practice*. London: DfES.

Further reading
Gardner, P. and Sandow, S. (eds) (1995) *Advocacy, Self Advocacy and Special Needs*. London: David Fulton Publishers.

Address
Citizen Advocacy Information and Training
162 Lee Valley Technopark
Ashley Road
London N17 9LN

Tel: 020 8880 4545
Fax: 020 8880 4546
e-mail: cait@teleregion.co.uk
www.citizenadvocacy.org.uk

Citizen advocates are unpaid, competent volunteers who, with the support of a citizen advocacy office, work on behalf of those who by virtue of their disability are not in a good position to exercise or defend their rights as citizens. Citizen advocates are independent of services and work on a one-to-one basis, building a relationship with their advocacy partner. Citizen Advocacy Information and Training provides information to individuals and organisations, and maintains a national database of local citizen advocacy schemes.

Age

Among the age considerations associated with special educational needs (SEN) are the following:

- the earlier the age of intervention (e.g. educational help, Portage work) for children with severe learning difficulties or severe disabilities, the better tends to be the child's progress. Early intervention does not guarantee later progress but it can give maximum opportunity for a child to make good progress;
- the physical and psychological changes associated with adolescence can pose difficulties for young people with SEN, as it can for all young people. For some young people with severe learning difficulties for example, frustrations can arise when independence is difficult to achieve. For those experiencing emotional

and behavioural difficulties, the physical, sexual, emotional and social changes of adolescence can exacerbate their difficulties. For anyone experiencing coordination difficulties, the growth spurt of adolescence and the temporary clumsiness which accompanies it can make coordination more difficult.

Age also raises issues of age-appropriateness, which is particularly relevant to the provision and resources made available for people with learning difficulties. Although a person's level of literacy or language attainment, for example, may be low compared with others of the same chronological age, this does not make it appropriate to use, with adults, resources designed for children. On the contrary, it is important to use materials suited to the chronological age of the learner, adapted to their attainment level. This relates to suitable teaching strategies.

National Curriculum levels and key stages for assessment were originally seen as age related. A more flexible view is now taken which enables pupils with SEN to be provided for more easily within the framework of the National Curriculum.

Further reading

Croll, P. and Moses, D. (2000) *Special Needs in the Primary School: One in Five?* London: Continuum.

Drifte, C. (2001) *Special Needs in Early Years Settings: A Guide for Practitioners.* London: David Fulton Publishers.

Aids to hearing

a)   Conventional hearing aids
A hearing aid has three main components:

- a microphone to receive sound
- an amplifier
- a receiver to transmit signals from the amplifier to the ear.

It is usually self-contained and worn either on the body or behind the ear and is powered by battery. **Hearing impairment** often affects certain frequencies more than others and the hearing aid does not compensate for this but simply amplifies sound from all frequencies. Hearing aids work best within two metres of the speaker.

b)   Cochlea implants
This involves using surgery to place an electronic device into the inner ear to increase sound perception. People who have become deaf as adults after previously having developed speech and language normally as children appear to have benefited from this technique. The use of the method with prelingually deaf children is much more controversial and some researchers have concluded that there is no evidence among children who have experienced implants of significantly improved speech or educational attainment (Cullington 2002).

c)   Radio aids
These comprise a microphone and transmitter worn by the speaker and a radio receiver worn by the listener. The speaker's words are picked up by the microphone, converted into a radio signal and broadcast to the receiver which is tuned at the appropriate frequency. A clear signal is picked up over a range of one

hundred metres irrespective of any background noise. This system has assisted the inclusion of children with severe hearing impairment into ordinary schools.

d) Induction loop system

This system may be used in schools to enable teachers and children with hearing impairments to communicate. The teacher wears a microphone which emits signals which are amplified and pass round a wire loop which goes around the classroom. Among the limitations of the system are that:

- it does not enhance communication between pupils
- the system may be picked up in other rooms
- there may be silent spots in the classroom.

Reference
Cullington, H. E. (ed.) (2002) *Cochlear Implants: Objective Measures*. London: Whurr.

Further reading
Tate-Maltby, M. (2002) (2nd edn) *Principles of Hearing Aid Audiology*. London: Whurr.

Address
Breakthrough Trust (Deaf-Hearing Integration)
Alan Geale House
The Close   Tel: 0121 472 6447
West Hill Campus   Fax: 0121 415 2323
Selly Oak   e-mail: midlands.manager@breakthrough-dhi.org.uk
Birmingham B29 6LN   www.breakthough-dhi.org.uk

Provides advice, aids and services for those with hearing loss, seeking to integrate deaf and hearing people.

Annual report and school prospectus

Governors' annual reports and school prospectuses for primary and secondary schools must include certain information concerning special educational needs (SEN) (Department for Education and Skills 2000a, 2000b). Assuming the annual report and the prospectus are published separately, both must include:

- a summary of the governing body's policy on children with SEN;
- any significant changes to that policy since the previous governors' annual report; and
- a statement on the success in implementing the governing body's SEN policy in the previous year.

The annual report only must include:

- a description of the admission arrangements for pupils with disabilities;
- details of steps taken to prevent pupils with disabilities from being treated less favourably than other pupils;
- details of existing facilities provided to assist access to the school by pupils with disabilities;
- the accessibility plan detailing the school's future policies for increasing disability access to the school.

References

Department for Education and Skills (2000a) *Governors' Annual Reports and School Prospectuses in Primary Schools*. London: DfES.

Department for Education and Skills (2000b) *Governors' Annual Reports and School Prospectuses in Secondary Schools*. London: DfES.

Address

Parents and Performance Division
Department for Education and Skills
Sanctuary Buildings
Great Smith Street
London SW1P 3BT

Tel: 020 7925 6124
Fax: 020 7925 5197
e-mail: dfes@prolog.uk.com
www.dfcs.gov.uk

Annual review

A review of a statement of special educational needs. The local education authority carries out such a review within 12 months of making a statement or within 12 months of any previous review (Department for Education and Skills 2001, ch. 9). The term annual review can therefore be misleading as it refers to the maximum period between reviews which may not always be the optimum period for a particular child.

Reference

Department for Education and Skills (2001) *Special Educational Needs Code of Practice*. London: DfES.

Anxiety

An acute anxiety state is a sudden response to a frightening/worrying situation, while a chronic anxiety state is an extended reaction to stress. Anxiety experienced by a person with learning difficulties may be exacerbated if the feelings or concerns related to the anxiety cannot be communicated effectively. Anxiety can also lead to learning difficulties because it is associated with such factors as poor concentration. In extreme cases it may be appropriate to treat anxiety through behaviour therapy or psychotherapy.

(See also *School phobia*)

Art therapist

Art therapists may be qualified and registered members of the British Association of Art Therapists (BAAT). Most have a knowledge of psychodynamic theory and practice enabling them to work with conscious and unconscious material which is associated with the art work produced within the therapeutic relationship.

Professional credibility was enhanced in 1982 when the Diploma in Art Therapy was recognised by the Department of Health as the qualifying course for working as an art therapist in the National Health Service. Four courses of training are approved and accredited by BAAT, the Department of Health and the National Joint Council (for local authority recognition).

Art therapists may be employed by the National Health Service, by schools or centres of adult education, by social services departments and others. Some principles of art therapy can be used by teachers in the classroom, for example where art is used as a means of communicating feelings such as grief or anger.

Address

The British Association of Art Therapists	Tel: 020 7383 3774
Mary Ward House	Fax: 020 7387 5513
5 Tavistock Place	e-mail: baat@ukgateway.net
London WC1H 9SN	www.baat.co.uk

The BAAT provides information to members and to the public on all aspects of art therapy. The Association publishes a journal, *Inscape*, and oversees standards of training and professional practice.

Art therapy

Art therapy is provided in a safe environment in a hospital, school, centre etc. It may involve the use of a variety of materials such as paint or clay. Clients use the materials to try to communicate feelings and thoughts in the presence of the therapist. Clients may be children or adults (including the very old). They may be mentally ill or have learning difficulties. Art therapy is also used with autistic children and adults and with those with communication difficulties. The therapy involves the therapist encouraging the client or clients to respond to what is being created. Suppressed feelings may be brought out and acknowledged.

Further reading

Case, C. and Dalley, T. (1997) *The Handbook of Art Therapy*. London: Routledge.

Asperger syndrome

While Asperger syndrome is regarded by some as a condition separate from autism, it is helpful to see it as part of a continuum of autism where the person has higher ability. Although the child with Asperger syndrome acquires speech that is complex and grammatical, it is not used for communicating in the normal way. Appropriate eye contact is not made. Speech tends to be used oddly and the topics of conversation tend to be fixed to the speaker's interest rather than taking account of the interest of the listener. The tone may be monotonous.

Because the features of the condition are less obvious than those of Kanner syndrome features of autism, Asperger syndrome may not be assessed early. Among the educational implications are the importance of understanding the condition and being challenging but realistic about what can be expected of a learner at different ages.

Further reading

Jones, G. (2002) *Educational Provision for Children with Autism and Asperger Syndrome*. London: David Fulton Publishers.

Address

The National Autistic Society	Tel: 020 7833 2299
393 City Road	Fax: 020 7833 9666
London EC1V 1NG	e-mail: nas@nasorg.uk
	www.oneworld.org/autism-uk/

Assessment (formative)

Much public attention has been directed at summative assessment, for example the need to achieve good results in statutory national tests. For all pupils, and particularly for those with special educational needs, the importance of formative assessment should be remembered. One example of a vehicle for formative assessment is the careful questioning of a pupil by the teacher to establish where learning has broken down. Another is the use of self-assessment worksheets giving learning objectives for classroom work against each of which a pupil records his or her view on whether the objective was reached.

Essentially, formative assessment requires teachers to maintain an ongoing knowledge of the state of their pupils' understanding and to use this information to help ensure learning. Formative assessment informs teaching and calls for action.

Further reading
Farrell, M. (2001) 'Assessment and its uses', in *Key Issues for Secondary Schools*. London: Routledge.

Assessment of special educational needs

For pupils with special educational needs (SEN), assessment is an important means of helping to ensure that their needs are met. Two important aspects of assessment are:

1. the assessment and recording processes by which a school monitors the progress of all pupils
2. the ways in which schools and other services assess the wide continuum of SEN, including statutory assessments and statements.

The two aspects are interrelated so that assessment procedures for SEN should emerge from and be a continuation of more general assessment procedures for all. A key document regarding assessment is the *Special Educational Needs Code of Practice* (Department for Education and Skills 2001). The Code states among its fundamental principles that: 'the special educational needs of children will normally be met in mainstream schools or settings' (1.5). It also stresses the importance of involving parents in assessment. The Code proposes a 'graduated response' to assessment and provision (4.9, 5.20, 6.22).

Reference
Department for Education and Skills (2001) *Special Educational Needs Code of Practice*. London: DfES.

Attention Deficit Hyperactivity Disorder (ADHD)

This term has emerged from attempts to clarify and define behaviours previously usually known as hyperactivity. If lack of attention is more evident than over activity then the term attention deficit disorder (ADD) is used. However, in instances where both lack of attention and over activity are evident, then ADHD is prefered. Both terms are diagnostic categories used by the American Psychiatric Association. Among factors apparently associated with ADHD and ADD are neurological damage, diet and poor socialisation.

Treatments have included modifications to the diet, **medication**, **behaviour therapy** and biofeedback. Among dietary treatments is the Feingold diet. The rationale for the diet is that

a)   some research has linked food additives to allergies; and

b)   hyperactivity may be a symptom of an allergic reaction.

The diet eliminates salicylates found in certain fresh fruit and vegetables, food flavourings, colourings and some preservatives. It appears to benefit a small proportion of children who are 'hyperactive'.

The use of medication has been controversial but has some strongly vocal advocates. Behaviour therapy can be successful and draws on the view that faulty learning in socialisation is a factor in ADHD and the inappropriate behaviour can be unlearned.

Biofeedback involves a person monitoring their own psychological processes. An instrument is used which responds to the relevant processes and emits a signal such as a sound tone. This in turn helps the person to respond to the physiological charges and control them. In the case of hyperactivity, muscle tension is monitored. The signal is activated when muscle tension is too high and this enables the child to control the tension and relax.

The implications for learning of ADHD and ADD are clear:

• the behaviour of children is inappropriate in itself
• it hinders learning and can lead to learning difficulties
• it can hinder the learning of others in a class group.

In schools, the teacher needs to draw on multidisciplinary help, for example, a doctor needs to be involved to look into possible physical causes of the behaviour. Parental involvement is important to try to ensure consistency in handling the child at school and at home. Behaviour therapy can be used at school and at home and psychological advice and support would enhance this. Particularly important for the inclusion of pupils with ADHD in the mainstream classroom are teacher attitudes, appropriate information and suitable in-service training with practical relevance.

Further reading
Cooper, P. and Bilton, K. (2002) (2nd edn) *Attention Deficit/Hyperactivity Disorder: A Practical Guide for Teachers*. London: David Fulton Publishers.

Address
ADD Information Services   Tel: 020 8905 2013
PO Box 340   Fax: 020 8386 6466
Edgware   e-mail: addiss@compuserve.com
Middlesex HA8 9HL   www.addiss.co.uk

Provides information and support to parents, teachers and others, and information on books, videos and support groups.

Audiologist

An audiologist is qualified in the study and evaluation of hearing and hearing impairment. Usually based in a hospital, the audiologist performs audiometric examinations. (S)he gives information for diagnosing **hearing impairment** and prescribing and monitoring hearing aids. An audiologist can help the teacher develop proper classroom procedures for children with hearing loss.

Further reading
Tate-Maltby, M. and Knight, P. (2000) *Audiology: An Introduction for Teachers and Other Professionals.* London: David Fulton Publishers.

Address
British Society of Audiology
80 Brighton Road
Reading RG6 1PS

Tel: 0118 966 0622
Fax: 0118 935 1915
e-mail: bsa@b-s-a.demon.co.uk
www.b-s-a.demon.co.uk

Audiology

An important aspect of audiology is audiometry, the measurement of hearing. This is achieved through the use of various instruments and procedures which include the following:

- a pure tone audiometer produces sounds of a known pitch and loudness to establish hearing thresholds. It prints the information graphically as an audiogram;
- a speech audiometer measures hearing for speech;
- in impedance audiometry, the audiologist measures the amount of sound reflected by the ear drum when a sound wave stimulates it. This yields information about the effectiveness of the middle ear and possible conductive hearing loss;
- in brainstem electric response audiometry or electric response audiometry, minute voltages produced in the nerves of the hearing system are measured as they respond to sound.

Further reading
Newton, V. (ed.) (2002) *Paediatric Audiological Medicine.* London: Whurr.

Autism

Autism was first identified as a separate condition in the 1940s by Leo Kanner, an American child psychiatrist. In earlier literature and sometimes still today, it is called Kanner syndrome or childhood schizophrenia.

Criteria for diagnosing autism are generally agreed to relate to: impairment of all modes of communication (language and body language) and their timing; impairment of social relationships; evidence of rigidity and inflexibility of thought processes; and onset before 30 months.

A central difficulty for autistic people appears to be their inability to make sense of the mind's own activities, thoughts, beliefs and feelings as indicated in the behaviour of others. Autistic people appear to lack a 'theory of mind'.

Early notions that autism had a psychological cause such as trauma have lost support and there is now a wide consensus that the cause of this lifelong condition is organic brain damage. Three times as many boys as girls are affected. While classic autism affects 4 to 5 children per 10,000, three times as many children again have autism-like difficulties. The concept of 'autistic spectrum disorder' has further widened the scope for identifying more children.

Some 75–80 per cent of autistic children experience severe or moderate learning difficulties. About a third of autistic people have epileptic fits at some time. Some autistic people have a talent in an area not requiring certain elements of social understanding (such as art or mathematics). Such instances are seized upon by the media giving many members of the public the impression that most autistic people have such abilities, an impression which is far from the truth. About 5–10 per cent of autistic children become independent as adults and 25–30 per cent will need continuing support. The remainder require lifelong help.

Effective education for the autistic person is likely to involve the following:

- bringing obsessional and inappropriate behaviours under control;
- structured work on communication and social skills;
- working particularly closely with parents/carers to ensure a consistent approach;
- a recognition that the literalness of an autistic person's understanding means that one cannot assume that skills learned in one context will be generalised to other similar contexts. This implies careful training (e.g. at work) in all aspects of what is required.

Asperger syndrome is regarded by some as a distinctive condition. Others view it as the higher-ability aspect of the continuum of autism.

Specific approaches with autistic people include the TEACCH Programme (**T**reatment and **E**ducation of **A**utistic and related **C**ommunication handicapped **CH**ildren) (e.g. Mesibov and Howley 2002). This is an approach oriented towards classroom-based skills but also involves collaboration with the home. It seeks to improve adaptation by both improving the skills of the learner through education and by modifying the environment to compensate for difficulties. Individual education programmes are based on assessment and identify emerging skills which then become the focus of work. Behavioural and cognitive perspectives inform the approach. Structured teaching is used.

Reference

Mesibov, G. and Howley, M. (2002) *Accessing the Curriculum for Pupils with Autistic Spectrum Disorders: Using the TEACCH Programme to Help Inclusion*. London: David Fulton Publishers.

Further reading

Powell, S. (2000) *Helping Children with Autism to Learn*. London: David Fulton Publishers.

Addresses

The National Autistic Society
393 City Road
London EC1V 1NG

Tel: 020 7833 2299
Fax: 020 7833 9666
e-mail: nas@nasorg.uk
www.oneworld.org/autism-uk/

The society includes parents of autistic children and professionally interested members. It runs schools and centres and produces literature on autism and on the education and care of autistic people. It organises conferences, day courses, seminars, workshops and study weekends. The NAS encourages research into the causes of autism, offers information and advice and publishes a journal.

Scottish Society for Autistic Children

Hilton House   Tel: 01259 720044
Alloa Business Park   Fax: 01259 720051
Whins Road   e-mail: autism@autism-in-scotland.org.uk
Alloa FK10 3SA   www.autism-in-scotland.org.uk

The SSAC exists to provide the best possible care, support and education for people of all ages with autism throughout Scotland.

Baseline assessment

Baseline assessment represents a starting point from which a pupil's current achievement can be determined and future progress can be judged. It also informs curriculum planning and educational provision. Baseline assessment needs to be meaningful to all children including those who may have special educational needs (SEN). In providing formative and diagnostic information, approaches to baseline assessment should identify early each child's learning needs, including SEN. It has the potential to contribute to **value added** measures. Statutory baseline assessment was replaced, in September 2002, by a different statutory assessment for the foundation stage, the 'foundation stage profile'.

Behaviour modification

In a behavioural model of intervention, measuring children's behaviour (e.g. challenging behaviour) is necessary before devising a suitable intervention programme. Behaviour needs to be clearly defined. For example, out-of-seat behaviour could be defined as 'the child's bottom ceases contact with the chair for five seconds or more'. The next step is to select an appropriate method of recording. This will depend on the rate of occurrence of the behaviour, duration and discreteness (whether it has a clear beginning and end).

One approach is to make a frequency count. This can be used most easily when the behaviour is fairly discrete and occurs at a medium rate. It involves observing the child and noting each time the behaviour occurs.

Another method of measuring the same behaviour is to look at its duration. Duration is also most useful when the behaviour is fairly discrete and not too frequent. By using a stopwatch one can time each occurrence. By measuring the duration of the behaviour it is possible to compare samples of unequal time length by calculating the percentage of time spent engaged in the behaviour. Instantaneous time sampling gives a less precise measure of behaviour. However, it is useful if the behaviour is very frequent or not discrete. Here a time interval of, for example, ten seconds is decided upon. At the end of each time interval the child is observed and a note is made of whether the behaviour is occurring or not. This involves observing every tenth second. This method allows the teacher to calculate the number of times a person is engaged in the behaviour as a percentage of the total number of intervals observed.

Event sampling is for behaviours that occur relatively infrequently. It allows the observer to focus on the behaviour's antecedents and consequences. It is also important to note the environment at the time of each occurrence of behaviour.

The teacher needs to consider what factors are influencing the behaviour. Insights may be gained by sampling behaviour in different settings and analysing the differences between settings. This leads to hypothesis testing. For example, if a teacher believes that a child is shrieking to escape doing a task then (s)he would expect that in a free play situation with a choice of preferred activities, the behaviour would decrease.

Behaviour modification has been effective with various learners including children with severe learning difficulties or those experiencing compulsive or obsessional behaviour. It aims to extinguish undesirable behaviour and/or to teach appropriate behaviour. A programme involves observing and defining the difficulty in behavioural terms; devising hypotheses to explain the observations, testing the hypotheses and evaluating the results. Behaviour analysis is important and includes observing defined behaviour in a defined environment. A careful record is kept and the information forms the baseline data, the foundation of a programme and its subsequent monitoring. Behaviour analysis focuses on: antecedents of the behaviour; behaviour (frequency and duration); and consequences of the behaviour. This is sometimes summarised as ABC analysis (antecedents–behaviour–consequences). Voluntary responses to antecedents ('operants') are instrumental in attaining goals. Events which are consequences of operants have a controlling effect on them in a process of operant conditioning. Behaviours are changed by changing their consequences. For example, a child may make noises in class (behaviour) which are followed by teacher attention which the child finds rewarding (consequence). The behaviour (noise) is expected to change if the consequences (teacher attention) are changed. Forms of intervention include the following:

1. *Chaining:* Chaining can be used to teach sequenced activities such as dressing or eating or certain occupational tasks. The sequence is divided into a series of links each taught in order and mastered before progressing onto the next. Help is given as necessary to complete the sequence but is phased out as the links are progressively learned. Backward chaining involves teaching a task by giving assistance as necessary for all but the last link in the sequence which is taught. The teacher then phases out help as the earlier links in the sequence are learned.

2. *Fading:* Verbal or physical prompts may be used in teaching one skill in behaviour modification and are faded out as the learner acquires the skills. In backward chaining prompts are usually faded out from the last link of the chain of behaviour progressively back to the first. Reinforcement fading involves reducing a reinforcement that has been originally used to encourage or discourage a behaviour in order that the reinforcement is no longer necessary.

3. *Generalisation:* Generalisation occurs when a behaviour learned in one situation happens spontaneously in another situation. For example, someone who is taught to queue in one self-service restaurant will eventually know how to queue in other similar venues. For children with severe learning difficulties, such generalisation may need to be encouraged by structured teaching in a variety of settings.

4. *Imitation:* Imitation is a powerful way of learning new behaviour. For people with learning difficulties it may be necessary to encourage imitation of desired behaviour by reinforcing their attempts to copy.

5. *Modelling:* Learning through observation and imitation is known as modelling. The required behaviour, perhaps a social skill, is demonstrated by another person (the model) and the learner is encouraged to observe then imitate the required behaviour.

6. *Prompting:* Verbal or physical prompts are given to help a learner to perform a required behaviour (e.g. putting on an item of clothing). Prompts are normally faded out once the desired behaviour is achieved.

7. *Reinforcement:* Concerns the consequences of a behaviour which will affect its frequency. Positive reinforcement (e.g. reward) tends to increase the frequency of the behaviour with which it is associated. Negative reinforcement involves the removal of an unpleasant stimulus when a desired behaviour occurs. The aim is for the learner to modify behaviour to avoid negative reinforcement. Punishment involves linking an unpleasant stimulus with an unacceptable behaviour. Extinction involves eliminating the reinforcers of unacceptable behaviour. For example, tantrums may be reinforced by adult attention. Denying adult attention (while ensuring the learner's safety) would tend to reduce the incidence of tantrums. Reinforcers may be primary (e.g. food) or secondary (e.g. praise). Successful reinforcers are immediate, consistent, and exclusively associated with the desired behaviour. The approach taken with learners with special educational needs may involve reinforcing desired behaviour and avoiding reinforcing undesirable behaviour.

8. *Shaping (or successive approximation):* Involves developing existing behaviour. If the behaviour required is say for a learner to lift a spoon to the mouth, reinforcement would be given for holding the spoon and lifting the hand slightly. Gradually closer approximation of the target behaviour would next be required until the target behaviour was achieved.

9. *Differential Reinforcement of Other Behaviour:* A programme which aims to reduce the rate of undesirable behaviour tends to be more effective when positive reinforcement is also given for other acceptable behaviour. Differential reinforcement of alternative behaviour involves reinforcing the learner for not exhibiting the undesirable behaviour. Differential reinforcement of incompatible behaviour means rewarding a behaviour incompatible with that desired (e.g. rewarding quiet behaviour when aiming to deter noisy behaviour). Differential reinforcement of a lower rate of undesirable behaviour involves gradually extending intervals at which lower rates of the behaviour are reinforced.

10. *Time out for positive reinforcement:* Attention from others may act as a positive reinforcement to undesirable behaviour. Temporarily removing that reinforcement through 'time out' (e.g. removing a learner from a group) immediately after the undesirable behaviour occurs can reduce the incidence of that behaviour. The period of removal should be short (e.g. two or three minutes) and the learner should be allowed to rejoin the group after showing, even if only briefly, desirable behaviour.

11. *Extinction:* Involves reducing the frequency of an undesirable behaviour by stopping reinforcements to that behaviour.

12. *Response cost:* A method of punishment sometimes used where a token economy is operated. Tokens are deducted when a specified undesirable behaviour occurs. It should be planned and monitored.

13. *Overcorrection:* When an undesirable behaviour occurs (e.g. physical assaults) a desirable behaviour is rehearsed repeatedly as a punishment. In restitutional overcorrection the learner removes or repairs any damage caused. 'Positive practice overcorrection' involves the learner practising types of appropriate behaviour. Overcorrection should be planned and monitored.

14. *Desensitisation:* May be used in behaviour therapy for managing fears such as dog phobia. The object or situation which evokes the fear is introduced in manageable phases. In the case of dog phobia for example a picture or a model of a dog may be introduced first. Behavioural approaches such as modelling are used to aid the control of the fear and the real feared object is gradually introduced.

Behaviour support plan

Under the Education Act 1996, section 527A, every local education authority is required to prepare, and from time to time revise, a plan which sets out the arrangements made or proposed by the authority regarding the education of children with behaviour difficulties. *Circular 1/98* (Department for Education and Employment 1998) offers statutory guidance in connection with this. LEAs had to publish their plan by the end of December 1998 and revise it subsequently at least every three years.

Documents should include details of strategic planning for pupils with behavioural difficulties including links to other plans such as Early Years Development Plans; and support to schools in improving the management of pupil behaviour including training and guidance. They should include details of support for individual pupils in mainstream schools including promoting regular attendance; and for pupils being educated outside mainstream schools including re-integrating pupils into mainstream schools and tracking educational progress. Regulations (Statutory Instrument No. 644) set out those whom an LEA are required to consult when preparing their plan (and revisions of it) and the manner of consultation. They also prescribe how the LEA must publish the plan and to whom copies must be provided; and the dates when plans are to be published.

References
Department for Education and Employment (1998) *Circular 1/98: LEA Behaviour Support Plans.* London: DfEE.
Statutory Instrument No. 644 *The Local Education Authority (Behaviour Support Plans) Regulations 1998.*
  www.dfee.gov.uk/circulars/1-98/contents.htm

Behaviour therapy

Behaviour therapy has much in common with **behaviour modification** as it uses such methods as operant conditioning. It also uses techniques such as aversion therapy. Behaviour therapy draws on these methods to treat difficulties and has been employed with some children with special educational needs.

Benchmarking

Benchmarking is the process of comparing the standards of performance achieved by members of a group who share similar characteristics, in order that individuals can see how well they compare with the others. The benchmark is the performance reached by the more successful members of the group. In the case of schools, benchmarks give comparative information about how well they are performing in relation to others. This information can be used to inform the setting of targets for improvement. Benchmarking in relation to special educational needs (SEN) is particularly difficult because of the contextual nature of the definition of SEN widely adopted which makes it difficult to know whether one is comparing like with like. Similarly, it is difficult to meaningfully compare special schools with other special schools in this way because the children whom they teach vary according to different factors such as the referral policy of the local education authority. Progress can be made in addressing these difficuties if there is a focus on standards of pupil achievement and pupils with SEN are compared with other pupils with SEN according to these standards.

Reference

Qualifications and Curriculum Authority/Department for Education and Employment (2001) *Supporting the Target Setting Process: Guidance for Effective Target Setting for Pupils with Special Educational Needs.* London: QCA/DfEE.

Further reading

Farrell, M. (2000) *Standards and Special Educational Needs.* London: Continuum.

Address

Qualifications and Curriculum   Tel: 020 7509 5555
   Authority   Fax: 020 7509 6666
83 Piccadilly   e-mail: info@qca.org.uk
London W1J 8QA   www.qca.org.uk

Birth difficulties

Special educational needs (SEN) may arise as a result of difficulties before, during or after birth and are considered as prenatal, perinatal and postnatal difficulties.

Prenatal factors

Prenatal factors relating to SEN include infections, chemicals and malnutrition.

1. Infections which can affect the foetus include the rubella (German measles) virus, and congenital cytomegalovirus infection (CMV). CMV, also known as cytomegalic inclusion disease, causes mild or no illness in adults. However, if a woman is infected with the virus during pregnancy, the foetus may be infected. In the UK it is estimated that about 1 per cent of live births are infected with the virus. About 10 per cent of those will experience learning difficulties. Other characteristics may be deafness, epilepsy and loss of vision. Research continues for an effective vaccine. Acquired Immune Deficiency Syndrome (AIDS) is an illness caused by a virus infection. In a minority of people it produces a clinical condition in which immunity is lowered and the infected person is prone to other infections. Babies can be infected in the womb if their mother is carrying human immunodeficiency virus (HIV).

2. Chemicals can lead to children having SEN. The excessive consumption by pregnant women of alcohol or nicotine and the accidental ingestion of metallic poisons such as methyl mercury have been associated with effects on the foetus. Foetal alcohol syndrome is a significant cause of learning difficulties. It is found in children whose mothers drink more than 80gms of alcohol per day during pregnancy. Among the characteristics are that growth is deficient before and after birth and brain development is abnormal. Learning difficulties occur in 85 per cent of children recognised as having the syndrome. The learning difficulties may be made worse by the psychosocial effects of the alcoholic household. Attempts to reduce the incidence of foetal alcohol syndrome include education and raising the general level of public awareness.

3. Prenatal malnutrition. Malnutrition is a complex phenomenon to assess in relation to SEN. For example, its relationship with severe and moderate learning difficulty is far from clearly defined. The child of a poorly nourished mother may also be ill-nourished in early life making it difficult to disentangle the influence of maternal malnutrition from neonatal malnutrition. The foetus of a malnourished mother may be at a greater risk from such noxious influences as alcohol, drugs and infections which can influence intellectual functioning. As well as broadly defined malnutrition, a lack of specific dietary ingredients is influential. For instance, iodine deficiency is linked to impairments in cognitive functioning.

Perinatal factors

Developments may occur in the process of birth and soon after causing conditions which lead to SEN. The perinatal period is from birth to four weeks.

Asphyxia (having insufficient air) can result in **brain injury**. **Cerebral palsy** can be caused by asphyxia. Asphyxia and 'mechanical' injury are often closely associated and are sometimes grouped together as 'birth injuries'. The proportion of births which are affected by either asphyxia or injury or both is not agreed, as research studies show varied results. The discrepancies probably reflect different views of the causes of the learning difficulties. Also, it is difficult to distinguish the effects of asphyxia in children because of the many confounding variables associated with it.

Hypoxia is the deprivation or reduction of the normal supply of oxygen just before, during and just after birth. If the supply of oxygen to the baby's brain is interrupted, this can be problematic. It may, for example, lead to cerebral palsy.

The incidence of injuries at birth may have declined because of various factors: improved perinatal monitoring and management, new diagnostic brain imaging techniques and new treatments.

However, improved facilities may result in the survival of babies who might previously have died. Babies at risk from birth injury and its consequences, because of premature birth and/or small size, have better prospects of progress than, say, 20 years ago.

Postnatal factors

Postnatal influences on learning difficulty include infection, malnutrition, poisoning and cerebral trauma.

Meningitis is an example of an infection of the nervous system. It is an inflammation of the membranes of the brain and/or spinal cord. Meningitis can be treated in some cases by chemotherapy. Another condition, encephalitis is caused by viral infections.

Malnutrition is difficult to link directly to learning difficulties because it tends to be linked to other adverse circumstances including socio-economic and psychological factors which can contribute to learning difficulties.

An example of poisoning is the ingestion of poisonous chemicals such as mercury, copper or lead. It has been found that persistently raised lead blood levels of 40mg/100ml may cause slight cognitive impairments. Research into the issue is complicated by the fact that people living in areas exposed to lead (e.g. near lead works) may be socially disadvantaged. Prevention of lead poisoning can be achieved through such measures as controlling industrial pollution and using lead-free petrol.

Cerebral trauma accounts for about 1 per cent of children with severe learning difficulties. Behaviour difficulties are also associated with cerebral trauma. Challenges in researching this area include the following:

- head injury could be 'caused' by the learning difficulty rather than vice versa, children with learning difficulties being more vulnerable to injury than others;
- both learning difficulties and head injury may reflect an uncaring background;
- severe learning difficulty may increase the chances of head injury through self-injurious head banging or through epileptic seizures.

Causes of cerebral trauma are accidental (e.g. traffic injuries) or non-accidental (e.g. battered children).

Boarding special school

Residential schools may offer:

- provision for rare disabilities where local provision is not feasible
- provision for disabilities which require fuller education and care than can be provided in a day school
- provision for children with damaging home circumstances.

On the other hand, residential provision has certain potential disadvantages. It separates pupils from the local community from which they come and to which often they have to return. While residential schools can plan transition arrangements for the pupil to return to his/her local community, this is difficult where the school and the pupil's community are far apart. Links with families tend to be difficult to maintain and there is a difficult shift in termly boarding schools from school to family and from family to school several times a year.

Alternatives in some cases include day special school placements combined with local care such as fostering. With such issues and with financial considerations in mind, some LEAs have looked carefully at their placements in residential schools outside their own boundaries. This has led to a reduction in the number of pupils in such schools and the closure of some residential special schools.

The single largest group of schools with residential provision is that for secondary age pupils with emotional and behavioural difficulties. Most boarding special schools cater for both boys and girls and boarding arrangements are most often weekly, although most schools offer some flexibility for example occasional respite care over the weekend for weekly boarders, if there are particular family problems.

A review of boarding special school inspections (Office for Standards in Education 1999) drew on a sample of 100 reports on maintained and non-maintained residential schools and also independent schools approved by the Secretary of State for Education and Employment. This review indicated that the great majority of heads of care led and managed their teams effectively. Close partnership between the head teacher and the head of care was associated with the best provision. Although staff training and induction programmes were satisfactory in the majority of schools, in over half of the schools for pupils with EBD they were unsatisfactory. Key worker schemes contributed to good standards of care.

Schools with high standards had care plans for pupils that set demanding targets and that related well to the planning of teachers. In good practice night staff were regularly supervised in their work, were suported by senior management on call and used effective proceedures for recording and for handing over. Child protection procedures were a priority for most schools although few provided an independent listener for pupils. The most common shortcomings were the absence of complaints procedures and of written policies for restraint. The quality and suitability of residential accommodation varied widely. Most schools communicated effectively with parents and most had good relationships with their local communities. Few had good links with local business and industry.

In brief, the quality of care was satisfactory or better in eight out of ten residential schools. Most care staff teams were well led, and close links between care and education enhanced the quality of care. Unsatisfactory standards were associated with weak leadership and poor accommodation.

(See also *Care staff*)

Reference
Office for Standards in Education (1999) *Special Education 1994–98: A Review of Special Schools, Secure Units and Pupil Referral Units in England*. London: The Stationary Office.

Further reading
Abbott, D., Morris, J. and Ward, L. (2000) *Disabled Children in Residential Schools: A Study of Local Authority Policy and Practice*. Bristol: Norah Fry Research Centre.

Braille

The well-known system of reading and writing used by blind people and based on touch, Braille is a system in which six raised dots are set in different positions to represent letters, punctuation, whole words etc. It takes a child about three times longer to read Braille than it does a sighted child of the same age to read print. Braille is written with a brailler which has six keys and impresses Braille dots on paper. Braillers linked with computers are improving communication for blind people. Versabraille is an electronic brailler which stores text on cassette or disc. It can:

- display text on a Braille display
- print text in Braille or in normal typeface
- reproduce as Braille a text which has been typed in using an ordinary computer keyboard.

Brain injury

The educational implications of brain injury are related to the location of the injury, its extent and the age at which it was suffered. Brain injury can affect emotional/social behaviour, motor skills, perceptual skills and intellectual skills. A diagnosis of brain damage cannot be made solely from psychological tests and inferring back from the results to such a diagnosis. What is important is an assessment of the child's abilities and disabilities and implementing a suitable educational programme.

Address

Children's Head Injury Trust
c/o Neurosurgery Department   Tel: 01865 224786
Radcliffe Infirmary   Fax: 01865 224786
Woodstock Road   e-mail: enquiries@chit.demon.co.uk
Oxford OX2 6HE   www.glaxocentre.merseyside.org/CHIT

Information, support and research for the parents of children with traumatic or acquired brain injury.

Building and design

The Schools Building and Design Unit of the Department for Education and Skills produce guidance on various aspects of building and design relating to special educational needs. Among these are 'Building Bulletins' concerning children with SEN in ordinary schools and in special schools.

There are also 'Design Notes' concerned with visual and hearing impairment and with access for disabled people. These documents guide architects and designers but are also useful to local education authorities and school staff working in liaison with architects and designers involved in building new schools or making alterations to existing buildings.

Further reading

Department for Education and Employment (1997) *Building Bulletin 84: Boarding School Accommodation: A Design Guide.* London: The Stationery Office.
Department for Education and Employment (1997) *Building Bulletin 87: Guidelines for Environmental Design in Schools (revision of Design Note 17).* London: The Stationery Office.

Address

Schools Building and Design Unit   Tel: 020 7273 6718
Department for Education and Skills   Fax: 020 7273 6762
Caxton House   e-mail: michael.bubb@dfes.gsi.gov.uk
Tothill Street   www.teachernet.gov.uk/schoolbuildings
London SW1H 9NA

Bullying

Associated with both psychological and physical intimidation, bullying may involve excluding a child from a group and physical violence or threats of violence. In general, in developing approaches to bullying, schools should lay the ground for consultation carefully, develop a clear and widely agreed policy, and make sure that procedures to deal with bullying are clear and understood by all concerned (Farrell 1999).

There are particular and diverse concerns with pupils having special educational needs. Children with emotional and behavioural difficulties may bully others and, while the bullying has to be tackled, such children will need help in understanding and changing their behaviour. Pupils with moderate or severe learning difficulties may be more vulnerable to bullying if they do not understand the nature of bullying and the action to take if they are being bullied.

Reference
Farrell, M. (1999) *Key Issues for Primary Schools*. London: Routledge.

Further reading
Young, S. (2002) *Solutions to Bullying*. Stafford: National Association of Special Educational Needs.

Address
Kidscape   Tel: 020 7730 3300
2 Grosvenor Gardens   Fax: 020 7730 7081
London SW1W 0DH   e-mail: contact@kidscape.org.uk
                                  www.kidscape.org.uk

Kidscape campaigns for childrens' safety.

Carer

Within the *Special Educational Needs Code of Practice* (Department for Education and Skills 2001), a carer is a person named by a local authority to care for a child for whom the social services department has parental responsibility. In such a case, the child is the subject of a care order and will have been placed in residential or foster care. If the carer qualifies as a parent in terms of the Education Acts because they have care of the child, they have a role in the consideration of any special educational needs the child may have.

Reference
Department for Education and Skills (2001) *Special Educational Needs Code of Practice*. London: DfES.

Care staff

Care staff in **boarding special schools** make an important contribution to the personal and social development of children and form a key part of the 24-hour curriculum. A review was reported in 1999 of special schools, including residential special schools, and other placements largely based on findings in the published reports on Office for Standards in Education inspections from 1994 to 1998 (Office for Standards in Education 1999). In the sample of schools whose reports were scrutinised, the quality of care was satisfactory or better in eight out of ten schools.

High-quality residential provision was marked by care programmes well matched to pupils' needs and planned with reference to the school curriculum. Daily handover meetings, briefings and staff meetings were well managed in most schools, making liaison between care staff and teaching staff effective. Care staff provided good role models for children, maintaining high expectations of behaviour and encouraging pupils to have good attitudes towards the school. About one in ten schools offered extra-curricular programmes leading to accreditation, such as the Youth Award Scheme, and such programmes were strongly associated with the most effective schools. Close partnerships between the head teacher and the head of care were associated with the best provision.

Where the quality of care was unsatisfactory, pupils lacked opportunities for the development of personal and social skills within the care programme and links between care and teaching staff tended to be weak.

Reference
Office for Standards in Education (1999) *Special Education 1994–98: A Review of Special Schools, Secure Units and Pupil Referral Units in England*. London: The Stationary Office.

Address
General Social Care Council   Tel: 020 7397 5100 (switchboard);
Goldings House   020 7397 5800 general information
2 Hays Lane   Fax: 020 7397 5801
London SE1 2HB   e-mail: info@gscc.org.uk
                                                          www.doh.uk/gscc

Along with equivalent bodies in Wales, Scotland and Northern Ireland, the General Social Care Council's aims are the development and promotion of education, training and qualifications for social work and social care staff in the statutory, voluntary and private sectors of the personal social services throughout the United Kingdom.

Cerebral Palsy

Cerebral Palsy (CP), the most frequent cause of permanent physical disability in children, is a disorder of movement and posture. Brought about by a permanent, static lesion of the brain in early life, CP may involve difficulties with vision, hearing, speech and intellectual ability. About one third of people with CP experience epileptic seizures. The combination and variety of brain lesions present different patterns in determining various types of CP. Various effects of CP are grouped together according to the impairments of movement associated with them; spastic, athetoid and ataxic.

About three quarters of people with CP have spastic movements due to the failure of muscles to relax. These are caused by damage to the motor cortex. One arm and one leg on the same side of the body may be affected (hemiplegia); all limbs may be affected (quadriplegia); all limbs may be affected with the legs being more affected (diplegia); or legs only may be affected (paraplegia). More rarely the arms may be more affected than legs or three limbs or one limb may be affected.

Athetoid CP, caused by damage to the basal ganglia, is typified by slow, writhing movements of the limbs which cannot be controlled.

Ataxia is associated with poor coordination and movement and disturbed balance and is caused by damage to the cerebellum.

CP can involve a mixture of spasticity, athetosis and ataxia. CP affects between two and five babies per 1,000 live births in developed countries. It can develop after birth and affects marginally more boys than girls. Among postnatal causes are meningitis, encephalitis (acute inflammation of the brain) or trauma such as a fractured skull and restriction of blood supply to the brain. However, CP is mainly caused by prenatal and perinatal factors. These include rhesus incompatibility, a condition now largely prevented by giving an affected baby a blood transfusion soon after birth. Other causes are maternal rubella, toxaemia or diabetes. A major cause is ataxia at birth which may be associated with prematurity and low birth weight. CP occurs in premature infants three times more often than in full term infants. There are difficulties in separating the relative contributions of physical disability and brain damage. Of course, physical disability is not necessarily linked with cognitive impairment. Although physical disability itself may not be restricting intellectually, it may have environmental consequences which are restricting (e.g. it may limit experience).

Among the educational implications of CP are the following:

- multidisciplinary assessment is necessary to ensure that all aspects of CP are taken into account when preparing an individual education plan;
- individual education programmes are particularly important because of the individual and varied nature of CP;
- the degree of impairments and difficulties should be taken into account; cognitive, physical, motor, speech, sight, hearing, perceptual and behaviour;
- attention should be paid to medical and motor aspects of CP (e.g. coordination, motor control) because these influence general educational development;
- special language programmes are important where there is language impairment;
- information and communications technology can be used to help difficulties with communication;
- for motor impairments, aids may include head pointers, individualised wheelchairs, electronic devices and a variety of adaptive equipment. Also, physical therapy within a daily programme may be critical;
- ongoing evaluation or at least periodic assessment is essential as the abilities and needs of children with CP change with development, medical treatment, therapy and teaching;
- the involvement of parents in programmes and early intervention are important.

(See also *Conductive education*)

Further reading
Parkes, J., Donnelly, M. and Hill, N. (2001) *Focusing on Cerebral Palsy*. London: Scope.

Address

SCOPE	Tel: 020 7619 7341 (library and information unit)
6 Market Road	Fax: 020 7619 7360
London N7 9PW	e-mail: information@scope.org.uk
	www.scope.org.uk

SCOPE provides a range of services for people with cerebral palsy and their families/carers (including schools, residential care, information and career advice). The Cerebral Palsy Helpline is available seven days a week on 0800 800 3333 (Mon. to Fri. 11 am–9 pm, Sat. to Sun. 2–6 pm). SCOPE has over 200 affiliated local groups.

Challenging behaviour

Challenging behaviour (CB) is behaviour which is socially unacceptable and significantly blocks learning. Its intensity, duration or frequency is such that the safety of the person exhibiting the behaviour or the safety of others is at risk. Such behaviour is likely to limit access to community facilities or completely prohibit it. Expressions used to indicate CB include 'problem', 'difficult', 'disturbing' and 'maladaptive' behaviour.

There is not always agreement on what constitutes CB because of varying standards of what is considered acceptable behaviour. Social class, culture, different chronological and developmental ages of children and different settings can all influence the assessment of the severity or even the existence of CB. Examples of CB are:

- self-injury
- injury to others
- damage to surroundings
- severe lack of compliance
- repeated absconding
- stereotyped behaviour (speech or movement)
- faecal smearing
- pica (habitually eating substances other than food such as paper or dirt)
- inappropriate sexual behaviour such as public masturbation or exposing the genitals to others
- persistent screaming
- repeated vomiting
- hyperactivity.

Work with people with CB draws on research in the areas of child development, psychiatry, medicine and psychology. In some cases CB is linked to specific clinical conditions such as Lesch-Nyhan syndrome which is associated with self-injurious behaviour and often violence to others, spitting and vomiting. Other factors which can contribute to CB are the side effects of drugs, pain, stress, anxiety and depression. Various factors can also contribute to the maintenance of CB. It can be viewed in a developmental context ranging from early rhythmical behaviour to the changes brought about by adolescence.

It is important to assess and measure the behaviour as part of the child's overall assessment. Hypotheses about the behaviour should be tested (e.g. its causes, antecedents and consequences). It is important to create optimum learning environments for children with CB and to work out intervention programmes which take full account of the child's needs and level of ability. Behavioural and psychotherapeutic approaches may he used. Individualised planning of specific programmes is necessary.

Interventions must be carefully planned, systematically implemented, and rigorously assessed then modified or changed if ineffective. Children with CB may need, from time to time, additional staff, experiences or equipment or a modified timetable.

CB may have a communicative function for the child making it important to have individual communication programmes devised in conjunction with a speech and language therapist. CB may be used to communicate one or several of the following:

- a request for social activities (e.g. attention or interaction)

- a request for items such as food or a toy
- a protest or refusal to comply with a request
- a wish to escape from a situation
- dissatisfaction
- a comment or declaration such as a greeting or compliance with a request
- boredom, pain or tiredness.

An analysis of the possible communicative function of CB can lead to effective interventions. Interventions may relate to events which precede the CB (antecedents) or events which follow the CB (consequences). Antecedent and consequent events may support the CB. Interventions may be selected on the basis of functional analysis. However, their long-term effectiveness may be impaired, for example, if the elimination of the unwanted behaviour is not supported by naturally occurring events which reinforce the new behaviour. One way of ensuring that natural contingencies are applied is to teach new functional behaviours. These must result in reinforcing consequences similar to those available following the unwanted behaviour. The new behaviour must be reinforced by the same consequences that reinforced the unwanted behaviour. Successful intervention depends on expanding the limited response repertoires of people with learning difficulties rather than just trying to eliminate the inappropriate behaviour. Among the forms of intervention are the following:

- ones designed to teach new communicative behaviours to replace unwanted behaviour, e.g. teaching a child desiring food to use a non-verbal sign rather than be disruptive;
- ones designed to teach other functionally related behaviours to replace the unwanted behaviour, e.g. teaching a child to listen to peaceful music on a headset to suppress an over-stimulating environment instead of exhibiting unacceptable behaviour such as shrieking;
- ones involving changing the events which lead up to the inappropriate behaviour. Such behaviour may indicate a wish to escape from a situation, for example, because it involved learning which the person found too difficult. If the tasks were simplified, and errorless learning was used, then the inappropriate behaviour might cease.

Early intervention is helpful. Children with CB may find change difficult, so this should be implemented in a planned way and with an acclimatisation period. Changes of staff, peers, school and the changes of environment involved in using respite care all need to be planned.

The support and training of staff working with children with CB is most important. Staff support groups and the active support of senior staff are necessary. Whole-school policies will help ensure consistency in working with children with CB. This involves developing and maintaining appropriate attitudes to work with CB. An open atmosphere in which difficulties can be shared and discussed is important. The development of management techniques and learning strategies must have a high priority for the whole school. Senior staff need to be closely involved. It has been found effective for a senior member of staff to have overall responsibility for coordinating and monitoring behaviour management programmes, working with classroom staff.

All staff need to be trained in behaviour management techniques so that children with CB are not denied free movement in the school because of lack of overall staff expertise. There should be opportunities for individual help with programme planning and chances to observe colleagues who are particularly skilled. Close links with parents/carers and between teachers, psychologists, speech therapists and others is vital. Links with other schools and agencies (especially staff who provide respite care for the individual and their families/carers) are equally important so that a common approach to the management of the children can be developed and maintained.

Further reading
Hewett, D. (1998) *Challenging Behaviour: Principles and Practices*. London: David Fulton Publishers.

Child and Adolescent Mental Health Services

Child and Adolescent Mental Health Services (CAMHS) form part of the range of service areas of National Health Service local trusts, perhaps as part of a wider mental health service. Referral is normally by a general practitioner and the CAMHS staff may include a clinical psychologist, social worker, occupational therapist, consultant psychiatrist, primary community mental health worker, community nurse, drama therapist and community psychiatric nurse.

Children with SEN are more likely to have mental health problems than are other children, making links between CAMHS and education services important. Many children with mental health problems may be identified as having emotional and behavioural difficulties.

The Health Advisory Service (HAS) outlined a strategic approach to commissioning and delivering a comprehensive child and adolescent mental health service. The model comprises four tiers of increasing specialisation. Tier 1 includes interventions by social workers, juvenile justice workers, school nurses, residential social workers, voluntary workers, general practitioners, health visitors and teachers. These workers are the first point of contact between a child or family and the childcare or health agencies. Tier 2 includes community child psychiatric nurses, community- and hospital-based paediatricians, child and adolescent psychiatrists, pupil support teachers, child psychologists, educational psychologists, social workers, psychotherapists and occupational therapists. Staff at tier 2 should be able to offer training and consultation to other professionals, assessment and onward referral as necessary. The first tier is linked to the more specialist tiers 2 and 3 by a primary mental health worker who is a member of a specialist service at tier 2. There are designated service level agreements and contracts between tiers 1 and 2. Tier 3 includes specialist assessment teams, a specialist eating disorder service, trauma service, family therapy teams, day unit teams, psychotherapy supervision teams and substance misuse teams. Tiers 2 and 3 are linked by designated service level agreements and contracts. Tiers 1 to 3 concern the district level of commissioning and delivery. Tier 4 includes very specialised outpatient services for young people with very complex and/or refractory disorders, in-patient child and adolescent mental health services, special units for sensorily impaired young people, special psychiatric liaison services, specialised neuro-psychiatric services and secure forensic mental health services.

Tier 4 services are provided on a regional basis. Tiers 3 and 4 are linked by contracts.

The Audit Commission (1999) indicated a range of concerns regarding CAMHS, including:

- a limited range of CAMHS available;
- the numbers and qualifications of the professional staff available;
- the quality of partnership between CAMHS and other services; and
- the need for more coordinated strategic planning.

References
Audit Commission (1999) *Children in Mind: Child and Adolescent Mental Health Services.* London: Audit Commission.

Further reading
Atkinson, M. and Hornby, G. (2002) *Mental Health Handbook for Schools.* London: Routledge Falmer.

Address
Association for Child Psychology and Child Psychiatry   Tel: 020 7403 7458
St Saviour's House   Fax: 020 7403 7081
39–41 Union Street   e-mail: accp@acpp.org.uk
London SE1 1SD   www.acpp.org.uk

The ACPP has as its objective the scientific study of all matters concerning the mental health and development of children, young people and their families. At meetings scientific matters are discussed, and in publications clinical findings, research projects and results are published. The ACPP publishes *The Journal of Child Psychology and Psychiatry, Child and Adolescent Mental Health* and *The Bridge* (a newsletter). It encourages a multidisciplinary membership.

Child psychiatrist

A child **psychiatrist** is normally employed by the Health Service and has specialised in the emotional and behavioural disorders of children. Usually based in a hospital, the child psychiatrist is a member of the **child and adolescent mental health services**.

Address
Association for Child Psychology and Psychiatry   Tel: 020 7403 7458
St Saviours House   Fax: 020 7403 7081
39 –41 Union Street   e-mail: acpp@acpp.org.uk
London SE1 1SD   www.acpp.org.uk

Child psychotherapist

A child psychotherapist helps children to recognise and respond to emotional conflicts. (S)he will have undergone training in psychotherapy or in psychotherapeutic counselling. A psychotherapist may be based at a hospital paediatric department, at a residential school for pupils with emotional/ behavioural difficulties or may have a private practice.

Child psychotherapists tend to work with very disturbed children. Trainees need a suitable personality, experience of working with children and an honours degree. Training takes a minimum of four years.

(See also *Psychoanalysis and psychotherapy*; *Play therapy*)

Address

Association of Child Psychotherapists   Tel: 020 8458 1609
120 West Heath Road   Fax: 020 8458 1482
London NW3 7TU   e-mail: acp@dial.pipex.com

The Association has the function of maintaining standards within the profession, of safeguarding the interests of its membership and is the designated authority for regulating entry into the profession under EC regulations. It is affiliated to a number of wider organisations within the field of mental health and child care. ACP organises regular meetings and lectures for members and allied professionals. The *Journal of Child Psychotherapy* is published for the Association.

Children in need

Government guidance (Department of Health 2000) is provided for staff involved in assessments of children in need and their families under the Children Act 1989. It indicates that in England there are between 300,000 and 400,000 children 'in need'. Within this group are two other slightly overlapping groups: 53,000 children who are looked after by a local authority ('looked after children') and 32,000 children on the child protection register. Under the Children Act 1989, section 17(10), children are 'in need' if:

- they are unlikely to achieve or maintain, or do not have the opportunity to achieve or maintain, a reasonable standard of health or development without provision made by the local authority; or
- their health and devlopment are likely to be significantly impaired, or further impaired, without provision being made by the local authority: or
- they are disabled.

Local social service authorities are required to promote and safeguard the welfare of these children. They must promote the child's upbringing by his or her family to the extent that this is consistent with the child's welfare.

In order to comply with these duties, local authorities must provide the following, as appropriate:

- advice, guidance and counselling;
- activities – social, occupational, cultural or recreational;
- home help;
- help enabling the child and family to have a holiday.

Local authorities also have to:

- take reasonable steps to identify how many children in the area are in need;
- keep a register of disabled children;
- publish information about services available; and
- ensure that this information gets to those whom it might help.

Advice, guidance and counselling are free but a charge may be made for other services except where families receive Income Support or Family Credit.

Government guidance (Department of Health 2000) is provided for staff involved in assessments of children in need and their families. The framework is structured to include the child's developmental needs, parenting capacity and family and environmental factors.

The child's developmental needs are seen as health, education, emotional and behavioural development, identity, family and social relationships, social presentation and self-care skills. Parenting capacity consists of basic care, ensuring safety, emotional warmth, stimulation, guidance and boundaries and stability. Family and environmental factors comprise family history and functioning, the wider family, housing, employment, income, the family's social integration and community resources.

Maximum timescales are set down for analysing the needs of the child and parenting capacity for children in need and for children where there are concerns of 'significant harm' that may lead to section 47 enquiries and child protection procedures. The roles and responsibilities of those concerned in the inter-agency assessment of children in need are outlined. The importance of education to the child in need is indicated and the roles of the educational welfare officer, educational psychologist and others are described.

Reference
Department of Health/Department for Education and Employment/Home Office (2000) *Framework for the Assessment of Children in Need and their Families*. London: The Stationery Office.

Address
Department of Health
Richmond House
Whitehall
London SW1A 2NL

Tel: 020 7210 4850
Fax: 020 7210 5661
e-mail: dhmail@doh.gsi
www.nhs.gov.uk

Chromosome abnormalities

A chromosome is a structure in the cell nucleus which carries the genes (which determine hereditary characteristics). There are normally 46 chromosomes in the nucleus of every living cell in the human body. Chromosomes are rod shaped and are arranged in 23 pairs. Twenty-two of these pairs are known as autosomes, the remaining pair are sex chromosomes.

Each member of a pair of chromosomes comprises two threadlike structures which touch but not at the midpoint. Each chromosome consequently has a long arm and a short arm. The long arm is labelled 'q' while the short arm is labelled 'p'. In a woman the sex chromosomes are a matching pair of so-called X chromosomes. In a man the pair are an X chromosome and a Y chromosome. The 22 pairs of autosomes are each different in shape and length. They are grouped accordingly and the groups are denoted by a letter. Each individual pair is designated a number 1 to 22. When female eggs and sperm are formed the chromosomes in each pair separate. This leaves 23 chromosomes in these cells rather than 23 pairs. When an egg is fertilised it receives the 23 chromosomes from the mother's egg and 23 chromosomes from the father's sperm. These then arrange themselves into pairs. When this process operates incorrectly, chromosome abnormalities occur. One in 200 live-born infants have such an abnormality. Some of these may cause physical and/or intellectual disability.

An additional chromosome to a pair making three is called a trisomy. The total number of chromosomes is 47 in such instances, rather than 46. The effects of this depend on which designated number chromosome pair the additional chromosome is associated with. If chromosome pair 21 is implicated, this is associated with **Down's syndrome** (trisomy 21). About 94 per cent of cases of Down's syndrome are associated with an extra chromosome at pair 21. Down's syndrome is the commonest chromosome abnormality in live-born infants. Partial trisomy (or duplication) is a wide range of chromosome disorders in which there is an extra part of a chromosome in each body cell. This may be duplication of part of a long arm of a chromosome (q) or of a short arm (p). The form and degree of the disorder appears to relate to the position of the duplication and its extent. The partial trisomy is referred to by the number of the arm of the chromosome concerned. For example, Rethore's syndrome (partial trisomy 9p) is caused by partial trisomy of the short arm (p) of chromosome 9. One feature of this condition is mild to severe learning difficulty (SLD).

If a chromosome segment breaks off and is lost, the effect depends on the particular chromosome affected, the site of the deletion and its extent. An example of a chromosome deletion is deletion 5p, a deletion of the short arm (p) of chromosome number five. It leads to Cri du-Chat syndrome. This rare condition is so-called because the baby has a rather catlike cry in the first few months. The syndrome is usually associated with SLD. Rarely both chromosomes in a pair break the ends which remain united forming a ring chromosome. An example is the formation of a ring in chromosome 13 which leads to Orbeli syndrome. Among the characteristics of this syndrome are slow development and often SLD.

In translocation, part of one chromosome becomes joined to another or becomes part of another. In a balanced translocation the amount of genetic material is presumed to be identical to that found in a normal cell and is simply redistributed. This does not usually lead to clinical changes. If the translocation is unbalanced this can affect development. For example, in 3 per cent of people with Down's syndrome translocation is the cause of the extra chromosomal material.

Where there is a chromosome mosaic, a number of cells contain chromosome abnormalities while the rest are normal. This is caused by abnormal chromosome separation in the later stages of cell division after the egg has been fertilised. The nature of the mosaic influences the extent of disorder.

Abnormalities of sex chromosomes relate to a higher than average incidence of speech and reading difficulties. More severe sex chromosome abnormalities can lead to learning difficulties. An example is Turner's syndrome which occurs in girls and is caused by the absence of one of the sex chromosomes, leaving only one X chromosome. Among the characteristics of the syndrome are left-right disorientation and difficulties with perceptual organisation.

Approaches have been developed which can help identify whether a baby in the womb is likely to be born with a chromosome abnormality (e.g. as in Down's syndrome). Amniocentesis involves drawing off a sample of the amniotic fluid in which the baby is suspended in the womb. If the analysis of this indicates a congenital defect such as chromosome abnormality, the mother may consider terminating the pregnancy. In chorionic villus sampling, chromosome abnormalities may be detected in an unborn foetus by analysing a sample of tissue taken from the placenta.

Further reading
Gilbert, P. (2000) *A–Z of Syndromes and Inherited Disorders*. London: Stanley Thornes.

Address

Contact-a-Family	Tel: 020 7608 8700; minicom 020 7608 8702
209–11 City Road	Fax: 020 7608 8701
London EC1V 1JV	e-mail: info@cafamily.org.uk
	www.cafamily.org.uk
	Helpline: 0808 808 3555 (freephone for parents and families 10 am–4 pm Mon.–Fri.)

A charity providing support and advice to parents whatever the medical condition of their child. Has a directory of rare and specific disorders.

Circle time

Quality Circles are used in industry and commerce to develop individuals in a group setting. Group therapeutic techniques also use the group to help individuals within it to develop emotionally. Developmental group work has been used, for example, in secondary school tutorial sessions and for personal and social education in primary schools. Such developments contributed to the evolution of circle time, an approach which seeks to develop individual potential and enable emotional and social development within a supportive, structured group setting.

Circle time involves activities, tasks and 'conferencing'. Everyone is an equal member of the circle and has an equal right to speak and to be heard. The games played are such that there are no winners or losers. Collaborative tasks are used. As members of the circle gradually get to know one another, different topics are explored such as feelings or problems associated with different times in the school day. Conference sessions follow the tasks.

Circle time aids communication, can be used to modify behaviour and encourages positive relationships. It can raise self-esteem and develop the understanding of interpersonal relationships and sensitivity towards them. Its positive effects can spill over into other aspects of school for example by improving the group skills in lessons. Among the benefits of circle time for pupils with special educational needs is its potential to offer opportunities to modify and understand difficult behaviour and increase the sense of self-worth.

Further reading
Mosley, J. and Tew, M. (1999) *Quality Circle Time in the Secondary School: A Handbook of Good Practice*. London: David Fulton Publishers.

Nash, M., Lowe, J. and Palmer, T. (2002) *Language Development: Circle Time Sessions to Improve Communication Skills*. London: David Fulton Publishers.

Clinical psychologist

A clinical psychologist is a psychology graduate who has undertaken further training including training in research methods to specialise in applying psychology to the clinical sphere. The clinical psychologist applies psychological principles to the treatment and management of people with emotional and behavioural difficulties and/or learning difficulties (particularly severe learning difficulties). He or she may work as an individual or as a member of a team and may treat clients as individuals or as members of a group. A clinical psychologist is usually employed by the health district's clinical psychology service.

Among the knowledge and skills a clinical psychologist can offer are:

- observation and assessment skills
- diagnostic skills
- treatment skills (e.g. the application of behaviour modification to unacceptable behaviour).

Address

British Psychological Society   Tel: 0116 254 9568
St Andrew's House   Fax: 0116 247 0787
48 Princess Road East   e-mail: bps1@le.ac.uk
Leicester LE1 7DR   www.bps.org.uk

The BPS is a professional body for psychologists in the United Kingdom. It has sub-groups and divisions and publishes *Psychologist* monthly. Its journals include the *British Journal of Clinical Psychology*.

Code of Practice

The *Special Education Needs Code of Practice* (Department for Education and Skills 2001), effective from 2002, developed from an earlier Code which it replaces. A summary of the new Code is given in the appendices of this volume. It concerns the identification and assessment of pupils with special educational needs but also has implications for provision. In addition to the guidance, an earlier draft of the Code helpfully provided a section outlining 'SEN thresholds', giving good practice guidance in decision-making on identification and provision for pupils with SEN. The Code gives guidance on the discharge of functions under the Education Act 1996, part 4, to:

- local education authorities
- the governing bodies of all maintained and non-maintained schools
- providers of government-funded early education
- those who help the above including health services and social services.

The Code provides guidance on policies and procedures intended to enable pupils with SEN to reach their full potential, to be included in their school communities and to make the transition to adult life successfully.

Reference

Department for Education and Skills (2001) *Special Educational Needs Code of Practice*. London: DfES.

Address

Special Educational Needs Division	Tel: 020 7925 5000
Department for Education and Skills	Fax:020 7925 6000
Sanctuary Buildings	e-mail: info@dfes.gsi.gov.uk
Great Smith Street	www.dfes.gov.uk
London SW1P 3BT	

Cognitive approaches

Psychological theories grouped as cognitive theories are sometimes contrasted with behaviourist theories. The latter view learning as essentially links between stimuli and response. Cognitive psychologists, however, place greater emphasis on brain functioning, and hypothesise internal thinking as well as processes. These internal phenomena include perception and memory which we acquire from experience and which influence our present behaviour. Personal awareness of the environment is considered important as is the ability to be flexible in our response to the environment. Cognitive theorists view the learner as an active participant in his or her learning, spontaneously activated to explore and learn. Intuition and insight are cognitive concepts which find no counterpart in behaviourist views.

The implications for special education will be apparent. An uncritical acceptance of behaviourist theory can lead to a view of the learner as exclusively a passive respondent to structured stimuli provided by the teacher. Such a view, taken to an extreme, would oversimplify the complexity of human life. Cognitive theories appear to encourage a view of the learner as more of an integral being in his/her own right, potentially active, spontaneous and curious.

It is easy, perhaps, particularly when working with people who have severe, profound or multiple learning difficulties, to use predominantly a behaviourist perspective when faced with the limited responses which may be evident. The cognitive perspective may help teachers remember the thinking, active element of all learners, including those with profound learning difficulties.

Learning difficulties may be understood according to the underlying cognitive basis of the learning difficulty because intervention aims to influence cognitive functioning. Assessment should determine the child's strengths and weaknesses in the pertinent cognitive domains. Three aspects are important:

- the processing demands of the task;
- the role of the environment;
- the processing skills of the learner.

The development of processing skills relate to:

- cognitive 'architecture' (the innate structure of the cognition system such as the organisation of the memory system);
- mental representations, that is, the structuring of information from the environment;
- task processes such as rehearsal; and
- executive processes, that is, those concerned with planning and regulating activities.

Such approaches may inform the understanding of a response to specific difficulties with language, reading (decoding and comprehension) and number as well as general learning difficulties (mild, moderate or severe). Children with general learning difficulties may experience difficulties with speed of information processing, attentional mechanisms and memory processes. Interventions focus upon correcting and compensating for missing or undeveloped skills and strategies of learning.

Assessments of cognitive development include norm-referenced tests, criterion-referenced tests and ordinal scales. Attempts to predict future cognitive development from assessments of current performance have limitations. Assessments involving proposed educational materials and programmes can be useful in that they can be used both to assess the child and to place the child on a progressive programme.

If criterion-referenced tests and ordinal scales are used to establish teaching goals in a similar way, they can also be useful. However, there are fundamental issues which are not always sufficiently considered when using a developmental programme. Among these are that such curricula are built upon an assumption of development which is sequential and progressive. The development of a child with special educational needs may be delayed. However, it may be different rather than delayed in areas relating to one or several aspects of the curriculum. This needs to be taken into account by viewing developmental approaches to the curriculum critically and being also guided by individual changes. Also important is the need for such approaches to be part of a broad and balanced curriculum, including the National Curriculum.

Further reading

Tilstone, C., Layton, L., Williams, A., *et al.* (2002) *Child Development and Teaching the Pupil with SEN.* London: Routledge Falmer.

College of further education

Three main forms of provision have emerged in colleges of further education:

1. support services to enable students to participate in the regular college courses;
2. bridging courses to prepare students for entry to regular courses;
3. special courses to develop personal, social and vocational skills.

Some colleges accept students part time from school to take part in certain activities. A common arrangement is a one or two year separate course of work preparation. Among the advantages of a place in a college of further education for people with special educational needs are the following:

- they have contact with contemporaries
- they are expected to behave maturely
- they have access to a wide range of social and vocational possibilities
- provided learners have support, when necessary, from specialist teachers, a period in a college can provide an important half-way stage to adult and working life
- even in the absence of work, further education can help to develop autonomy and a range of interests.

Further reading
Lifetime Careers Publishing (annually) *Compendium of Post 16 Residential Education and Training for Young People with Special Needs.* West Sussex: Lifetime Careers Publishing.

Address
Learning and Skills Council
101 Lockhurst Lane
Foleshill
Coventry CV6 5SF

Tel: 024 7658 2761
Fax: 024 7658 2738
e-mail: info@lsc.gov.uk
www.lsc.gov.uk

Community home with education

Community homes with education on the premises are managed by local social services authorities. With regard to 'looked after' children, a local education authority may conclude that suitable arrangements have been made and that they are relieved of their duty to arrange the provision specified in the child's statement of special educational needs if the child is placed in a community home with education. The LEA may also take the same view if the child is placed with another children's home that provides education or with an independent fostering agency providing education (Department for Education and Skills 2001, section 8.100)).

Reference
Department for Education and Skills (2001) *Special Educational Needs Code of Practice.* London: DfES.

Conductive education

Conductive education is a special form of education for people with motor disorders, such as those associated with cerebral palsy, Parkinson's disease, multiple sclerosis, head injuries and strokes. It was developed in Hungary by Andras Peto, founder of the Peto Institute in Budapest. Orthofunction is the aim of conductive education and is the ability to carry out functional movements independently.

Conductive education is provided by specially trained staff called conductors, two or more of whom work throughout the day with a small group of children in a residential setting. The conductor teaches the child skills, such as walking, feeding and grasping, and also teaches reading and number. Parents are involved from an early stage so that they can take over from the Institute when the child leaves. Several comparative studies have indicated that conductive education is less effective than conventional methods of teaching and therapy used in special schools in the United Kingdom.

Further reading
Read, J. (1995) *A Different Outlook: Service Users' Perspectives on Conductive Education.* Birmingham: Foundation for Conductive Education.

Address
The National Institute of Conductive Education
Cannon Hill House
Russell Road
Moseley
Birmingham B13 8RG

Tel: 0121 449 1569
Fax: 0121 449 1611
e-mail: foundation@conductive-education.org.uk
www.conductive-education.org.uk

The Foundation for Conductive Education is a registered charity founded in 1986 to establish the science and skill of conductive education in the United Kingdom. The Foundation provides continuous and sessional services for children with cerebral palsy aged 0 to 16 years. Services are provided at The National Institute of Conductive Education in Birmingham. The Foundation publishes *The Conductor* quarterly.

Connexions Service

The Connexions Service (CS) is responsible for working with all year groups aged 13 to 19 in England, providing guidance and support to help them make the most of their educational and vocational choices and development opportunities and to prepare for successful transition to work and adult responsibilities. The local education authority works in partnership with the CS to ensure that the needs of young people are served.

CS is delivered mainly through Personal Advisers linking with specialist support services, including services for young people with special educational needs (SEN). The CS plays an important role in the transition process for young people with SEN from year 9 onwards. For pupils with SEN, the CS must attend the year 9 annual review meeting and should be invited to all subsequent annual reviews. Personal advisers provide information, guidance and advice whether the recipient is at school, in further education, in work or out of work.

Further reading
Department for Education and Skills (2002) *Working with Connexions.* London: DfES.

Addresses
Connexions Service National Unit (CSNU)
Department for Education and Employment
Room W407   Tel/Fax: see website for contact numbers of local offices
Moorfoot   e-mail: patraining.connexions@dfes.gsi.gov.uk
Sheffield S1 4PQ   www.connexions.gov.uk

The National Association of Careers and Guidance Teachers (NACGT)
9 Lawrence Leys   Tel: 01295 720 809
Bloxham   Fax: 01295 720 809
Banbury OX15 4NU   e-mail: nacgt@freeuk.com
                           www.nacgt.org.uk

The NACGT is a professional organisation for teachers and others practitioners involved in careers education and guidance (CEG). It aims to promote the highest professional standards by supporting professional development, lobbying nationally to raise standards in CEG, providing information and disseminating details of initiatives, and providing publications and other services for members.

Continuing professional development

While the implementation of continuing professional development (CPD) resides mainly with schools and colleges, central and local government and their associated agencies seek to contribute leadership, strategic planning, support and funding. Higher education institutions make a significant contribution to the provision of

SEN training. This includes providing SEN training on and off campus; servicing or supporting SEN courses organised and taught by providers from schools or local education authorities (LEAs); and being a channel for teachers to gain access both to higher degrees in SEN-related areas and to research knowledge in the SEN field.

Specialist distance learning courses are available in topics such as **autism** or **hearing impairment**. These can comprise local tutorials and regional residential courses to supplement the distance learning. Open University specialist courses involve distance learning packs, television and radio programmes, local tutorials and regional/national residential sessions.

In-service education and training (INSET) enables appropriate levels of educational knowledge and skills to be passed to all teachers, to teachers with special educational responsibilities and to specialist teachers and advisers. The Standards Fund is one mechanism for supporting INSET. The range of grants reflects the government's priority of raising standards as set out in the White Paper *Excellence in Schools*. Centrally important is school improvement through targets agreed with the LEA and written into the school and LEA development plans. Most of the Standards Fund is allocated to schools, while LEAs support schools in raising standards. Among the areas supported by recent Standards Fund grants are SEN, inclusion and improving attendance and behaviour.

Address

Teacher Training Agency
Portland House
Stag Place
London SW1E 5TT

Tel: 020 7925 3700
Fax: 020 7925 3792
e-mail: through on-line advice form
www.canteach.gov.uk

Counselling

Counselling may range from the involvement of a teacher and a pupil in talking over some issue of concern to in-depth counselling by a professionally trained and qualified counsellor. Some special schools for pupils with emotional/behavioural difficulties (EBD) use counselling as a means of encouraging pupils to articulate their feelings. In some cases counselling may be psychotherapeutic, having aspects in common with psychotherapy. There are several approaches to counselling including:

- humanistic-existential, e.g. person-centred counselling
- behavioural
- cognitive and cognitive-behavioural
- career development
- integrative.

Also, psychotherapy and psychoanalysis can be seen as part of a wider area of counselling psychology. Counselling may focus on careers and vocational issues, learning difficulties or EBD.

Further reading

British Association of Counselling and Psychotherapy (2001) *Good Practice Guidance for Counselling in Schools* (3rd edn). Rugby: BACP.

Counsellor

The term 'counsellor' is commonly used to refer to a specialist counsellor. However, a teacher takes on the role of counsellor from time to time within the pastoral care system of a school. In large schools counsellors may be employed solely by the institution or otherwise may be peripatetic, working for several schools. A teacher-counsellor is often a qualified, experienced teacher who has taken extra training in counselling. Such a staff member spends part of the time teaching and part of the time seeing pupils by arrangement for individual counselling.

Address
British Association for Counselling and Psychotherapy (BACP)
1 Regent Place   Tel: 0870 443 5252
Rugby   Fax: 0870 443 5160
Warwickshire CV21 2PJ   Minicom: 0870 443 5162
                                              e-mail: bacp@bacp.co.uk
                                              www.bacp.co.uk

The BACP promotes counselling, and maintenance of standards of training and practice. It provides information on training and lists of local counsellors on receipt of a self-addressed, stamped envelope, or via the BACP website. Counselling in Education, a specialist division, provides support for those working in school and youth services.

Curriculum

1. The National Curriculum and pupils with special educational needs
The Foundation stage of education is a phase from a child's third birthday to the end of the reception year. Early learning goals set out what most children are expected to achieve by the end of the Foundation stage. They are organised into six areas of learning: personal, social and emotional education; language and literature; mathematical development; knowledge and understanding of the world; physical development; and creative development. By the end of the Foundation stage most children will have had at least three terms of full-time education in reception class as well as their nursery and/or preschool experience.

The National Curriculum sets out a statutory entitlement to learning for all pupils, determining the content of what is taught and setting attainment targets for learning. Underpinning the school curriculum is a belief that education is a route to equality of opportunity, and part of its aims includes that it should promote equal opportunities.

The National Curriculum applies to pupils of compulsory school age in community, foundation and voluntary schools. It is organised in four key stages: Key Stage 1 for pupils aged 5 to 7 (years 1–2), Key Stage 2 for pupils aged 7 to 11 (years 3–6), Key Stage 3 for pupils aged 11 to 14 (years 7–9) and Key Stage 4 for pupils aged 14 to 16 (years 10–11).

In all key stages, the National Curriculum core subjects of English, mathematics and science, and the three foundation subjects of design and technology, information and communications technology and physical education are statutory.

Other foundation subjects are statutory at different key stages. History, geography, art and design, and music are statutory in Key Stages 1, 2 and 3 but not in Key Stage 4. Modern foreign languages and citizenship are statutory in Key Stages 3 and 4.

At Key Stage 4, schools may 'disapply' for any one pupil up to two National Curriculum subjects. Schools may disapply two subjects from science, design and technology or modern foreign languages to provide wider opportunities for work-related learning. They may disapply design and technology and/or modern foreign languages to allow: (a) a pupil making significantly less progress than peers to consolidate learning across the curriculum; or (b) a pupil with individual strengths or talents to emphasise a particular curriculum area.

For each subject and key stage, programmes of study set out what pupils should be taught in terms of knowledge, skills and understanding and breadth of study. Attainment targets set out expected standards of pupil performance. Four general teaching requirements apply across the programmes of study: inclusion; the use of language across the curriculum; the use of information and communications technology across the curriculum; and health and safety.

Attainment targets set out expectations for pupils at the end of each key stage. Except for citizenship, attainment targets comprise eight level descriptions of increasing difficulty plus a description of exceptional performance above Level 8. Each level description describes the type and range of performance that pupils working at that level should typically demonstrate. For citizenship, end-of-key stage descriptions set out expected performance for the majority of pupils at the end of Key Stage 3 and 4.

The great majority of pupils are expected to work within certain ranges: at Key Stage 1, Levels 1 to 3; at Key Stage 2, Levels 2 to 5; and at Key Stage 3, Levels 3 to 7. The majority of pupils are expected to attain Level 2 at the end of Key Stage 1, Level 4 at the end of Key Stage 2 and Level 5/6 at the end of Key Stage 3. At Key Stage 4, national qualifications are the main way of assessing attainment in National Curriculum subjects.

National targets have been set for the percentage of pupils achieving particular levels: the percentage of 11-year-olds achieving Level 4 in English and mathematics at the end of Key Stage 2; and 16-year-old pupils expressed as a percentage of pupils gaining:

- five or more A* to C grades in General Certificate of Secondary Education or its equivalent,
- one or more A* to G grades at GCSE or its equivalent; and
- the average GCSE/General National Vocational Qualification point score per pupil.

At the end of Key Stage 1, some aspects of statutory assessment in English and mathematics at Level 2 have been subdivided into 2a, 2b and 2c to help differentiate between the attainment of different groups.

To aid target setting for pupils achieving significantly below age-related expectations, performance criteria have been developed in English, and mathematics and science, leading to Level 1 and within Levels 1 and 2 (Department for Education and Employment/Qualifications and Curriculum

Authority 2001). Also, performance criteria have been developed for personal and social development.

Other requirements include that schools must provide religious education for pupils, although parents can withdraw their children. Also primary schools must provide an up-to-date written statement of their policy on sex education. In secondary schools, sex education must be taught. Secondary schools must provide a programme of careers education in years 9, 10 and 11.

Learning across the National Curriculum includes promoting spiritual, moral, social and cultural development. This embraces explicit opportunities to promote pupils' development in these areas in religious education and in personal, social and health education and citizenship. There is a non-statutory framework for personal, social and health education at all key stages and a non-statutory framework for citizenship at Key Stages 1 and 2, citizenship being statutory at Key Stages 3 and 4.

Promoting skills across the National Curriculum includes developing six key skill areas which are embedded in the National Curriculum: communication; the application of number; information technology; working with others; improving own learning and performance; and problem solving. Thinking skills, which are also embedded in the National Curriculum, are also important. They comprise skills in information processing, reasoning, enquiry, creative thinking and evaluation. Other aspects of the National Curriculum include financial capability, enterprise education and education for sustainable development.

Frameworks for literacy and mathematics have been established to support strategies to raise standards for all in primary schools. The National Curriculum documents also include non-statutory guidelines for personal, social and health education and citizenship at Key Stages 1 and 2 and for modern foreign languages at Key Stage 2.

2. Inclusion

Concerning the general teaching requirement of inclusion, this concerns providing effective learning opportunities for all pupils. Three principles are involved: setting suitable learning challenges, responding to pupils' diverse learning needs, and overcoming potential barriers to learning and assessment for individuals and groups of pupils. These should help ensure that only very few pupils will need to be disapplied from the National Curriculum. Also schools can provide other curricular opportunities outside the National Curriculum to meet pupils' needs, such as speech and language therapy.

In setting suitable learning challenges, teachers can, as appropriate, choose knowledge, skills and understanding from earlier or later key stages so that pupils can progress and demonstrate what they can do.

Responding to pupils' diverse learning needs requires, among other things, that teachers act to: create effective learning environments; secure pupil motivation and concentration; provide equality of opportunity through teaching approaches; use appropriate assessment approaches; and set targets for learning.

Overcoming potential barriers to learning and assessment for individuals and groups of pupils involves teachers taking action to provide access to learning for pupils with special educational needs (SEN). These actions include providing for pupils needing help with communication, language and literacy; planning to develop pupils' understanding through the use of all available senses and experiences; and planning for pupils' participation in learning and in physical and practical activities. Also, important are helping pupils to manage their behaviour, to participate in learning effectively and safely and, at Key Stage 4, to prepare for work; and helping individuals to manage their emotions and take part in learning.

Concerning pupils with disabilites, not all will have SEN. Teachers should take action to enable the effective participation of pupils with disabilities. These include planning appropriate amounts of time to allow tasks to be completed satisfactorily; planning opportunities for the development of skills in practical aspects of the curriculum; and identifying aspects of the programmes of study and the attainment targets that may present difficulties for individuals.

References

Department for Education and Employment/Qualifications and Curriculum Authority (2001) *Supporting the Target Setting Process.* London: DfEE/QCA.

Department for Education and Employment/Qualifications and Curriculum Authority (1999a) *The National Curriculum: Handbook for Primary Teachers in England.* London: DfEE/QCA.

Department for Education and Employment/Qualifications and Curriculum Authority (1999b) *The National Curriculum: Handbook for Secondary Teachers in England.* London: DfEE/QCA.

Further reading

Byers, R. and Rose, R. (2002) *Planning the Curriculum for Pupils with Special Educational Needs.* London: David Fulton Publishers.

Address

Qualifications and Curriculum Authority (QCA)
83 Piccadilly
London W1Y 7PD

Tel: 020 7509 5555
Fax: varies according to enquiry
e-mail: info@qca.org.uk
www.qca.org.uk

Dental care

Dental care is part of the school health service and in some areas there is associated orthodontic treatment. Dental hygiene is particularly important for children and young people with severe learning difficulties who may not understand the purpose of dental treatment. As a part of personal and social skills, dental hygiene is also important. Some conditions associated with learning difficulties involve teeth abnormalities. For example, in Down's syndrome, teeth develop late and may be abnormal in shape and size and may not be in alignment. Teeth grinding may be associated with learning difficulty and if not controlled it leads to excessive wear of the protective enamel covering the teeth.

Address

British Dental Association
64 Wimpole Street
London W1G 8YS

Tel: 020 7563 4195
Fax: 020 7935 6492
e-mail: enquiries@bda-dentistry.org.uk
www.bda-dentistry.org.uk

Deprivation/disadvantage

Cultural deprivation is the deprivation in childhood of the necessary range of experiences conducive to normal development, because of various family and social conditions. These may include poverty, overcrowding at home, poor health care, inadequate adult models at home, and poor language stimulation. Such deprivation can result in limited intellectual and physical development. In school, culturally deprived children may be difficult to motivate and may need particular help developing the language skills necessary to get the most out of their education.

Regarding maternal deprivation some earlier views on the potentially detrimental effects of maternal deprivation have been challenged. However, it is still widely accepted that mother–child relationships are very important for future child development and that short-term effects of separation on young children can be detrimental.

Further reading
Cox, T. (2000) *Combating Educational Disadvantage.* London: Routledge Falmer.

Designated medical officer

The 'designated medical officer' (community medical officer or clinical medical officer) is a medical doctor who, as part of the community health services, plays an important role in preventative medicine. (S)he also has several roles which affect special education.

(S)he:

- liaises with the medical and education services regarding preschool children with special needs;
- is a member of a Community Team for People with Learning Difficulties which serves children with special needs;
- draws together medical assessment and advice given to the local education authority; and
- advises teachers and parents regarding health factors that might impinge on a child's educational difficulties.

Developmental delay

Children who develop slowly, physically or intellectually may be assessed using developmental schedules. These allow comparisons to be made with 'statistically normal' developments at a specified age in areas such as motor, social, language and emotional development.

It is important to remember that schedules are norm referenced and not all differences below the norm necessarily indicate difficulties; the size of the difference below the norm is important. Delay may be indicated in one area (e.g. motor development) and not others, or it may be more general across several or all areas. Also, there is an expectation that development progresses in the same way for the average child and children with special educational needs (SEN). However, the development of some children with SEN does not appear to progress in the same way.

Another issue is that developmental delay in predominantly one area may affect development in other areas. For example, delayed motor development can affect the ability to handle objects and explore, therefore, affecting the child's cognitive development.

Diet

Malnutrition is generally associated with reduced intellectual capacity. Also, diet is associated with several areas of special need as the examples below indicate:

The Feingold diet has been tried in an attempt to reduce hyperactivity. Based on the belief that hyperactivity is caused by food allergy, the diet excludes such things as synthetic colours and flavours.

Phenylketonuria is a condition in which the appropriate diet can reduce the effects which include the risk of developing severe learning difficulties. It is caused by a deficiency of the enzyme phenylalanine hydroxylase. Phenylalanine cannot be converted into the amino acid tyrosine. Instead phenylalanine undergoes alternative metabolic pathways producing toxins that damage the brain. Tests indicate the presence of phenylketonuria in infants and a low phenylalanine diet is followed, often until the teenage years, to reduce considerably the effect of the condition.

Ketogenic diets have been followed for cases of severe epilepsy which do not respond to anticonvulsant drugs. The diet involves reducing the intake of protein and carbohydrates and providing 80 per cent of calorie intake through fats.

Further reading
Buttriss, J., Wynne, A. and Stanner, S. (2001) *Nutrition: A Handbook for Community Nurses*. London: Whurr.

Difficulty in learning

If a child has a significantly greater 'difficulty in learning' than the majority of children of the same age that child is considered to have a learning difficulty under the Education Act 1996, section 312. If the learning difficulty calls for special educational provision to be made then the child is considered to have SEN. It will be seen that a child may have a 'difficulty in learning' but (if it is not significantly greater than most children of the same age) not a learning difficulty.

Disability

The World Health Organisation (2000) has sought to reposition earlier concepts such as disability, impairment and handicap. The earlier classification was the International Classification of Impairments, Disability and Handicap (ICIDH), which was first published by the WHO in 1980 for trialing purposes. Although the new classification is the International Classification of Functioning, Disability and Health, the WHO proposes to use the earlier acronym of ICIDH, and the classification is to be ICIDH-2. Components of ICIDH-2 are, in summary: body functions and structures; activities; participation; and contextual factors. Each of these may be expressed in terms of: construct of concern; characteristics; positive aspect; negative aspect; and qualifiers.

In a matrix of these parameters the intersection of 'negative aspect' and the four components produce the following:

- body functions and structures–negative aspect–*impairment*;
- activities–negative aspect–*activity limitation*;
- participation–negative aspect–*participation restriction*;
- contextual factors–negative aspect–*barriers/hindrances*.

Impairment is seen as 'problems in body function and structure as a significant deviation or loss' (ICIDH-2, p. 11). *Activity limitation* is similar to the term 'disabilities' as used in the earlier ICIDH of 1980. *Participation restriction* is defined as 'problems an individual has in execution of task or involvement in life situations in current environment' (ICIDH-2, p. 14) and this concept is similar to the former one of handicap. *Barriers/hindrances* refers to an interaction of personal and environmental factors having a negative effect on performance. These constructs of health-related experiences are intended to replace earlier terms such as 'disability' and 'handicap'.

Disability is defined in several ways in legislation; it forms part of the definition of SEN in England and Wales, carried forward into later Education Acts including the Education Act 1996, which emphasises the link with learning. It states that:

a child has special educational needs... if he has a learning difficulty which calls for special educational provision to be made for him.   (Education Act 1996, section 312)

It follows from this definition that the 'learning difficulty' has to be specified. The Act does this stating that a child has a learning difficulty if:

a) he has a significantly greater difficulty in learning than the majority of children of his age;

b) he has a disability which either prevents or hinders him from making use of educational facilities of a kind generally provided for children of his age in schools within the area of the local education authority; or

c) he is under the age of five and is, or would be if special educational provision were not made for him, likely to fall within paragraph (a) and (b) when of, or over that age.
(section 312 (2))

The Children Act 1989 states that a child is disabled if he is blind, deaf or dumb or suffers from mental disorder of any kind or is substantially or permanently handicapped by illness, injury or congenital deformity or other such disability as may be prescribed.

The Disability Discrimination Act 1995 defines a disabled person as someone who has: 'a physical or mental impairment which has a substantial and long term adverse effect on his ability to carry out normal day-to-day activities'. In the 2001 SEN and Disability Rights Act, (Department for Education and Employment 2001) the definition of disability used is that given in the Disability Discrimination Act 1995.

Regarding the relationship between disability and SEN under the Education Act 1996, not all children with a disability will have a learning difficulty (because the disability may not 'prevent or hinder him from making use of educational facilities' as described). Also, a difficulty in learning and a disability are not always separate. A pupil with a difficulty in learning, leading to a learning difficulty such as severe learning difficulties, may also experience a disability such as blindness.

References

SEN and Disability Rights in Education Act 2001.

World Health Organisation (2000) *International Classification of Functioning, Disability and Health.* Madrid: WHO.

Addresses

Disabled Living Foundation	Tel: 020 7289 6111; 0845 130 9177 helpline
380–4 Harrow Road	Fax: 020 7266 2922
London W9 2HU	e-mail: dlfinfo@dlf.org.uk
	www.dlf.org.uk

Provides impartial advice and information on daily living equipment for disabled and elderly people through a helpline, equipment centre and publications.

Disability Rights Commission	Tel: 08457 622 633
Freepost MID 02164	Fax: 08457 778 878
Stratford upon Avon	e-mail: enquiry@drc-gb.org
CV37 9HY	www.drc-gb.org

The Disability Rights Commission is an independent body seeking to eliminate discrimination against disabled people and to promote equality of opportunity. It has a helpline, a Disability Conciliation Service and various teams dealing with casework, legal issues and practice development. It also offers publications and carries out research and policy work.

Disagreement arrangements

Arrangements provided by an LEA to help prevent or resolve disagreements between the parents of a child with SEN and the LEA or a school. Intended to bring together the parties informally to try to resolve the disagreement through discussion, the arrangements must have an independent element. These voluntary arrangements do not effect the right of parents to appeal to the SEN and Disability Tribunal.

Disapplication

A maintained school has to provide access to the National Curriculum for all pupils on its school register including those being temporarily taught at home, in a hospital school or in a pupil referral unit. When it is not possible to offer a pupil the full National Curriculum, aspects can be disapplied. Disapplication and modification may apply to the following:

- a programme of study;
- attainment target;
- assessment;
- any other components of the National Curriculum;
- any combination of the above including entire subjects or the whole National Curriculum.

Two forms of disapplication and modification are available. The first is through the Education Reform Act 1988, section 18. This states that some or all of the National Curriculum may be modified or disapplied by a child's Statement of special educational needs. The second way is through the Education Reform Act, section 19, which states that some or all of the National Curriculum may be temporarily disapplied for a child. Such disapplication should be rare. It may be contemplated, for example, for a child whose emotional or physical circumstances are considered to be unsuitable for participation. Under section 19, head teachers can make two types of temporary disapplication: general or special directions. General directions are for children without a Statement or not requiring a Statement but for whom temporary disapplication is needed. Special directions are for children who may need a Statement or who are undergoing the process of having a Statement made.

Disapplication from teacher assessment will be necessary only in rare circumstances. Where a single attainment target has been disapplied, an overall subject level can still be calculated using the attainment targets which remain and their weighting. Where more than one attainment target has been disapplied subject levels must not be awarded. Regarding disapplication from tasks or tests, a level cannot be awarded when a child is disapplied.

Further reading
DES (1989) *Circular 15/89: Temporary Exceptions from the National Curriculum.* London: Department for Education and Science.

Disorder

The term disorder appears to imply that a condition is related to factors within an individual rather than to a combination of factors including social factors. It may also suggest permanence (the word difficulty does not seem to carry these suggestions). Disorder also carries with it a medical perspective. Among conditions referred to as disorders listed in this Handbook are: *attention deficit hyperactivity disorder; genetic disorders; perceptual disorder and its assessment;* and *psychiatric disorders*.

Down's syndrome

First clearly described by Langdon Down in 1866, Down's syndrome has up to 300 distinguishing characteristics. Among the physical characteristics are a flat nasal bridge, a small mouth often with a protruding tongue and often transverse single palmar creases. Clinical findings associated with Down's syndrome are a high incidence of cardiovascular anomalies, bowel malformations, reduced stature, predisposition to infections and leukaemia and almost always learning difficulties. There are about 14 to 20 cases of Down's syndrome per 10,000 live births and more boys than girls are affected.

Down's syndrome is caused by **chromosome abnormalities** first identified in 1959. In about 95 per cent of instances of Down's syndrome the cause is the nondisjunction of an additional chromosome. Chromosome 21 occurs three times instead of twice (trisomy). In 3 per cent of cases chromosome structure is the cause. The major part of an additional chromosome is fixed to another chromosome of a different group (translocation). Often chromosome 21 adheres to 14. In 2 per cent of cases a mosaic chromosome structure is the cause (nondisjunction).

The prevention of the birth of children with Down's syndrome is being approached in several ways. In genetic counselling couples can be given an age-related risk of having a child with Down's syndrome. Screening programmes of amniocentesis identify instances. An important factor is maternal age, the incidence of Down's syndrome being around 10 per 10,000 live births for women under 28 years and about 470 per 10,000 live births for women over 40 years.

Further reading
Lorenz, S. (1998) *Children with Down's Syndrome: A Guide for Teachers and Learning Support Assistants in Mainstream Primary and Secondary Schools*. London: David Fulton Publishers.

Address
Down's Syndrome Association   Tel: 020 8682 4001
155 Mitcham Road   Fax: 020 8682 4012
London SW17 9PG   e-mail: hcopeland@downs-syndrome.org.uk
                                www.downs-syndrome.org.uk

The Association exists to support parents and carers of people with Down's syndrome and improve the lives of people with the condition. The national office provides information and advice on all aspects of the condition.

Drama therapy

Drama therapy has been effective in helping children with emotional and behaviour difficulties, particularly adolescents. It can be used with a therapist working with groups or individuals. Role play and enactment are sometimes used by teachers in the context of therapeutic work. Counsellors, occupational therapists and psychiatric nurses may also use the techniques.

(See also *Psychoanalysis and psychotherapy*)

Further reading
Jennings, S. (ed.) (1994) *Drama Therapy with Children and Adolescents*. London: Routledge.

Address
Division of Arts and Play Therapy Tel: 020 8392 3709
University of Surrey Roehampton   Fax: 020 8392 3709
Roehampton Lane   www.roehampton.ac.uk/arthum/arts/prog/
London SW15 5PH   dramatherapy_ma.asp

The Institute offers certificate and diploma courses in drama therapy.

Dual sensory impairment

The dual sensory impairments referred to are those of vision and hearing which are so severely affected that the person cannot simply use services offered to those with hearing impairments or visual impairments. The combination of deafness and blindness profoundly affects the person's perception of the environment and the term multisensory deprivation is sometimes used. One of the major causes is maternal rubella.

Important issues in the education of children with dual sensory impairment are as follows:

- early and accurate assessment including assessment of any residual vision or hearing;
- support and education of parents in communicating with their child;
- special provision and teaching.

Further reading

Aitken, S., Buultjens, M., Clark, C., Eyre, J. T. and Pease, L. (eds) (2000) *Teaching Children Who are Deafblind.* London: David Fulton Publishers.

Address

Sense
The National Deafblind and Rubella Association   Tel: 020 7272 7774
11–13 Clifton Terrace   Fax: 020 7272 6012
Finsbury Park   Minicom: 020 7272 9648
London N4 3SR   e-mail: enquiries@sense.org.uk
                                                  www.sense.org.uk

Sense offers advice, help and information to deafblind young people and their families; supports families through a national network of parents' self-help groups and runs holidays for deafblind children and young adults. It advises teachers and local authorities on education and provision for deafblind people; provides further education and rehabilitation for deafblind young adults and runs rehabilitation courses for people with Usher syndrome. Sense provides long-term residential care in group homes for deafblind adults; works with local authorities and voluntary organisations to develop services for deafblind people; seeks to raise awareness of deafblindness and provides information on the main causes. The organisation provides training for those working with deafblind people and campaigns to ensure that legislation recognises the needs of deafblind people.

Dyslexia

A child experiencing dyslexia, according to one perspective, tends to have significant difficulties in reading, writing, spelling or manipulating number which are not reflective of the child's general intellectual ability. While oracy may be well developed, difficulty may be experienced in acquiring literacy and numeracy skills. Such views of dyslexia are known as 'discrepancy' definitions. A child's frustration at this discrepancy may lead to withdrawn or disruptive behaviour or poor concentration.

In terms of SEN legislation, it would be expected that the child had a 'difficulty in learning' greater than children of the same age. An indication of this would be that a child with dyslexia would be behind children of the same age in attainment in reading, spelling and perhaps number. If this difficulty in learning was sufficient to lead to a 'learning difficulty' then the child might be considered to have SEN.

Estimates of the prevalence of dyslexia vary but it is sometimes judged that as many as 10 per cent of children may experience dyslexia to some degree with possibly 4 per cent of all children being severely affected. Dyslexia is not thought to be caused by general intellectual impairment, emotional factors or sociocultural constraints. There appear to be differences in the brain morphology of dyslexic people which are related to areas of the brain which affect language development.

The first reference in medical literature to congenital word blindness, or what would now be called developmental dyslexia, is that by Hinshelwood and Kerr in 1895. Believing that 'word blindness' was owing to defective development of the visual memory centre, Hinshelwood proposed a multisensory method of teaching which would stimulate many cerebral centres. Such multisensory methods continue to be common, although it is not clear in the light of subsequent research whether or not visual defects are an important contributing factor.

Early identification and assessment is important. The identification of dyslexia is partly based on a significant discrepancy between assessments of 'normal' cognitive ability or lower attainment in oral comprehension, reading, spelling or number. Other factors include clumsiness; left–right confusion; problems with sequencing or visual perception; difficulties with working memory; or significant delays in language functioning.

Phonological coding is important in the development of reading. Poor readers may have a level of general ability higher than would be expected from their reading performance in which case they would tend to be included in the discrepancy definition of dyslexia. Other poor readers may not have a discrepancy between their reading attainment and their general ability. However, poor readers, irrespective of any discrepancy with general ability, tend to have difficulty reading pseudo words. This has been linked to the reader's inability to break words into sound patterns. Because phonological difficulties underlie the reading difficulties of many children, it appears that phoneme awareness and the ability to understand phoneme segments may underlie difficulties with the phonological coding of written language (an important feature of dyslexia). Therefore a phonographic method of teaching reading and spelling may be helpful. Another consequence of a perspective which relates phonological awareness to subsequent reading failure is that early intervention in developing phonological awareness may have a positive impact on the later development of reading skills.

It is important that provision is tailored to the particular needs and difficulties of the child and that as far as is practicable, there should be an explicit and explainable link between the assessment and subsequent provision. Provision should follow an assessment of particular strengths and weaknesses.

However, some approaches appear to be broadly appropriate. Individual, direct, structured, sequential teaching which is phonics based and multisensory and involves over-learning and repetition is considered effective.

A structured reading programme, including phonics teaching, and a structured spelling programme are appropriate. Approaches such as those recommended for the primary school literacy hour offer a helpful framework. The use of multisensory teaching strategies aimed at developing skills in reading, spelling and number has already been mentioned. Information and communications technology is a useful tool (e.g. Keates 2002), most obviously through the use of computers with word processing and spell checking software. It is important that the pupil who benefits from such provision is properly trained to use it and that parents and teachers can support the child so that there is a consistent approach both at home and at school.

Any emotional and behavioural factors should be identified and addressed as far as possible. For example, anxiety may be eased by giving the pupil the opportunity to talk about his difficulties and by offering practical curriculum support such as that outlined above. Opportunities to praise small steps of success should be taken to help raise self-esteem.

Individual education plans should be drawn up to support provision and to help ensure that progress is systematically monitored. If satisfactory progress is not made, then as with all children with SEN, further consideration should be given to the provision being made. It may be that the methods being used require refining, or that more time needs to be spent on support, or that support should be sought from a specialist teacher of children with dyslexia or from an educational psychologist. In any event, the careful monitoring, recording and reporting of progress or lack of it is essential.

The Joint Council for General Certification of Secondary Education allow examination concessions for GCSE candidates with dyslexia if a report from an educational psychologist is provided. This may allow the candidate extra time.

Reference
Keates, A. (2002) *Dyslexia and Information and Communications Technology: A Guide for Teachers and Parents* (2nd edn). London: David Fulton Publishers.

Further reading
Thompson, M. (2001) *The Psychology of Dyslexia: A Handbook for Teachers*. London: Whurr.

Addresses
British Dyslexia Association (BDA)   Tel: 0118 966 8271
98 London Road   Fax: 0118 935 1927
Reading   e-mail: info@dyslexia.help-bda.demon.co.uk
Berkshire RG1 5AU   www.bda-dyslexia.org.uk

Its work includes a national helpline; early identification, working with professionals and parents; and education, working closely with schools, local education authorities and others. The BDA offers advice to students in further and higher education and to all dyslexic adults; promotes the needs and talents of dyslexic people in employment; arranges befrienders to assist parents in securing suitable educational help for their child; and offers a computer advice service.

Dyslexia Institute (DI)   Tel: 01784 463 851
133 Gresham Road   Fax: 01784 760 747
Staines   e-mail: spane@connect.bt.com
Middlesex TW18 2AJ   www.dyslexia-inst.org.uk

A non-profit making charity, the DI is a national independent educational body. It is involved in many assessments carried out by psychologists. It develops screening techniques and provides psychological advice for statutory, legal and professional bodies. The Institute is involved in teaching children and adults in centres and outposts and workers for the Institute may visit schools to give specialist help. The Institute provides a national postgraduate course and short courses for teachers. It is involved in research and development including the use of information and communications technology for people with dyslexia. The Dyslexia Institute Guild offers an information service for members, provides an annual symposium and produces a journal, *Dyslexia Review*.

Dyspraxia

In the *Special Educational Needs Code of Practice* (Department for Education and Skills 2001), dyspraxia is noted as a specific learning difficulty (Code 7.58). This relates to the fact that performance in day-to-day activities requiring motor coordination is substantially below what is expected given the child's chronological age and general intelligence. Also, the child may have good oral skills but be unable to reach commensurate standards in literacy or in recording skills.

Dyspraxia is a developmental disorder of the organisation and planning of physical movement, making physical activities difficult to learn, retain and generalise and their performance awkward and hesitant. Also known as developmental dyspraxia or developmental coordination disorder, dyspraxia is less commonly referred to as minimal brain dysfunction, perceptuo-motor dysfunction or motor learning difficulty.

Its cause is unknown but may relate to immature neurone development in the brain. Dyspraxia may be associated with difficulties with speech and language, perception and cognition. In the early years, speech may be immature or difficult to understand. Language may develop late or may be impaired. For some children, the main problem is in making and coordinating the movements used in producing speech, resulting in severe and persistent difficulties. This condition, known as developmental verbal dyspraxia, may occur on its own or together with general motor difficulties. Perception difficulties may show themselves as poor understanding of the messages conveyed by the senses and difficulty relating these messages to action. Cognition difficulties may relate to the planning and organising of thought.

Estimates of the incidence of dyspraxia vary from 2 per cent to 10 per cent in part related to the severity of impairment at which the condition is judged to exist. Of those diagnosed, 80 per cent are male.

In the early years, indications of dyspraxia may include that the child:

- reaches developmental milestones late;
- may not demonstrate the same gross motor skills as children of the same age;
- has difficulties with some personal and social skills;
- has limited understanding of positional concepts (e.g. 'on', 'in'); and
- is slow and hesitant in most actions.

At primary and secondary school, the child may retain some of the difficulties experienced in the early years. The child may also:

- write immaturely and with great effort;
- avoid physical education and games;
- have difficulty with mathematics and in writing structured stories; and
- have difficulty copying from a blackboard or overhead projector slide.

While dyspraxia is not curable, there may be improvements with growth and maturity and early identification, treatment, practice in certain activities and practical ways of minimising difficulties can help.

Reference
Department for Education and Skills (2001) *Special Educational Needs Code of Practice*. London: DfES.

Further reading

Portwood, M. (2001) *Developmental Dyspraxia* (2nd edn). Hitchin: Dyspraxia Foundation.
Ripley, K., Daines, B. and Barrett, J. (2000) *Dyspraxia: A Guide for Teachers and Parents*.
  Hitchin: Dyspraxia Foundation.

Address

The Dyspraxia Foundation   Tel: 01462 454 986 (helpline)
8 West Alley   (Mon.–Fri. 10 am–2 pm);
Hitchin   01462 455 016 (administration)
Hertfordshire SG5 1EG   Fax: 01462 455 052
                                  e-mail: dyspraxia@dyspraxiafoundation.org.uk
                                  www.dyspraxiafoundation.org.uk

The Dyspraxia Foundation aims to: support individuals and families affected by dyspraxia; promote better diagnostic and treatment facilities for those who have dyspraxia; help professionals in health and education to assist those with dyspraxia; and promote awareness and understanding of dyspraxia. It offers contact with other families, local activities, meetings and social events and publishes a newsletter and other publications.

Early education

Wherever it takes place, early education provision is part of the Foundation stage of education for children aged 3 to 5 years. The *Special Educational Needs Code of Practice* (Department for Education and Skills 2001) states that the management group of these settings should work with practitioners 'to determine the setting's general policy and approach' to SEN provision. The head of the setting is responsible for the day-to-day management of all aspects of the work of the setting including provision for children with SEN. All practitioners should be involved in the development for the SEN policy and be 'fully aware' of the procedures for identifying, assessing and providing for children with SEN. The SEN coordinator has responsibility for the day-to-day operation of the SEN policy and for coordinating provision for children with SEN (Code 1.39).

Identification, assessment and provision in early education settings involves a graduated response which may include 'early years action', 'early years action plus', statutory assessment or a statement of SEN.

Reference

Department for Education and Skills (2001) *Special Educational Needs Code of Practice*.
  London: DfES.

Further reading

Wall, K. (2003) *Special Needs and Early Years: A Practical Guide*. London: Paul Chapman
  Publishing.

Early education setting

Early education settings are providers of early education who receive government funding (Department for Education and Skills 2001, section 4.2). Such early education may be provided by:

● maintained mainstream and special schools;

- maintained nursery schools;
- independent schools;
- non-maintained special schools;
- local authority daycare providers such as day nurseries (provided by local social services authorities, voluntary organisations and others) and family centres; and
- other registered daycare providers (e.g. preschools; playgroups and private day nurseries; local authority Portage schemes; and accredited childminders working as part of an approved National Childminding Association network).

Early education settings are important for children with special educational needs because it is widely accepted that early intervention can improve cognitive and social development.

Reference
Department for Education and Skills (2001) *Special Educational Needs Code of Practice.* London: DfES.

Early years action and early years action plus

Early years action involves the early years practitioner, who works with the child day-to-day, or the SEN coordinator, identifying that the child has SEN. The practitioner and the SENCO together then provide interventions that are additional to or different from the curriculum and strategies normally provided by the setting.

Early years action plus involves the early years practitioner, who works with the child day-to-day, and the SENCO, being provided with advice or support from 'outside' specialists. This enables alternative interventions and strategies that are additional to or different from those provided through early years action to be put in place.

Economics

Economics relates to how societies organise the production and consumption of goods and services. It seeks to understand and explain the goods and services that societies produce; how societies produce them and for whom they are intended.

An important question in the economics of special education is, 'Where does the funding for special education come from and how is it allocated?' Nationally, the funding for special education comes from taxes and is redistributed to local education authorities (LEAs) and, to some degree, to schools, directly by government.

Schools receive direct government funding through such mechanisms as the Standards Fund for SEN (and other matters). For example, funds have been allocated under the heading of 'inclusion' to support SEN training and professional development of teachers and other staff and to support parent partnership and conciliation services for parents of children with SEN. It has been used to develop and support inclusive education systems by enabling more placements of pupils with SEN in mainstream settings, support special school outreach work and to improve speech and language therapy provision for children with communication difficulties.

More generally, the Department for Education and Skills allocates funds relating to SEN to LEAs according to a formula based on the eligibility of pupils in the area for free school meals. While this is a broad proxy indicator of SEN in a local area, it has the advantage of being simple to administer. This funding is in turn allocated by LEAs to schools in various ways.

An element is passed to schools under a formula based on pupil numbers. This simply assumes that among any population of children, there will be a certain proportion who have SEN. Another element of school funding is allocated according to local formulae and is often called the additional educational needs (AEN) element. This might also be based on eligibility for free school meals. It might be related to the standards of pupil achievement in particular schools; or there may be a formula allocating funds according to both of these criteria, and perhaps others. There may have been local consultation between the LEA, schools and parents seeking a system that all consider fair. The AEN element is not considered solely for pupils with SEN but also for others, including Travellers and 'looked after' pupils.

Next, an element of centrally held funding is allocated to schools in the form of support from centrally funded staff. For example, educational psychologists seek to allocate their time according to a system ensuring that they visit schools that require their services most. They may take into account the number of children with SEN and the nature of their SEN. Where support teachers and others are centrally funded a similar principle applies. Some LEAs are devolving funds to schools for some teacher support. This may be associated with schools working in clusters to decide how the time and support of such staff might be allocated across several schools.

Further funding to schools is attached to statements of SEN. Again, many LEAs seek to link statements for certain SEN to particular amounts of money translated into support time of teachers and learning support assistants. For example, funding for a statement for a pupil with profound and multiple learning difficulties would be likely to be greater than that for a pupil with moderate learning difficulties. A review of the different approaches taken by various LEAs is provided by the National Foundation for Educational Research (Hendy 2000).

If there is no agreement about when a statement of SEN should be provided, then distortions may occur because of pressure from more articulate parents, schools or pressure groups. Gross (1996), for example, concludes that resources are unfairly allocated to children whose parents are more literate, persistent and articulate than others and he therefore supports formula funding for greater fairness. An attempt to give guidance on what levels of learning difficulty and what degrees of disability might justify a statement (or other intervention) was made in the Threshold Document originally appended to the *Draft Special Educational Needs Code of Practice* (Department for Education and Employment 2000).

A project was established by the Department for Education and Skills in September 2000 concerning the distribution and delegation of resources to schools for SEN provision (Beck 2002). Pupils with SEN were regarded as a group within a wider group of pupils with AEN. In evaluating resource distribution models, criteria were set. These included that models should: support the inclusion of children with AEN in mainstream schools where possible and allow schools to manage the use and distribution of resources to aid efficiency. The models should support early identification and intervention strategies; allow flexibility to meet the needs of children with complex particular disabilities; be developed in partnership with schools and others; and involve accountability, including monitoring how resources are used and the outcomes for children. Although LEAs in the study used combinations of arrangements, three models were identified: the use of proxy indicators; direct pupil audit; and using school clusters to distribute resources for pupils with complex needs.

A study by the European Agency for Development in Special Needs Education, involving countries in the European Union, Iceland and Norway, considered the financing of special education (Meijer 1999). Important factors in budget allocation were the destination of the budget; forms of funding; and criteria for effective funding models.

The identification of certain conditions has an economic (and a political) element. The growth of some conditions may be seen as related to particular groups seeking to benefit from a redistributive society. There is a continuing growth of pupils with SEN and increasing cost. Where, lacking clear guidance from central government, local authorities allow SEN to be defined in a relativist way, leverage may be used to extract benefits for pupils who in broad terms require it less than many who receive no benefits.

References

Beck, C. (2002) 'The distribution of resources to support inclusive learning', *Support for Learning*, **17**(1).

Department for Education and Employment (2000) *Draft Special Educational Needs Code of Practice*. London: DfEE.

Department for Education and Skills (2001) *Special Educational Needs Code of Practice*. London: DfES.

Gross, J. (1996) 'The weight of evidence', *Support for Learning*, **11**(1).

Hendy, J. (2000) *Who Holds the Purse? Funding Schools to Meet Special Educational Needs: Information and Management Exchange Report No. 57*. Slough: National Foundation for Educational Research.

Meijer, C. (ed.) (1999) *Financing of Special Needs Education: A seventeen-country study of the relationship between financing of special needs education and inclusion*. Middelfart: European Agency for Development in Special Needs Education.

Office for Standards in Education (1999) *Pupils with specific learning difficulties in mainstream schools: a survey of the provision in mainstream primary and secondary schools for pupils with a statement of special educational needs relating to specific learning difficulties*. London: Ofsted.

Education Supervision Order

Under the Children Act 1989, section 36, a local education authority may apply for a child of statutory school age who is not being properly educated to be put under the LEA's supervision. The aim is to ensure that the child receives efficient full-time education suited to the child's age, aptitude, ability and any special educational needs, and that the parents are provided with sufficient support, advice and guidance.

Education Welfare Officer (EWO)

The EWO (sometimes called an education social worker) is employed by a local education authority to fulfil various duties. These may include the following:

- to ensure that parents take up their child's right to education through attendance at school or otherwise;
- to advise parents of their rights (e.g. regarding welfare grants);
- in some authorities, to undertake casework with children and families;
- to liaise with others (e.g. social services, schools, psychological services);
- to deal with free school meals applications;
- to license children for part-time employment;
- to provide advice and training to schools to develop an effective attendance policy;
- to arrange alternative education for pupils not educated at school; and
- to work with excluded pupils.

Address

For an example of a local education authority website concerning an Education Welfare Service (Staffordshire) see: www.sln.org.uk/specialneeds/ews.htm

Educational psychologist

A professional qualified psychologist who offers advice on the education of children with educational problems caused by difficulties with learning and/or behaviour. The educational psychologist may be called upon during the process of identifying special educational needs (SEN) and of the statutory assessment process which can lead to a child having a Statement of SEN and may work as a member of a team of other professionals; teachers, speech therapists and others.

As well as observing children and discussing any educational problems with parents, teachers and others, the educational psychologist may test and otherwise assess children. (S)he may advise schools on certain educational issues such as the provision for pupils with SEN and on the use of standardised tests.

Parents can contact an educational psychologist through the school, or by contacting their local educational psychology service directly. The Association of Educational Psychologists supplies information on psychologists in different geographical areas. An educational psychologist must be a qualified teacher and must have taught before (s)he begins training in psychology. The training is both theoretical and practical. The British Psychological Society offers 'chartered' status to psychologists, including educational psychologists who have undergone the requisite professional training and a register is available.

Further reading

Shorrocks-Taylor, D. (ed.) (1997) *Directions in Educational Psychology.* London: Whurr.

Addresses

Association of Educational Psychologists (AEP)   Tel: 0191 384 9512
26 The Avenue   Fax: 0191 386 5287
Durham DH1 4ED   e-mail: aep@aep.org.uk
                                                  www.aep.org.uk

The AEP is the professional association for educational psychologists in England, Wales and Northern Ireland.

The British Psychological Society (BPS)
St Andrew's House
48 Princess Road East
Leicester LE1 7DR

Tel: 0116 254 9568
Fax: 0116 247 0787
e-mail: mail@bps.org.uk
www.bps.org.uk

The BPS is a professional body for psychologists in the United Kingdom. It has sub-groups and divisions and publishes *The Psychologist* monthly. Its journals include *The British Journal of Educational Psychology*.

Emotional, behavioural and social difficulties (EBSD)

Pupils with emotional, behavioural and social difficulties (EBSD) may in some cases, but certainly not all, disrupt the education of others. EBSD may stem from various causes such as abuse or neglect, physical or mental illness, sensory or physical impairment or psychological trauma. Sometimes EBSD may arise from features of the school setting or may be made worse by them. EBSD may also be associated with other learning difficulties.

EBSD can be understood from various perspectives. From an educational viewpoint, EBSD are on a continuum above occasional naughtiness to below what would be considered mental illness. Children with EBSD may tend to be withdrawn, depressive, aggressive or self-injurious. They may be excessively anxious, phobic (a form of anxiety) or demonstrate obsessive and compulsive behaviours. Deciding whether a child has EBSD is influenced by the nature, persistence, severity, abnormality or cumulative effect of the behaviour, in comparison with what is normally expected for a child of the same age.

Among the educational implications of EBSD are that an appropriate venue is important. For particularly disruptive children, and for especially vulnerable children, this may be a special school or a separate unit. Such provision may be necessary for the child with EBSD. It may also be needed to ensure that children in mainstream schools can continue their education without the disruption that may be created by a child with EBSD. This provision can effectively concentrate the necessary teaching and therapeutic approaches. Residential provision can remove the child from what is sometimes an intolerable home situation, which can in itself improve matters. The behaviour of a child who is in specialist provision may well improve. However, the improvement may not be sustained when attempts are made to include the child back into mainstream school. Also, when children reach school leaving age they may find it particularly difficult to sustain work or community life. Support is needed to aid such transfer.

Whether provision is in special or mainstream school, it is important to recognise that many children with EBSD also have other learning difficulties and other needs that have to be addressed. Partnership with parents is important, but parents may be unable, or disinclined, to support the child. Psychotherapy, behavioural approaches or counselling need to be built into the school's provision as appropriate. Children with EBSD may benefit from various forms of therapy including play therapy, music therapy, drama therapy and art therapy. Also they may benefit particularly from aspects of the school curriculum which allow emotions and emotional conflicts to be expressed and examined. These include drama, art, role play and dance. On the other hand, insecure children may be drawn to the more controllable and predictable areas of the curriculum such as aspects of mathematics and science.

Further reading

Ayers, H. and Prytys, C. (2001) *An A to Z Practical Guide to Emotional and Behavioural Difficulties*. London: David Fulton Publishers.

Address

Association of Workers for Children with Emotional and Behavioural Difficulties (AWCEBD)

Charlton Court	Tel: 01622 843 104
East Sutton	Fax: 01622 844 220
Maidstone	e-mail: awcebd@mistral.co.uk
Kent ME17 3DQ	www.mistral.co.uk/awcebd/

The AWCEBD is a multidisciplinary association for teachers, residential social workers, psychologists, psychotherapists, researchers and others working with children and young people experiencing emotional and behavioural difficulties. The association offers training and policy development to members and publishes the journal *Therapeutic Care and Education*.

(See also *Psychiatric disorders; Residential therapy*)

Epilepsy

Epilepsy is a condition in which the affected person tends to have recurrent seizures ('fits') because of an altered state in the brain. A chemical imbalance leads to excessive electrical discharges in the nerve cells. Where these discharges occur determines the type of seizure.

The condition affects about one person in every 200 and usually develops before the age of 20 (although it can occur at any age). In many cases, epilepsy can be controlled by medication. However, anticonvulsant drug treatment can have the side effect of making a child feel sleepy which in turn can affect education. The attainment levels of children with epilepsy tend to be lower than average. This may be because of the effect of drugs or petit mal seizures which may go unnoticed and lead to temporary loss of attention which inhibits learning. The frustration created by this lower attainment may be linked to emotional and behavioural difficulties which some children with epilepsy experience.

Most children with epilepsy attend ordinary schools. Teaching strategies need to take account of individual needs. Drowsiness or inattention should not necessarily be interpreted as boredom or uncooperativeness. Where attention has been lost, missed material will need repeating. Difficult behaviour may be reduced if the teacher is aware of possible lapses in attentiveness and can compensate for it. Particular care is needed with potentially dangerous physical pursuits. Careers guidance for people with epilepsy also needs to take account of restrictions which the condition may impose.

Further reading

Johnson, M. and Parkinson, G. (2002) *Epilepsy: A Practical Guide*. London: David Fulton Publishers.

Addresses

British Epilepsy Association
New Anstey House
Gate Way Drive
Yeadon
Leeds LS19 7XY

Tel: 0113 210 8800
Fax: 0113 391 0300
e-mail: epilepsy@bea.org.uk
www.epilepsy.org.uk

The British Epilepsy Association works to improve the quality of life for people with epilepsy in the community. It provides information, a freephone epilepsy helpline and works with the government and other bodies to bring about improvements in services. It has a network of branches nationwide.

National Society for Epilepsy
Chesham Lane
Chalfont St Peter
Gerrards Cross
Buckinghamshire SL9 ORJ

Tel: 01494 601 300
Fax: 01494 871 927
www.erg.ion.ucl.ac.uk/nsehome

The National Society for Epilepsy is the oldest epilepsy charity in the UK. It provides a comprehensive range of services for people with epilepsy including longer-term care, rehabilitation, daytime activities centres, sheltered employment and training and a full information and education service.

Epilepsy Association of Scotland
48 Govan Road
Glasgow G51 1LJ

Tel: 0141 427 4911
Fax: 0141 419 1709
e-mail: admin@epilepsyscotland.org.uk
www.epilepsyscotland.org.uk/epilepsy

Facilitated communication

A controversial and unproved approach, facilitated communication (FC) seeks to help non-verbal people to communicate by typing or by pointing to alphabet board letters. It has been used with adults and children with physical disabilities, with autism and with severe learning difficulties. 'Facilitators' guide the person's arm, hand or finger to allow them to tap the keyboard or point to letters. The majority of research studies into FC have found little evidence of genuine communication. There is evidence that the majority of apparently new communication comes from the facilitators themselves.

Further reading
Hornby, G., Atkinson, M. and Howard, J. (1997) *Controversial Issues in Special Education.* London: David Fulton Publishers.

Foundation stage of education

Early years development and childcare partnerships draw together providers from the maintained, voluntary and private sectors with local education authorities, social services, health services and parent representatives in planning and providing services in early education. Many education providers are eligible for government funding. These include maintained mainstream schools, maintained and non-maintained special schools, maintained nursery schools, independent schools, local authority care providers (e.g. day nurseries and family centres), preschools, playgroups, private day nurseries, local authority Portage schemes and accredited childminders working as part of an approved network.

The Foundation stage of education is a phase from a child's third birthday to the end of the reception year (the year in which most children are admitted into the reception class of an infant or primary school). Early learning goals set out what most children are expected to achieve by the end of the Foundation stage. They are organised into six areas of learning: personal, social and emotional education; language and literature; mathematical development; knowledge and understanding of the world; physical development; and creative development. By the end of the Foundation stage most children will have had at least three terms of full-time education in reception class as well as their nursery and/or preschool experience.

It is important that early years practitioners work closely with partners including parents, speech therapists, district nurses, speech and language therapists, health visitors, Portage workers and teachers of children who have visual or hearing impairments. A few children at the Foundation stage with special educational needs (SEN) will require specific provision such as specialist teaching, adapted equipment or adult support for certain activities. Practitioners should, whenever possible, work with other professionals such as those from community health services.

All providers of government-funded early education must have regard to the Code of Practice (Department for Education and Skills 2001) and are expected to have a written SEN policy. Early education providers, except specialist SEN providers, identify a special educational needs coordinator (SENCO). The Code sets out a model of graduated action and intervention to SEN. In the early years setting, a level of intervention known as 'early years action' is initiated if there is concern; for example, if a child makes little or no progress, even when teaching approaches are targeted to improve the child's area of weakness. Appropriate intervention at this point may include the provision of different learning material or equipment or other approaches. Provision that is different from or additional to what is already provided is recorded on an individual education plan.

In certain circumstances the setting may initiate 'early years action plus', which is characterised by the involvement of external support services. The triggers for this include that, despite receiving an individualised programme and/or specialist support, the child continues working at an early years curriculum substantially below age expectations. Intervention at this stage may include external support services giving advice on new IEPs and targets, providing more specialist assessments, advising on new and specialist materials or strategies, or providing direct support. If concerns continue, the child may be referred for a statutory assessment that may lead to a statement of SEN.

Ofsted inspect SEN in the early years using a consistent framework across different establishments.

References

Department for Education and Skills (2001) *Special Educational Needs Code of Practice.* London: DfES.

Qualifications and Curriculum Authority (2000) *Curriculum Guidance for the Foundation Stage.* London: QCA.

Address

Qualifications and Curriculum Authority (QCA) Tel: 020 7509 5555
83 Piccadilly Fax: 020 7509 6666
London W1Y 7PD e-mail: info@qca.org.uk
  www.qca.org.uk

Foundation Stage Profile

A 'Foundation Stage Profile' formed the statutory assessment for the Foundation stage from September 2002, replacing the previous statutory baseline assessment.

Fragile X syndrome

Fragile X syndrome, the commonest cause of learning difficulties after Down's syndrome, is an inherited condition associated with a fragile site at the end of the X chromosome. While it affects both males and females, it is more common in boys. Both men and women can be carriers and genetic counselling is important for families in which there is Fragile X syndrome. Diagnosis is established by a Fragile X DNA test which is usually done on a blood sample. Its effects are very varied. Intellectual functioning is usually characterised by mild to moderate learning difficulties but up to one-third of children can have severe learning difficulties while others may have subtle cognitive impairments.

In the area of cognitive development, the child will have relatively better verbal skills than reasoning skills. Abstract reasoning tends to be diverted by the child paying heed to inconsequential features of tasks or events. Children with Fragile X find the concept of number and understanding arithmetical processes exceptionally difficult, while there may be relative strengths in vocabulary and reading for children at that level. Behaviour may be typified by a short attention span, distractibility, impulsiveness and over-activity. Shyness and social withdrawal may be found in girls. Many have autistic-like features – a lack of eye contact, difficulty in relating to other people, anxiety in social situations often leading to tantrums, insistence on familiar routines and hand flapping or hand biting. The child may be over-sensitive to perceived criticism or rejection and may overreact to comparatively small upsets. There may be a seeming need for frequent reassurance and security and the child may be overwhelmed by 'busy' environments. Speech and language may involve litany-like speech (up and down swings of pitch), and cluttering (a combination of rapid and dysrhythmic speech). The child may repeat the last word or phrases spoken to them or repeat their own words or phrases. Speech may also involve unrelated comments, digressions, jargon and stereotyped vocalisation. Physical features associated with Fragile X syndrome include a long narrow face and prominent ears but these are rarely obvious in young children. About 20 per cent of children with Fragile X have epilepsy.

Successful teaching approaches involve curriculum-referenced assessment (assessing what has been taught), straightforward teaching methods, rewards and praise for appropriate behaviour and learning, but insistence on appropriate behaviour, and structured teaching taking account of the child's level and extending new learning realistically. Learning outcomes should be clear to the child. The learning environment should be calm and uncluttered and a close partnership should be established with parents. Behaviour management may involve the principles of behaviour modification, for example being aware of the antecedents and consequences of the child's behaviour. Speech and language therapy is valuable.

Further reading
Saunders, S. (2001) *Fragile X Syndrome: A Guide for Teachers*. London: David Fulton Publishers.

Address
The Fragile X Society   Tel: 01424 813147
53 Winchelsea Lane   e-mail: lesleywalker@fragilex.k-web.co.uk
Hastings   www.fragilex.org.uk
East Sussex TN35 4LG

Formed in 1990 by the parents of children with Fragile X, the Society aims to improve the quality of life of those affected by the syndrome. It provides information and mutual support for families, raises public and professional awareness of Fragile X and encourages research.

Genetic disorders

1.   Genes and genetic disorders
Genes are the biological units of heredity arranged along the length of the chromosomes. At fertilisation half the chromosomes in the new organism come from the male and half from the female. A gene from the father will be matched by a gene from the mother. In the simplest cases, if both genes are disease bearing then the disease will be inherited by the child. If only a gene from one parent carries the disease then whether the child inherits the disease depends on whether the affected gene is dominant or recessive. If the gene is dominant the child will inherit the disease while if the gene is recessive the child will not. Where the situation is more complex, patterns of genes rather than single genes are involved. A single gene is involved in the inheritance of phenylketonuria (a metabolic disorder) which, if untreated, leads to severe learning difficulties. A pattern of genes is involved in the inheritance of certain neural tube defects such as spina bifida in which part of the spinal column does not close properly leaving part of the spinal cord insufficiently protected.

2.   Genetics
Genetics is concerned with the origins of the characteristics of an individual and the study of hereditary characteristics carried by genes. It includes the study of chromosome abnormalities. Genetics studies the process by which certain conditions are inherited. As these processes are made clear it is possible to identify genes which are responsible for conditions giving rise to special needs.

3.   Genetic counselling
Genetic counselling draws on family history, specific tests and knowledge of the relevant research literature. It involves discussing with prospective parents the probability of a particular condition being present in any children they may have in the future. Techniques have developed which bear on genetic counselling. One example is chorionic villus sampling in which chromosome abnormalities may be

detected in an unborn foetus by analysing a tissue sample from the placenta. With such techniques the possibility of terminating a pregnancy to avoid giving birth to a child having special needs arises. This requires specialised counselling exploring all the implications.

Further reading
Genetic Interest Group (2000) *Getting Involved in Research: A Guide for Individuals, Families and the Groups that Support Them.* London: Genetic Interest Group.
Marinker, M. and Peckham, M. (1998) *Clinical Futures.* London: BMJ Books.

Address
Genetic Interest Group   Tel: 020 7704 3141
Unit 4D   Fax: 020 7359 1447
Leroy House   e-mail: mail@gig.org.uk
436 Essex Road   www.gig.org.uk
London N1 3QP

An umbrella group for organisations involved with genetic disorders. Provides lists of genetic clinics and services.

Gentle teaching

Gentle teaching is an approach to dealing with severe problem ('challenging') behaviour, e.g. self-injurious behaviour. It emerged because of the perceived inadequacy of psychoactive medication and applied behaviour analysis in relation to challenging behaviour. Important aspects of gentle teaching are: non-aversiveness and the aim of teaching/bonding interdependence through gentleness and respect. Four interacting core themes characterise gentle teaching.

1. unconditional valuing
2. teaching the client to return value to others
3. need for staff to develop an attitude reflecting solidarity and mutuality
4. human engagement.

The approach has been presented as contrasting with aversive procedures. While gentle teaching differs from applied behaviour analysis in important ways, it does use certain behaviour change techniques.

A national support network for gentle teaching is coordinated through the Royal College of Nursing. Little evaluative work has been done but it appears that while gentle teaching is not universally effective, it may be effective in specific cases. The aspects of the approach which contribute to effectiveness and the factors of challenging behaviour which may respond to gentle teaching have yet to be determined.

Further reading
Hornby, A., Atkinson, M. and Howard, J. (1997) *Controversial Issues in Special Education.* London: David Fulton Publishers.

Governor

The duties of governing bodies are summarised in the *Special Educational Needs Code of Practice* (Department for Education and Skills 2001, e.g. 1.16–1.22).

Governing bodies, with the head teacher, should 'decide the school's general policy and approach to meeting pupils' special educational needs'. They must set up 'appropriate staffing and funding arrangements and oversee the school's work' (Code 1.16).

Under the Education Act 1996, section 317, governors of community, voluntary and foundation schools, and LEAs regarding maintained nursery schools, must 'do their best to ensure that the necessary provision is made for pupils with special educational needs' (Code 1.17).

Reference
Department for Education and Skills (2001) *Special Educational Needs Code of Practice.* London: DfES.

Further reading
Gordon, M. and Williams, A. (2002) *Special Educational Needs and Disability in Mainstream School: A Governors' Guide.* Stafford: National Association for Special Educational Needs.

Address
National Association of Governors and Managers (NAGM)
Suite 1
4th Floor
Smallbrook Queensway   Tel/Fax: 0121 643 5787
Birmingham B5 4HQ   e-mail: governorhg@nagm.org.uk
                                www.nagm.org.uk

The NAGM aims to enable school governors to play their part in promoting the best possible education for all pupils in schools.

Graduated response

In the *Special Educational Needs Code of Practice* (Department for Education and Skills 2001), a graduated approach concerns action and intervention in schools and early education settings to help pupils with special educational needs (SEN). Recognising that there is a continuum of SEN, the approach indicates that, as necessary, greater levels of specialist skills should be introduced.

In early education settings, where a pupil appears not to be making progress it may be necessary to 'present different opportunities or use alternative approaches to learning' (Code 4.9). Continuing difficulties may necessitate help at a level above that normally available in the setting. These approaches are termed, respectively, 'early years action' and 'early years action plus'. Decisions are informed by whether the child's current rate of progress is adequate or not (Code 4.13).

In the primary phase, similar approaches involve 'school action' and 'school action plus' (5.21). If a pupil with SEN is at 'serious risk of disaffection and exclusion', the individual education plan should reflect strategies to meet the needs of the pupil (5.52). In secondary school, the approach also involves 'school action' and 'school action plus' (6.23), and a similar approach to pupils at risk of disaffection and exclusion (6.60). In a few cases the local education authority makes a statutory assessment and then considers whether or not to issue a statement of SEN (7.1).

Reference
Department for Education and Skills (2001) *Special Educational Needs Code of Practice*. London: DfES.

Group education plan

It has been suggested that where pupils in the same class, group or subject lesson have common targets 'and hence common strategies' (Department for Education and Skills 2001: 203), a group education plan may be used rather than individual education plans for each child. However, this makes the sometimes false assumption that common targets are reached appropriately by all children by common strategies. Also, as an attempt to reduce paperwork it is weak, as once pupils start to progress at different rates, individual education plans are likely to provide a clearer picture of the child's progress.

Reference
Department for Education and Skills (2001) *Special Educational Needs Code of Practice*. London: DfES.

Head teacher

Within the *Special Educational Needs Code of Practice* (DfES 2000) the head teacher (or the appropriate governor) is the 'responsible person'. The responsible person must be informed by the LEA when the LEA decides that a pupil has special educational needs (SEN). The responsible person must then ensure that all those who will teach the child know about his or her SEN. The head teacher has duties under the Code annual review system. These can be delegated to a teacher at the school.

Reference
Department for Education and Skills (2001) *Special Educational Needs Code of Practice*. London: DfES.

Addresses

National Association of Headteachers
1 Heath Square
Boltro Road
Haywards Heath
West Sussex RH16 1BL

Tel: 01444 472472
Fax: 01444 472473
e-mail: info@naht.org.uk
www.naht.org.uk

The National Association of Headteachers is a registered trade union for head teachers and deputies of all types of schools. Special education conferences have been run for many years and professional support is provided through a national network of regional officers, backed up by headquarters staff, who include solicitors, professional advisers and specialists in educational, salaries, pensions and conditions of service matters. A range of support documents published by the Association are prepared with the specific needs of head teachers and deputies in mind. The NAHT offers unlimited legal support and gives members ready access to support and advice.

Secondary Heads Association
130 Regent Road
Leicester LE1 7PG

Tel: 0116 299 1122
Fax: 0116 299 1123
e-mail: info@sha.org.uk
www.sha.org.uk

The Secondary Heads Association represents the majority of heads and deputies in all types of secondary schools including special schools. It offers a range of professional services, including a personal 'hotline' advisory service to every member. SHA is the only association which speaks exclusively for secondary education.

Health service

Healthcare in England can be understood in terms of national, regional and local responsibilities. At the national level, the Department of Health is responsible for the health services and the personal social services in England. The Secretary of State for Health is responsible to Parliament for the provision of health services and is assisted by a Policy Board and the National Health Service (NHS) Executive. The Policy Board sets the broad strategic direction of the NHS while the NHS Executive deals with operational issues within this strategy.

At the regional level, there are regional offices (e.g. London, North West, West Midlands) of the NHS Executive with responsibilities for such things as monitoring the performance of local health authorities and trusts.

Locally, important parts of the structure are:

- health authorities;
- NHS Trusts; and
- primary care groups, or primary care trusts.

Health Authorities provide strategic leadership and are responsible for seeing that primary care groups (and primary care trusts) take forward improvements in care. They also have responsibility for enabling NHS Trusts and local authorities to take a full role in improving local health.

NHS Trusts provide most hospital services and community services. They are responsible to the local health authorities and to the primary care groups for the services that they deliver and to the NHS Executive for their statutory duties.

Primary care groups comprise all general practitioners (GPs) in the locality and community based professionals. These groups are responsible for commissioning local services and work closely with local social services departments. Primary care groups may be free-standing primary care trusts with the extra responsibility of running community hospitals and community health services. GPs have the status of independent contractors.

Contact with healthcare professionals differs in different circumstances. Early education practitioners should get advice from their local Early Years Development and Childcare Partnership about what partnership arrangements are in place with local agencies.

For schools, the initial contact with health services is likely to be through school health services represented by a school doctor or nurse. These health professionals will be likely to be able to advise the school and, if a problem is identified, should inform the medical officer designated to work with children with SEN that the school has asked for advice. Other healthcare professionals such as speech and language therapists also give advice and support to pupils with SEN.

When they consider that a child has SEN, health authorities and trusts must provide parents with information on local statutory services and voluntary services that might be able to help them.

Should a school be concerned about the educational progress of a child it should, in cooperation with parents, consult the school health service or the child's general practitioner about whether a medical condition may be contributing. If the child's difficulties indicate that he may require a statutory assessment, the health professional consulted should, with parental consent, notify and give necessary medical information to a particular colleague. This colleague is the medical officer designated by the health authority to work with the LEA on behalf of children with SEN and to lead the contribution of the health authority to the statutory assessment.

The health authority should agree with the primary care groups and trusts how its contribution to statutory assessment and to meeting the medical needs of children will be carried out. Primary Care Trusts and Community Trusts may employ the staff from whom the health authority designate the medical officer for SEN. This officer has strategic and operational roles in coordinating activity across health authorities, NHS trusts, primary care groups and general practitioners. These roles are outlined in the *Special Educational Needs Code of Practice* (Department for Education and Skills 2001). They include that the designated medical officer should ensure that all schools should have a contact, usually with the school health service, for seeking medical advice on children who may have SEN (Code 10.26).

Reference
Department for Education and Skills (2001) *Special Educational Needs Code of Practice.* London: DfES.

Address
Department of Health   Tel: 020 7210 4850
Richmond House   Fax: 020 7210 5661
Whitehall   e-mail: dhmail@doh.gsi
London SW1A 2NL   www.nhs.gov.uk

Health visitor

A health visitor is a State Registered Nurse who has undergone extra training and who is a member of the community health team. With a focus on preventive medicine, the health visitor:

• visits all homes having a child under five years old
• screens children for special needs
• provides information on health and welfare services
• provides counselling and support for parents.

The health visitor is an important bridge between a family which has a child with special needs and the health service and education service.

Address
United Kingdom Central Council for Nursing (UKCC)   Tel: 020 7637 7181
Midwifery and Health Visiting   Fax: 020 7436 2924
23 Portland Place   www.ukcc.org.uk
London W1N 3AF

The UKCC is the regulatory body of nursing, midwifery and health visiting professionals throughout the United Kingdom. The principal duties of the Council are to establish and improve standards of training and professional conduct of nursing, midwifery and health visiting. The UKCC deals with policy and not directly with the operational aspects of training.

Hearing impairment

Under this entry, frequency and intensity, two important aspects of sound are considered, along with screening tests of hearing; conductive hearing loss; sensori-neural hearing loss; the effects of hearing impairment; and the educational implications.

1.   Frequency
Frequency concerns the rate at which sound waves vibrate and are usually measured in cycles per second (cps). Sound frequency is perceived as pitch, with rapidly vibrating sound waves creating a perception of high pitch and slowly vibrating waves being perceived as low-pitched sounds. The normal human ear is responsive to sounds between 60 and 16,000 cps and most responsive to sounds between 500 and 4,000 cps. Speech sounds occupy the most responsive band and particular speech sounds often involve several frequencies. Vowels tend to occupy the lower frequency range while sibilants and fricatives (e.g. s, f, th, sh) tend to occupy the higher ones. Hearing losses rarely affect all frequencies equally, so hearing is usually distorted. With high frequency hearing loss, the ability to hear sibilants and fricatives is reduced. In low frequency hearing loss, the ability to hear vowels is impaired. Because consonants make speech intelligible, high frequency hearing loss is usually the more serious.

2.   Intensity/amplitude
The intensity of a sound is experienced as loudness. Intensity is measured on the decibel scale. The quietest audible sound is given a value of 0. The loudest sound attains a value of 140. Normal speech is about 60 decibels (dB). Hearing impairment can be measured on the decibel scale in terms of dB loss. The system recommended by the British Association of Teachers of the Deaf has four categories of hearing impairment.

   a) slight; not exceeding 40 dB loss
   b) moderate; 41 to 70 dB loss
   c) severe, 71 to 95 dB loss, and postlingual losses, greater than 95 dB
   d) profound; at least 96 dB loss, acquired prelingually.

The distinction in categories (c) and (d) between prelingual and postlingual loss, is important for future communication. A child who has experience of hearing and using speech, may already be speaking and may wish to continue. However, a child with a similar loss which occurred prelingually, would find speech communication more difficult.

3.   Screening tests of hearing
The cooperative test of hearing is used with children aged 18 to 30 months and requires the child to understand language and follow instructions using toys. The distraction test is used with children aged 6 to 18 months. Two testers are involved.

The first gets the baby's attention. The second tester provides a controlled sound signal outside the baby's vision. The baby is expected to turn his or her head to the sound. The test is repeated for each ear at around 35 decibels and for high and low frequencies.

4. Conductive hearing loss

Two forms of hearing loss are usually distinguished; conductive and sensori-neural, with the latter usually being more serious. Conductive hearing loss is caused when there are difficulties in sound being transmitted into the ear canal or across the middle ear system. It affects all levels of sound frequency which impairs hearing sensitivity to all levels of pitch (rather than sound distortion). About one in five children are affected with conductive hearing loss and most instances do not cause lasting difficulties. Causes of conductive hearing loss include otitis media (an infection or inflammation of the middle ear), malformations of the outer and/or inner ear, and obstructions in the middle ear (e.g. wax). Glue ear, caused by inflammation of the middle ear, may be treated with antibiotics if it is caused by infection. Decongestants are used to dry out the middle ear. In chronic cases, the fluid can be drained and a grommet (a tiny tube) placed in the ear drum to keep the middle ear ventilated. Conductive hearing loss may be associated with delayed language development perhaps affecting language structure, as well as speech; difficulty in discriminating sounds which may make learning to read more difficult; and poor concentration.

5. Sensori-neural hearing loss

This is caused by damage to the inner ear and/or auditory nerves. It may have various causes:

- congenital
- inherited
- maternal illness during pregnancy (e.g. rubella)
- anoxia (a state in which the body lacks oxygen) during birth
- postnatal e.g. effects of certain viral illnesses (e.g. meningitis)

Severe sensori-neural hearing loss occurs in about one child in every one thousand and many affected children experience conductive loss also. Often hearing of higher frequencies is more affected than that of lower frequencies leading to distorted hearing for which a hearing aid offers limited help. The potential impact that sensori-neural hearing loss has on a child's education may be mitigated by early diagnosis.

6. Effects of hearing impairment

The effects of hearing impairment depend on various factors including: the size of dB loss; the frequencies affected and the speech sounds which will be difficult; any perceptual damage; past experience including teaching; the age at which the hearing impairment occurred; and parental support given to the child.

7. Educational implications

The child with HI may be educated in a special school, a unit attached to an ordinary school or in a mainstream classroom. If education is in a mainstream classroom, support for both child and teacher may be provided by advisers, peripatetic specialist teachers, **audiologists** and others. The appropriate form of communication should be used which may be speech, sign language or both. Sign language is usually chosen where the hearing impairment is greater. Particular attention needs to be given to encouraging and aiding language development and to the teaching of reading. In the 1990s, support grew for 'bilingualism' which involves deaf children being taught their native sign language as their first language. English is then taught as a second language.

(See also *Aids to hearing, Sign language, Total communication*)

Further reading
Gravell, R. and Johnson, R. (2001) (eds) *Ballantyne's Deafness* (6th edn). London: Whurr.
Watson, L., Gregory, S. and Powers, S. (1999) *Deaf and Hearing Impaired Pupils in Mainstream Schools.* London: David Fulton Publishers.

Address
British Association of Teachers of the Deaf (BATOD) Tel: 01494 464 190
21 The Haystacks   Fax: 01494 464 190
High Wycombe   e-mail: secretary@batod.org.uk
Buckinghamshire HP13 6PY   www.batod.org.uk

BATOD promotes the educational interests of all hearing impaired children, young people and adults and safeguards the interests of teachers of the deaf. Conferences are organised nationally to develop the professional expertise of Association members and to promote issues connected with the education of hearing impaired children. Seven regions organise workshops and activities locally. Courses and conferences are open to non-members. Associate membership is open to those who are not qualified teachers of the deaf.

Higher education
The Special Educational Needs and Disability Act 2001 places duties on further and higher education institutions and local education authorities in respect of adult education and youth services. There is a duty not to treat disabled students less favourably, without justification, for a reason relating to their disability. There is also a duty to make reasonable adjustments to ensure that people who are disabled are not put at a substantial disadvantage to people who are not disabled in accessing higher education, further education and LEA secured education.

The Open University, for example, encourages students with special needs through open entry arrangements on a first come first served basis; open learning and home study, and special provisions for disabled students such as special induction courses for students with disabilities.

Further reading
Skill: The National Bureau for Students with Disabilities (1998) *Higher Education and Disability.* London: NBSD.

Address
Office for Students with Disabilities   Tel: 01908 274 066
Open University   Fax: 01908 653 744
Walton Hall   e-mail: ces-gen@open.ac.uk
Milton Keynes MK7 6AA   www.open.ac.uk

The Open University supports its 5,000 disabled students through a range of services including alternative course materials, special study equipment, human resources (e.g. helpers, interpreters, lipspeakers) and locally-based counselling and teaching staff. Services are coordinated at the OU's headquarters by the Office for Students with Disabilities.

History of special education

For most non-specialists, views of the history of special education are obtained from texts concerning such history rather than from primary sources. When considering such texts, therefore, among the questions that may be asked are:

- Who was being educated? (e.g. rich, poor, blind, deaf, 'idiots').
- By whom were they being educated? (e.g. private tutors, school teachers, men, women, the State, charities, the Church, industrialists).
- To what purpose were they being educated? (e.g. for independence, for work).
- When were they being educated? (e.g. in the nineteenth century, the twentieth century).
- Where were they being educated? (e.g. England, France, countryside, industrial towns).
- For whose benefit were they being educated? (e.g. for society, for themselves, for industrialists).

Each of these questions taken in different combinations reveal different perspectives. There is a balance to be struck between facts and interpretation or what has been called 'an unending dialogue beween the present and the past' (Carr 1987). This applies to any history of special education. Any approach to history is shaped by the historian's access to, selection of and interpretation of so-called historical facts. Also, history remains important because it is not solely to do with gathering 'incontrovertible' facts about the past but also about the re-interpretation of the past through the concerns of the present. These current preoccupations affect not just the way we see facts, but also the selection of the facts considered relevant. When a particular perspective is taken in advance, it is beneficial if the perspective is made clear and explicit, but it remains a difficulty that readers are not party to the 'facts' that have been sifted out because they were not considered pertinent.

Texts may seek to offer a broad history of special education (e.g. Safford and Safford 1996) or a thematic history (e.g. Cole 1989). They may explicitly take a particular viewpoint such as a sociological one (e.g. Tomlinson 1982) or focus on a particular country and period of time (e.g. Pritchard 1963).

References
Carr, E. H. (1987) *What is History?* London: Penguin.
Cole, T. (1989) *Apart or a Part? Integration and the Growth of British Special Education.* Milton Keynes: Open University Press.
Pritchard, D. G. (1963) *Education of the Handicapped 1760–1960.* London: Routledge & Kegan Paul.
Safford, P. L. and Safford, E. J. (1996) *A History of Childhood and Disability.* New York: Teachers College Press, Colombia University.
Tomlinson, S. (1982) *A Sociology of Special Education.* London: Routledge & Kegan Paul.

Home education

Home education may overlap with the education of sick children in that such children may be educated at home. Also, children with emotional and behavioural difficulties who are unable to attend school may be taught at home. Home education (or home tuition) is provided by local education authorities. Home teachers usually work for an agreed number of half days a week with a pupil, liaising with the pupil's school to assist the pupil's return to school when appropriate.

Further reading

Department for Education (1994) *Circular 11/94: The Education by LEAs of Children Otherwise than at School*. London: DFE.

Hospital school

A hospital school, a special school maintained by a local education authority on hospital premises, is subject to the School Standards Framework Act 1998, section 31 and schedule 6. These relate to the establishment of such schools, their 'discontinuance' and making prescribed alterations. While hospital schools are not legally obliged to offer the National Curriculum, guidance (Department for Education and Skills 2001, para 8.10) indicates that they should 'make every effort' to offer a full National Curriculum where the hospital situation allows. Hospital schools have delegated responsibility for their budget. The age range of pupils in hospital schools is from those under five years old to students in further education colleges studying for examinations. Most pupils are in-patients. Some chronically ill children attend daily from home. Some are admitted for a few days, others for much longer. Some pupils attend hospital school for a few days a week and go back home for the remaining days.

Further reading

Department for Education and Skills (2001) *Access to Education for Children and Young People with Medical Needs*. London: DfES.

Identification (of special educational needs)

Identification of special educational needs (SEN) is a key part of the *Special Educational Needs Code of Practice* (DfES 2001). Among the essential functions of the local education authority are that: 'the needs of children and young people with SEN are identified and assessed quickly and matched by appropriate provision' (1.11). In early years settings, the initial identification of a child's SEN may be made by the early years practitioner or the SEN coordinator; in the primary phase initial identification is by the class teacher or the SENCO and in the secondary phase by the subject teacher, member of the pastoral team or the SENCO. This has clear implications that all teachers need an awareness and knowledge of SEN. Screening and assessment tools and the assessment of children within the National Curriculum may be used to assist the identification of SEN.

It is acknowledged that SEN is contextual in that the learning environment and the child interact. At the same time, assessments are used to give an indication of a child's performance against national norms or against diagnostic criteria. Reading tests may be used to give an indication of difficulties. Such tests may be a useful screening device particularly in large secondary schools. However, the next step is to focus on children who appear to be having difficulty in a more individual way, through diagnostic assessment and through formative assessment which inform teaching.

With children under two years old it is more likely that any SEN will have been first identified by parents, the child health services or social services.

Reference

Department for Education and Skills (2001) *Special Educational Needs Code of Practice*. London: DfES.

Address

Department for Education and Skills
Sanctuary Buildings
Great Smith Street
London SW1P 3BT

Tel: 020 7925 5000
Fax: 020 7925 6000
e-mail: info @dfes.gsi.gov.uk
www.dfee.gov.uk

Impairment

Impairment refers to personal limitations brought about by the loss of physical, sensory or mental functioning. Examples are dual sensory impairment, hearing impairment, language impairment, visual impairment and motor impairment.

Under the Disability Discrimination Act 1995, section 1(1), a person has a disability if 'he has a physical or mental impairment which has a substantial or long-term adverse effect on his ability to carry out normal day-to-day activities'. This impairment relating to disability does not necessarily mean that if that person is a child he will have SEN. For although the legal definition of SEN in the Education Act 1996, section 312, includes the term 'disability', this has to be such that it 'prevents or hinders them from making use of the educational facilities of a kind generally provided for children of the same age in schools within the area of a local education authority'. Even then, the disability may be seen as leading to a learning difficulty but that learning difficulty, would have to be such that it 'calls for special educational provision' to be made in order for there to be an SEN.

Inclusion

Inclusion is a broader concept than one relating only to special education. But the implications of an inclusive perspective for pupils with special educational needs (SEN) may be considered as an aspect of wider inclusion. An inclusive approach is sometimes associated with a more subjective, sociologically influenced view of education which seeks to avoid labelling and potential stigma, the categorisation of children and an overly technocratic and mechanistic approach to teaching. In this respect it is sometimes contrasted with an extreme, more objective medical-psychological perspective concerned with diagnosis and treatment. Whereas someone taking a medical-psychological view might think in terms of identification, assessment and provision for pupils, one taking an inclusive approach might see an opportunity to celebrate diversity.

An attempt to recognise the breadth of the concept of inclusion was made in the *Programme of Action* (Department for Education and Employment 1998) which stated that the term can include:

- the participation of young people in the full range of social experiences and opportunities once they have left school;
- the participation of all pupils in the curriculum and social life of mainstream schools and in learning which leads to the highest level of achievement; and
- the placement of pupils with SEN in mainstream schools.

                                                    (adapted from Chapter 3, paragraph 3)

Taking a slightly different approach to the *Programme of Action*, three strands of inclusion are evident that relate to pupils with SEN, although the three may interrelate.

First, the approach to social inclusion reflected in such documents as *Circular 10/99* (Department for Education and Employment 1999a) and *Circular 11/99* (Department for Education and Employment 1999b). *Circular 10/99* mentions that among children at risk of exclusion from school are those with SEN who develop challenging behaviour. *Circular 11/99* suggests that LEAs consider legal remedies to compel the attendance of non-attending pupils. The inclusion of some of these children may involve providing education in a pupil support unit or pupil referral unit.

Secondly, there is a concern to include children who are already in mainstream schools. This involves developing a culture of inclusion in mainstream schools. It implies encouraging schools to reconsider their structure, teaching approaches, pupil grouping and use of support so that they respond to the diverse learning needs of all their pupils. Teachers need to develop opportunities to look at new ways of involving all pupils and draw on experimentation and reflection. For the school, a central necessity for inclusion is providing planned access to a broad and balanced curriculum which is developed from its foundations as a curriculum for all pupils. Teachers are likely to hold values that provide a rationale for inclusive practice, believing that pupils with SEN belong in mainstream classes. There will be a commitment to reviewing performance and a commitment to change. Teachers will draw on a variety of instructional approaches, for example providing choice in tasks and activities and encouraging different ways for pupils to access and express knowledge and skills. Collaborative problem solving is important to seek solutions to challenges that arise when teaching a diverse group of pupils.

Thirdly, inclusion may relate to increasing the proportion of pupils in mainstream schools in relation to those in specialist provision, such as that provided by a special school or a pupil referral unit. This view of inclusion was evident in the 'SEN Green Paper' (Department for Education and Employment 1997: 43) which stated that:

> The ultimate purpose of SEN provision is to enable young people to flourish in adult life. There are therefore strong educational, as well as social and moral, grounds for educating children with SEN with their peers. We aim to increase the level and quality of inclusion within mainstream schools, while protecting and enhancing specialist provision for those who need it.

If it is the intention of government to reduce 'segregated' provision, it is not clear why the intention should be to reduce segregated provision in special schools while not doing so in other provision segregated according to religion (Jewish, Muslim schools), ability (Beacon schools), and gender (single-sex schools).

References

Department for Education and Employment (1997) *Excellence for All Children: Meeting Special Educational Needs*. London: DfEE.

Department for Education and Employment (1998) *Meeting Special Educational Needs: A Programme of Action*. London: DfEE.

Department for Education and Employment (1999a) *Circular 10/99 Social Inclusion: Pupil Support*. London: DfEE.

Department for Education and Employment (1999b) *Circular 11/99 Social Inclusion: The LEA Role in Pupil Support*. London: DfEE.

Further reading

Booth, T. and Ainscow, M., with Black-Hawkins, K. (2000) *Index for Inclusion: Developing Learning and Participation in Schools*. Bristol: Centre for Studies for Inclusion in Education.

Cheminais, R. (2001) *Developing Inclusive School Practice: A Practical Guide*. London: David Fulton Publishers.

Lorenz, S. (2001) *First Steps in Inclusion: A Handbook for Teachers, School Governors and Managers and LEAs*. London: David Fulton Publishers.

Address

Centre for Studies on Inclusive Education (CSIE)
Room 2S 203
S Block   Tel: 0117 344 4007
Frenchaz Campus   Fax: 0117 344 4005
Cold Harbour Lane   www.inclusion.org.uk
Bristol BS16 1QU

The CSIE is a charity pressing for the inclusion of disabled pupils in mainstream schools.

Incontinence

Incontinence of urine (enuresis) is more common at night as bed-wetting than during the day. By the age of four most children are dry both day and night. Only at about the age of five is regular incontinence of urine seen as problematic. Night time bed-wetting creates extra work at home and restricts visits away from home. In residential schools it can be a source of shame and embarrassment with peers. Day time enuresis can create difficulties with teachers and peers at school.

The treatment of enuresis consists of addressing any physical reasons, restricting fluid intake, encouragement and behavioural training. The most widely known form of behavioural treatment of bed-wetting is the bell and pad method. A battery operated bell/buzzer is placed under the bottom bed sheet and a rubber sheet is placed beneath the bell. When the child passes urine the pad becomes wet and completes an electrical circuit which sounds the bell. This wakes the child who has to get out of bed to switch off the alarm. The child then goes to the toilet. Eventually, in many cases, the bladder pressure which preceded the alarm, acts as the trigger to wake the child who then visits the toilet.

Incontinence of faeces (encopresis) usually ceases around three years of age. If soiling continues after four years old, it is seen as problematic. It creates similar difficulties to enuresis. Its treatment involves tackling any physical causes first, providing effective toilet training and, if the condition appears to be related to emotional problems, providing therapy involving the family.

Address

Enuresis Resource and Information Centre   Tel: 0117 960 3060
34 Old School House   Fax: 0117 960 0401
Britannia Road   e-mail: enuresis@compuserve.com
Kingswood   www.enuresis.org.uk
Bristol BS15 2DB

Independent parental supporter

All parents who wish it should have access to an independent parental supporter. They must be able to support parents through, for example, attending meetings, helping parents understand the SEN framework and encouraging parents to participate. They are independent of the decision-making process determining the type and level of support for a child with SEN. Often they will be from a voluntary organisation or a parent partnership service or they may be another parent or a friend.

Independent school

An independent school is not maintained by a local education authority and is registered under the Education Act 1996, section 464. Conditions exist under which the Secretary of State may approve an independent school as being suitable to admit children with statements of SEN. These are set out in the Education Act 1996, section 347.

Concerning statutory assessment of SEN, where a child attends an independent school, the LEA may only hear about the child when a parent or the school requests an assessment. The *Special Educational Needs Code of Practice* (DfES 2001) states that the procedures that the LEA follows and the factors to be considered in deciding whether to make an assessment 'should be the same as if the child were in a maintained school.' (Code 7.24)

One of the exceptions to the eight-week time limit for making a statement of SEN is set out in The Education (Special Educational Needs) (Consolidation) Regulations 2001, section 17 (4)(e). This arises where the LEA sent a written request to the Secretary of State seeking consent that a child be educated in an independent school which is not approved by the Secretary of State. If the consent is not received by the LEA within two weeks of the request being made an exception to the eight-week time limit is allowed.

Parents may place a child with a statement in an independent school or in a non-maintained special school at their own expense. However, the LEA must still be satisfied that the school is able to make the provision set out in the statement before they are relieved of their duty to arrange that provision.

References

Department for Education and Skills (2001) *Special Education Needs Code of Practice.* London: DfES.

Address
Independent Schools Council Information Service (ISCis)
Grosvenor Gardens House   Tel: 020 7798 1500
Grosvenor Gardens   Fax: 020 7798 1531
London SW1W 0BS   e-mail: info@iscis.uk.net
                                www.iscis.org.uk

ISCis carries out the information, public relations and media activities of the Independent Schools Council. It produces publications for parents and *mISC*, the magazine of the Independent Schools Council. ISCis answers requests for information from parents, schools, researchers and others.

Individual Education Plan (IEP)

An IEP is a working document relating to planning, teaching and reviewing progress. It records short-term targets and strategies for individual pupils that are different from, or additional to, those applying to the rest of the class or group. IEPs are used for early years action, early years action plus, school action, school action plus and for pupils with statements of SEN.

Much of good practice relating to IEPs is common to the earlier development of individual programme planning (IPP). A particular application of IPP was an approach to individualised teaching of priority needs used especially with people with severe or profound and multiple learning difficulties. It began with an assessment of an individual pupil's needs and strengths and a critical consideration of whether existing curriculum provision met those needs. Where an aspect of need was not met, an IPP was devised as an integrated part of programme and curriculum delivery to help ensure that the necessary learning took place.

The IPP contributed to the development of school programmes and the school curriculum. IIPs drew on a combination of information processing, cognitive and behavioural approaches. Communication with the pupil and with carers and other colleagues was vital.

Practical steps included:

- Initial assessment.
- Identifying a 'need' and a specific, achievable goal.
- Establishing a baseline of performance/behaviour/understanding.
- Diagrammatically indicating how the skill to be taught related to the overall teaching aims of the pupil concerned. This comprised showing in the curricular area to be covered (e.g. social skills) the final aim and large steps to be covered eventually (e.g. pupil eats appropriately); and showing the specific task to be taught (e.g. picks up and holds a spoon correctly for eating) and the increments leading to this skill and their relationship with each other.
- Planning a teaching method to get from the baseline to the target. Steps and methods were explicit and it was clear how they applied to the learner concerned. Reinforcers were used as necessary.
- Deciding on the time scale and reviewing it in the light of progress.
- Recording progress so that the direction of learning was clear and so it was apparent when the IPP needed to be modified. Ensuring that the records were clear to the pupil and to colleagues.

- Evaluating the IPP and the success or otherwise of the teaching.
- Making evaluation both formative and summative.

Formative evaluation involved amending the IPP as teaching progresses to ensure, for example, that the most appropriate method was being used, that the steps were correctly sequenced and neither too small nor too large, that progress was being made and that the learning was being generalised.

Summative assessment concerned such issues as checking that what was achieved was what was intended, whether IPP was the correct and most appropriate approach for the task and considering the implications for curriculum organisation and delivery.

It was important to build into the IPP procedures that helped ensure generalisation of learning. If teaching the use of a spoon, for example, the programme included such variations as different sized spoons and spoons of different materials and colours and using a spoon in various venues. This ensured that the learner was not limited to one particular spoon in one setting. Part of the assessment included 'probes' to ensure that generalisation was taking place. A related aspect was discrimination and this was built into the teaching. It was important (using our example) that a spoon was used in the appropriate circumstances. For instance, the learner should not take and use a spoon from someone else's table place setting.

Clearly, much of the approach associated with IPP is directly relevant to the development of effective IEPs. IPP was often delivered in discrete sessions of say 15 minutes, twice per day. IEPs may be approached in a similar way. However, they may also be applied in a more general way. For example, a target on an IEP may be tackled in a discrete session but also worked on as need arises. Also, specific sessions may be devoted to improving an aspect of number work, but this may be reinforced in a planned way in general classroom work.

A weakness of IEPs is that it is difficult to determine whether targets are sufficiently challenging.

Further reading
Department for Education and Skills (2001) *SEN Toolkit Section 5: Managing Individual Education Plans*. London: DfES.

Individualised teaching

Individualised teaching in a class or group context involves the teacher being aware of the special educational needs of each pupil and using a variety of methods to meet those individual needs. At the same time, the teacher should encourage each child to communicate with others in the group so that social and personal skills are not lost in the focus of individual need.

Induction period (newly qualified teacher)

In relation to special educational needs (SEN), newly qualified teachers are expected to refine and develop the skills, knowledge and attitudes associated with the requirements of qualified teacher status and initial teacher training. Standards for determining whether an NQT has satisfactorily completed an induction period are set out in Annex A of *The Induction Period for Newly Qualified Teachers*

(Department for Education and Skills 2002). The head teacher, to recommend that an NQT has satisfactorily completed the induction period, has to be satisfied on two points. First, the NQT should have continued to meet the standards for the award of qualified teacher status, 'consistently in teaching at the school'. Secondly, the NQT should have met all the induction standards.

In the section of these standards concerning 'planning, teaching and class management', the NQT must demonstrate that he or she 'plans effectively, where applicable, to meet the needs of pupils with special educational needs'. Regarding 'monitoring, assessment, recording, reporting and accountability', the NQT has duties relating to all pupils – such as liaising effectively with parents – that are particularly important for pupils with SEN. Under 'other professional requirements', again there are duties to all pupils such as deploying support staff effectively who have particular relevance to pupils with SEN.

Reference
Department for Education and Skills (2002) *The Induction Period for Newly Qualified Teachers*. London: DfES.

Further reading
Cheminais, R. (2002) (ed. Gains, C.) *Special Educational Needs for Newly Qualified and Student Teachers: A Practical Guide*. London: David Fulton Publishers.

Address
General Teaching Council for England
344-54 Grays Inn Road
London WC1X 8BP

Tel: 0870 001 0308
Fax: 020 7841 2909
e-mail: tqhelpdesk@gtce.org.uk
www.gtce.org.uk

Information and Communications Technology (ICT)

ICT is used in relation to a wide range of special educational needs (SEN). It may enhance the communication of people with motor and/or sensory disabilities. It can refine the discrimination practicable for individual pupils to work at a pace and level appropriate for them. Virtual reality developments have also found innovative applications. Architectural simulations of a pupil's school have been used to help pupils in wheelchairs plan and practise routes through the school and gain 'experience' of them before physically attempting the routes themselves. Software has been designed which improves access to learning (e.g. to literacy). Speech input and speech output devices are available. Peripherals, devices and software utilities can open up 'ordinary' software to learners with disabilities. CD-ROM technology can be made more accessible to learners with physical or sensory impairments. Software is available to improve visual and auditory skills, spelling, early language, reading for meaning and to support writing and keyboard skills. Some software is suitable for pupils with dyslexia. ICT is also used to support learners with severe learning difficulties. ICT has been used to support vocational work in colleges using strategies which include overlay keyboards for topic vocabulary, digitised images and symbols for understanding and communicating, and simplified spreadsheets.

Among ICT provision that may be particularly helpful for different aspects of SEN are the following:

- learning difficulties: word processing facilities, overlay keyboards and software speech output, on-screen word banks;
- severe or profound and multiple learning difficulties: progressive, developmentally based activities (for both assessment and teaching) – these may include experimental visual and auditory stimulation; cause and effect through pressing a switch or touching a screen to create or change shape, pattern and object animation, phased switch building, timed activation, and making choices through row scanning;
- specific learning difficulties: word processing facilities including spell checkers and other software, direct speech input, voice output, word prediction software;
- emotional and behavioural difficulties: word processing facilities, painting programs and other software which encourages communication and self-expression, desktop publishing, spreadsheets;
- physical disabilities: special keyboards and switch input to allow access to word processing facilities and software, adaptations to overcome problems using a mouse, speech input, on-screen 'keyboards', Internet;
- hearing difficulties: word processing facilities, painting programs and other software which uses the visual power of the computer;
- visual difficulties: voice synthesisers linked to computers, speech input and screen magnification software to gain access to standard software, Braille input and output systems;
- speech and language difficulties: word processing facilities, painting programs, software which encourages communication and self-expression, speech output technology for pupils with severe language difficulties, a graphic capability such as icons and symbols.

Further reading
Hardy, C. (2000) *Information and Communications Technology for All.* London: David Fulton Publishers.

Address
British Educational Communications Technology Agency (BECTA)

Milburn Hill Road	Tel: 024 7641 6994; Dialcom: 84: MTT 005
Science Park	Fax: 024 7641 1418
Coventry CV4 7JJ	e-mail: becta@becta.org.uk
	www.becta.org.uk

BECTA aims to develop and promote the use of ICT in every area of education and training. It researches and evaluates the relevance of new technologies to enhance learning and raise standards in teaching and learning. It promotes their effective use across all sectors of education. It also produces publications relating to special education. BECTA is responsible for developing the National Grid for Learning.

Initial teacher training (student teacher)

The government has set out professional standards for qualified teacher status (QTS) and requirements for initial teacher training (ITT) (Department for Education and Skills 2002). The standards for the award of QTS are 'outcome statements', setting down the knowledge, understanding and skills necessary. They represent the minimum legal requirement, and trainers may provide additional training by offering a specialised area of study such as the teaching of pupils with SEN (ibid.: 3). The standards are organised in three interrelated sections describing the criteria for the award:

- professional values and practice;
- knowledge and understanding; and
- teaching.

Within the section on 'professional values and practice', the requirements relating to all pupils naturally concern pupils with SEN; for example that the teacher must demonstrate that 'they understand the contribution that support staff and other professionals make to teaching and learning' (p. 6). In the 'knowledge and understanding' section are requirements that apply to all pupils, including those with SEN, and also a particular requirement that the teacher must show that, 'They understand their responsibilities under the *Special Educational Needs Code of Practice* and know how to seek advice from specialists on less common types of SEN' (p. 8). In the section on 'Teaching' are sub-sections concerning, 'planning, expectations and targets', 'monitoring and assessment' and 'teaching and class management'. Again, as well as requirements applying to all pupils, including those with SEN, there are specific requirements. They include being able to identify and support pupils 'who experience behavioural, emotional and social difficulties' (3.24) and differentiating teaching to meet the needs of pupils, including 'those with SEN'.

The requirement for ITT providers concerns the management of ITT partnership and quality assurance.

Reference
Department for Education and Skills (2002) *Qualifying to Teach: Professional Standards for Qualified Teacher Status and Requirements for Initial Teacher Training*. London: DfES.

Further reading
Farrell, M. (2003) *Understanding Special Educational Needs: A Guide for New and Student Teachers*. London: Routledge.

Inspections

Office for Standards in Education (Ofsted) inspections aim to identify strengths and weaknesses in provision so that schools can improve the quality of education which they provide and raise the standards achieved by pupils. In 'mainstream' schools, the inspection team will have certain expectations including the following:

- The school should be fully aware of the *Special Educational Needs Code of Practice* (DfES 2001) and have taken heed of its recommendations.
- The school's SEN policy should be current and accurate and should be being implemented.
- All documents (e.g. Individual Education Plans) should be up to date and sufficient.
- SEN should concern the whole school including governors, not only the designated person.
- Statements of SEN should be fully implemented, parents and pupils should be involved in decisions and annual reviews should be thorough.

- Extended curricular activities should contribute to the experiences offered to pupils with SEN.

Special schools are subject to the same inspection procedure as mainstream schools, but there is also specific guidance to inspectors concerning special schools.

Schools draw up action plans after an inspection and guidance has been provided on this process. For special schools, guidance has been developed on writing and implementing an action plan (Department for Education and Employment 1998). This includes action planning for special schools requiring special measures or those with serious weaknesses. The proportion of special schools requiring special measures (7%) and those special schools with serious weaknesses (20%) is much higher than for mainstream schools.

References

Department for Education and Employment (1998) *Effective Action Planning After Inspection: Planning Improvement in Special Schools*. London: DfEE.
Department for Education and Skills (2001) *Special Education Needs Code of Practice*. London: DfES.

Address

Office for Standards in Education (Ofsted)   Tel: 020 7421 6800
Alexandra House   Fax: 020 7421 6707
33 Kingsway   e-mail: info@ofsted.gov.uk
London WC2B 6SE   www.ofsted.gov.uk

Inspector

An inspector may be one of *Her Majesty's Inspectors*, or may be self-employed or employed by a Local Education Authority (LEA) or a company. An LEA inspector reviews school progress, assesses the content of courses, teaching methods, working conditions, health and safety and other issues. (S)he may be a subject specialist, a phase specialist (e.g. nursery, primary) or have another specialism (e.g. special educational needs). Like other inspectors, the inspector for special educational needs may:

- give advice/support to schools and sometimes to parents
- inspect and report on schools for the LEA
- organise and help deliver in-service education courses
- be involved in inspections for the Office for Standards in Education (Ofsted).

Further reading

Landy, M. and Gains, C. (1996) *Inspecting Special Needs Provision in Schools*. London: David Fulton Publishers.

Address

National Association of Educational Inspectors Advisers and Consultants
Woolley Hall   Tel: 01226 383 428
Woolley   Fax: 01226 383 427
Wakefield WF4 2JR   e-mail: jill@naeiac.co.uk
                                                    www.naeiac.co.uk

Intelligence

Intelligent activity involves seeing the essentials in a given situation and responding appropriately to them. The possible structure of intelligence has been the source of much research and debate. Various methods of 'factoring' the correlations between tests through the statistical technique of factor analysis have led to various interpretations of the structure of intelligence, including a hierarchical structure involving group factors. Guilford identified some 120 intellectual skills. Such structures have led to tests being developed which aim to assess children's performance in different areas of mental ability (spatial, verbal, reasoning, etc). Another approach is that of the theory of multiple intelligence in which various intelligences are regarded as different from each other. Mathematical intelligence is fundamentally different from linguistic intelligence in this view. Such a view seems to explain some effects of brain damage and also the rare occasions when autism is accompanied by a high level of attainment in one area of functioning against a background of general low attainment.

Some intelligence tests may be administered to groups while others are administered individually. The latter are sometimes used as part of the assessment of children with special educational needs (SEN). The use of intelligence tests has limitations in its use with minority groups and those whose first language is not that of the test nor the population upon which the test was standardised.

An important concept related to intelligence tests is intelligence quotient or IQ. Most modern intelligence tests have a deviation quotient. They are standardised to produce distributions of IQs with a mean of 100 and standard deviation of 15 points. Intelligence test scores can also be expressed as percentile ranks or other measures.

An example of an intelligence test which can be administered as a group test is Raven's Progressive Matrices. A standard form comprises 60 designs in groups of 12. Each design has a piece omitted and several possible missing pieces are shown from which the correct one has to be chosen. As one progresses through the test, the logical relationships on which the correct judgement is based, becomes progressively more difficult. A coloured form is used for 5–11 year olds or for people with learning difficulties. There is an advanced form for the very able. Children whose physical or motor impairment may make some intelligence tests difficult to administer, may be able to be assessed using Raven's Progressive Matrices because the correct response can be given merely by pointing.

An example of an individually administered intelligence test is The British Ability Scales. This is a standardised battery which measures cognitive ability in the age range $2^1/_2$ to $17^1/_2$ years. It covers six process areas: speed of information processing, reasoning, spatial imagery, perceptual memory, short-term memory and retrieval and application of knowledge. These give an ability profile and a general IQ score. The scales are used for assessing children, including children with SEN.

Internet: World Wide Web sites and e-mail

The Internet is being increasingly used by those with an interest in special educational needs (SEN). It is impossible to list all the sites of interest but an hour or so spent exploring some of the better known sites will reveal links which will point towards the wealth of information available on other sites. Among the main sites are the following:

National Association of Special Educational Needs
www.nasen.org.uk/mainpg.htm

Contents pages of the *British Journal of Special Education*
www.ncet.org.uk/senco/sources/journals/bjse/bjsecon.htm/

This 'page' gives links to other journals: *Special!*, *Special Children* and *Support for Learning.*

Internet Resources for Special Children
www.irsc.org/

The SENCO Information Exchange
www.ncet.org.uk/senco/

Special Education Resources on the Internet
www.hood.edu/seri/serihome.htm

VOIS the Voluntary Organisations Internet Server
www.vois.org.uk/a2z.html/

As well as World Wide Web sites such as those listed above, increasingly electronic mail is being used to aid communications for those involved in special education. Many organisations list their e-mail address, and journal articles often include the author's e-mail so that speedy contact can be made.

The Internet is also being selectively used to facilitate the learning of and increase the inclusion of pupils with SEN.

Further reading
Abbott, C. (2002) *Special Educational Needs and the Internet: Issues for the Inclusive Internet.* London: Routledge Falmer.

Journals and other publications

Among publications concerned with special educational needs are the following:

As We See It
The Dyslexia Institute   Tel: 01784 463851
133 Gresham Road   Fax: 01784 760747
Staines   e-mail: spane@connect.by.com
Middlesex TW18 2AJ   www.dyslexia-inst.org.uk

British Journal of Special Education
NASEN House   Tel: 01827 311500
4–5 Amber Business Village   Fax: 01827 313005
Amber Close   e-mail: welcome@nasen.org.uk
Amington   www.nasen.org.uk
Tamworth
Staffordshire B77 4RP

Viewpoint (a fully accessible national newspaper for and by people with learning disabilities)

Royal MENCAP Society	Tel: 020 7696 5599 editor
123 Golden Lane	Fax: 020 7454 9193
London EC1Y 0RT	e-mail: viewpoint@mencap.org.uk
	www.mencap.org.uk

Special!
(as for *British Journal of Special Education*)

Support for Learning
(as for *British Journal of Special Education*)

(See also journals and other publications mentioned in appropriate entries. For example, under Educational psychologist reference is made to the *British Journal of Educational Psychology*.)

Learning difficulty

The *Special Educational Needs Code of Practice* (Department for Education and Skills 2001) defines special educational needs (SEN) in terms of the Education Act 1996, sections 312(2) and (3). A child has learning difficulty if:

a) he has a significantly greater difficulty in learning than the majority of children of this age
b) he has a disability which either prevents or hinders him from making use of educational facilities of a kind provided for children of the same age in schools within the area of the local education authority
c) he is under five and is, or would be if special educational provision were not made for him, likely to fall within paragraph (a) or (b) when of, or over that age.

A child with a learning difficulty does not necessarily have SEN under the Act which states that 'A child has special educational needs...if he has a learning difficulty which calls for special educational provision to be made for him' (section 312).

Reference

Department for Education and Skills (2001) *Special Educational Needs Code of Practice*. London: DfES.

Learning mentor

Learning mentors for pupils are members of school staff working with teaching and pastoral staff. They assess, identify and work with pupils who need extra help to overcome what are seen as barriers to learning, whether these are inside school or outside. They act as the single access point for specialist support services, such as social services, education welfare service, the youth service and others.

Pupil mentoring may be used as part of approaches to social inclusion (Department for Education and Employment 1999). Older pupils sometimes support pupils who need help and guidance, perhaps after poor behaviour, or where they risk failure at school because of bullying by others. Teachers, learning support assistants and volunteer mentors from business and the wider community may also support pupils at risk.

Reference

Department for Education and Employment (1999) *Circular 10/99 Social Inclusion: Pupil Support*. London: DfEE.

Address

School Inclusion Division
Department for Education and Skills
Sanctuary Buildings
Great Smith Street
London SW1P 3BT

Tel: 020 7925 5000
Fax: 020 7925 6000
e-mail: info@dfes.gov.uk
www.dfee.gov.uk

Learning support unit

Learning support units, sometimes known as in-school centres, provide teaching and support to pupils with very difficult behaviour. They may be used by the school on whose site they are situated or by neighbouring schools. These units aim to keep 'disaffected and unruly pupils' working (Office for Standards in Education 2001), address their behaviour problems and return them to mainstream classes as soon as possible, keeping disruption in the unit and in the schools to which the pupils return to a minimum. Admission procedures for pupils are agreed between the head teacher and the head of the unit. Before a pupil starts in a unit, staff should plan the learning and behaviour strategies to be used and agree how the pupil will be re-integrated into mainstream lessons.

Reference

Office for Standards in Education (2001) *Inspecting New Developments in the Secondary Curriculum*. London: Ofsted.

Lifelong learning

Lifelong learning refers both to the capacity and the opportunity to learn throughout one's life and implies that one's present learning is forward looking and encourages further learning later. It relates not just to formal educational systems but to the wider role of society and the learning potential of pursuits such as sports and leisure activities. It relates to learning before school, in school, after school, in further and higher education, within the family, at work and in the community. Important is an approach which develops the skills and attitudes necessary for self-motivated learning such as problem solving and research skills. It applies to all areas of development including spiritual, moral, physical, cognitive and artistic development.

For people with severe learning difficulties, lifelong learning will in part be a continuing preparation for increasingly independent living. Where learners with severe or profound and multiple learning difficulties live in communities especially developed for them, such communities strive to encourage the role of wider society as a lifelong learning society to the benefit of its own community members.

When lifelong learning is considered for those with emotional and behavioural difficulties, the importance of the role of wider society is also important. If such children learn from society as a whole, the negative values learned from peers and perhaps parents with similar difficulties needs to be balanced by a school with very powerful values of its own. The values conveyed by the more lurid aspects of the media would also be questioned, particularly as they may be interpreted or sought out by emotionally and behaviourally disturbed people. If society is to be a source of lifelong learning and it is agreed that certain moral values are desirable in that society, this may suggest a greater degree of control by government and others than is at present exercised.

One approach has been to help adults with learning difficulties and/or disabilities to acquire skills through good teaching and learning. A working group established by the Department for Education and Employment reported in 2000. The report stated that there would be an entitlement to lifelong learning 'which will enable learners to acquire new skills and to maintain those already learned' (Department for Education and Employment 2000, executive summary para. 12). Among recommendations to improve provision were:

- developing alternative ways of enabling learners to demonstrate achievement;
- developing a flexible and coherent curriculum at pre-entry level to enable learners at pre-entry level to progress to entry level.

A potentially negative consequence of a lifelong learning view of education is that, in the formal education system, it may lower the school's necessary sense of urgency about what it should achieve in a child's school career. Also, a school may feel that it should provide a narrower curriculum than it might otherwise offer because the breadth will be offered at later stages of the learner's life. Such a view would, of course, limit the opportunities offered and would reduce the chances of a child finding and developing an area of learning in which he can do comparatively well.

The use of information and communications technology is important. Also, preparation where possible for productive work is an aspect of lifelong learning and this includes housework, voluntary work and community service as well as paid employment.

Reference
Department for Education and Employment (2000) *Freedom to Learn: Basic Skills for Learners with Learning Difficulties and/or Disabilities*. London: DfEE.

Further reading
National Advisory Group for Continuing Education and Lifelong Learning (1998) *Creating Learning Cultures: Next Steps in Achieving the Learning Age*. London: DfEE.

Address
Access to Participation Division   Tel: 0870 011 2345
Department for Education and Skills   Fax: 020 7925 6000
Sanctuary Buildings   e-mail: info@dfes.gov.uk
Great Smith Street   www.lifelonglearning.dfes.gov.uk
London SW1P 3BT

Life skills

Life skills are those skills which lead towards a person being able to function autonomously in adult society. They include self-help skills (e.g. feeding, dressing, general hygiene and health care); household skills (shopping, cooking, cleaning etc.); social skills (dealing with regular social tasks such as using a post office, bank, travel etc.). Life skills are part of education leading towards independence. Part of their purpose is to prepare a young person for their role as an adult. However, pupils with profound and multiple learning difficulties are taught life skills while there is no expectation of their being independent. The aim for such pupils is to aim for comparative independence in particular skills, e.g. feeding.

An example of the accreditation of life skills is the Award Scheme Development and Accreditation Network (ASDAN) Youth Award Scheme Bronze or Silver Award. Used in schools with Year 10 students, it is employed either within a tutorial/personal social education programme for all students or as an option for students who require more support. In special schools, the Award is used to complement the National Curriculum and other programmes and enables tutors to involve students in relevant life skills.

(See also *Accreditation of achievement*)

Address

ASDAN Central Office   Tel: 0117 941 1126
Wainbrook House   Fax: 0117 935 1112
Hudds Vale Road   e-mail: info@asdan.co.uk
St George   www.asdan.co.uk
Bristol BS5 7HY

Literacy

The National Literacy Strategy aims to raise the standards of literacy in primary schools in line with national expectations. The definition of literacy adopted is, at its simplest, the ability to read and write. Other aspects of literacy include the following:

1.   Reading difficulties
Learning to read involves a developing range of skills which mean that the nature of the reading process changes as the pupil's proficiency increases. This overall pattern of development is informed by phonological skills, whole word recognition and the effective use of contextual cues.

Where there are difficulties in learning to read, there may be a variety of factors involved. These include visual and/or auditory perceptual difficulties and difficulties in integrating visual and/or auditory perceptions. Another factor may be intellectual development which is insufficient for a child to comprehend text. There may be difficulties with attention, memory or motivation which may affect learning generally, including reading. Social and cultural influences are also associated with reading difficulties. These include a cultural background and/or a family background, which places low value on literacy. Anti-educational peer group pressures are another influence. Educational factors include school absence, frequent changes of teacher and low teacher/parent expectations. Inadequate reading material which is inappropriate to the ability and interests of the learner is another feature. In any event, reading difficulties should be identified, assessed and addressed in an ongoing way and using appropriate materials and methods.

2.   Assessment of reading difficulties

a)   Fog Index
The level of difficulty of a text can be assessed and represented as a grade to help ensure that materials are pitched appropriately for a child. One approach is to combine two indices: a measure of word difficulty and a measure of sentence difficulty. The Fog Index uses several sample passages of 100 words and calculates the number of words in an average sentence (a), and the percentage of words with three or more syllables (b).

These indices are added and multiplied by 0.4 to give the Fog Index. This is converted into an approximate reading age in years by adding 5.0.

Approximate reading age level = (a)+(b)×0.4+5.0 years.

Such estimates give only broad guidance and have shortcomings including that other factors are influential such as the interest of the material to the child. Also, measures such as the Fog Index are based on samples of text which may or may not be representative. Consequently, such indexes should be treated with caution, forming only a part of the information from which a professional judgement of appropriateness of reading material is made.

b)   Cloze procedure
Cloze procedure involves the child's response to samples of text. Fluent reading is assumed to require the use of contextual clues and comprehension skills to predict missing material. Samples of the text to be assessed are taken and words are omitted, say every fifth word (except the first word in each sentence, proper nouns and numbers). Depending on the percentage of deletions which are guessed correctly, a judgement is made of the difficulty level of the text for the particular child. This indicates whether the text is too hard, is suitable for instruction or for independent reading.

c)   Informal Reading Inventory (IRI)
IRI is a criterion-referenced assessment of the difficulty level of a text in relation to a child's reading skills. Guidelines are provided to help a teacher to establish the reading level. There are four levels.
   i)   Independent level: the child reads for pleasure and does not require supervision. S(he) makes less than 1 per cent mistakes, reading individual words in context and less than 1 per cent errors answering comprehension questions.
   ii) Instructional level: the child needs some help from the teacher. S(he) makes less than 5 per cent word errors and less than 25 per cent comprehension mistakes.
   iii) Frustration level: the text is too difficult and the child becomes frustrated with failure. The child makes more than 5 per cent word mistakes and more than 25 per cent comprehension errors.
   iv) Capacity level: to assess this, the teacher reads parts of the text and asks the pupil questions on it. A child listening comprehension error of more than 25 per cent suggests that the material is too difficult for the child to reach.
   IRI aims to ensure that reading material used by a child is neither frustratingly difficult nor boringly easy.

3.   Examples of approaches to the teaching of reading

a)   Companion reading
Children are paired so that the least and most able are matched. The teacher demonstrates the required skill and learners respond in unison. A period of study follows when members of each pair take a turn to tutor each other using pause, prompt, praise techniques. This is followed by a short period of individual study then mastery checking.

b)   Gillingham Method
A **multisensory teaching method** for reading, used with children with reading difficulties, including dyslexia. It takes a phonic approach in which certain letter sounds are learned in a set order. Three letter words are then spelled out orally while being written.

4.   Writing difficulties
Some writing difficulties arise when children are starting to form letters which are appropriate in size and shape but which are constructed wrongly. Closer supervision of the order and direction of strokes tends to help. Pupils with fine motor coordination difficulties will find handwriting particularly difficult. A progressive developmental approach may be used for some pupils.

   In more severe cases, neuromuscular difficulties may give rise to writing difficulties (dysgraphia) or the inability to write (agraphia). Where writing is impracticable, communication can be achieved through word processors operated in ways other than by finger movements (e.g. by breath or by dictation).

5.   Spelling difficulties
Among strategies for spelling are the following, all of which can be used as appropriate. As progress or otherwise is monitored, the teacher should be able to identify approaches which are particularly helpful to an individual child.

a)   Phonics: For regular simple words a written unit (grapheme) can be directly linked to a sound unit (phoneme) in words such as 'big' or 'top'.

b)   Rules: The difficulty with rules such as 'i before e except after c when the sound is ee' is that there are exceptions.

c)   Simultaneous oral spelling: This technique is useful for irregular words. The approach is as follows:
   i)   identify the area of difficulty
   ii) write the word correctly from a dictionary once using lower case letters and naming the letters as the word is written
   iii) cover the word
   iv) write the word again spelling it audibly as it is written
   v)   check back to the original
   vi) repeat steps (iv) and (v) until the word is spelled correctly three consecutive times. Check each time with the original.
   Also, **multisensory teaching methods** are used.

Further reading
Duncan, H. and Parkhouse, S. (2002) *Improving Literacy Skills for Children with SEN.* London: Routledge Falmer.

Literacy hour

The National Literacy Strategy aims to raise the standards of literacy in line with national expectations.

Part of the approach is that there should be a 'literacy hour' for primary children each day. There are concerns among some teachers who seek to implement the strategy. The suggested time allocations within the literacy hour include half an hour in which children are expected to interact with the teacher in a whole-class grouping. This may be difficult for some children with special educational needs (SEN), for example those who have difficulty in concentrating for more than a relatively short period and some flexibility will be needed with such children. Where whole-class teaching, led by the teacher, takes place for extended periods of time it will be particularly important that the roles of learning support staff and other adults in the classroom have a clear and constructive role in contributing to the learning of the children. Legitimate roles for such adults could include helping contain potentially disruptive behaviour or encouraging contributions from a child who finds communication difficult.

The structured work includes the recommendation that certain words be taught within specified periods, for example that a number of high frequency words be taught as sight recognition words through the reception year to Year 2.

The abstract nature of many of these words may not make them the most suitable to be taught to some pupils with SEN. Some more 'concrete' words, words with easily distinguishable shapes and words which draw on the child's interests, will be more likely to be learned by some children and would help to build their confidence to prepare for more abstract yet important words.

There is provision for setting pupils and this could be done for the whole or for a part of the literacy hour on some days of the week if not all. In special schools and classes, it is recognised that adjustments may be necessary to the literacy hour, for example because of the more individualised approach to teaching. In mainstream schools, strategies for increasing the inclusion of children in the literacy hour include preparation teaching for some children, the support of learning support assistants and the use of information and communications technology.

Further reading

Berger, A. and Morris, D. (2000) *Implementing the Literacy Hour for Pupils with Learning Difficulties*. London: David Fulton Publishers.

Address

The National Centre for Literacy and Numeracy
London House
59–65 London Street
Reading RG1 4EW

Tel: 0118 952 7500
Fax: 0118 952 7507
e-mail: l&n@cfbt-hq.org.uk
www.standards.dfee.gov.uk

Local Education Authority (LEA)

In England and Wales, a local education authority (LEA) is an elected council of local government which from its members forms an education committee. The committee is served by a permanent chief education officer (sometimes called a director of education) who has a permanent staff to administer local education. In Scotland the responsibility for education is with regional councils and island councils which are known as education authorities. In Northern Ireland, education is the responsibility of the Education and Library Boards.

Under the Education Act 1996, LEAs have important responsibilities in meeting children's special educational needs (SEN). LEAs make statutory assessments and Statements, review Statements, publish information on their SEN policies and review their arrangements. The LEA may supply SEN support services to schools in their area and elsewhere.

Further reading
SEN Policy Options Group (1996) *Bucking the Market: LEAs and Special Needs*. Stafford: National Association of Special Educational Needs.

Address
Confederation of Education Service Managers   Tel: 0161 275 8810
Humanities Building   Fax: 0161 275 8811
University of Manchester
Oxford Road
Manchester M13 9PL

Local education authority policy framework

The Special Educational Needs (Provision of Information by Local Education Authorities) (England) Regulations 2001 require LEAs to publish their policy on SEN. They must also publish, with regard to children with SEN, information on how the authority is:

- promoting high standards of education for these children;
- encouraging these children to participate fully in their school and community and to take part in decisions about their education;
- encouraging schools in the area to share practice in providing for these children; and
- working with other statutory and voluntary bodies to provide support for these children.

LEAs must also publish general arrangements. These include any plans setting out objectives, targets and timescales concerning local arrangements for:

- identifying children with SEN;
- monitoring the admission of children with SEN to maintained schools in their area;
- organising the assessment of children's statements including any local provision for doing this;
- providing support to school concerning making provision for children with SEN;
- auditing, planning, monitoring and reviewing provision for children with SEN in general and with regard to individual pupils;
- supporting pupils with SEN through 'school action' and 'school action plus';
- securing training, advice and support for staff working in SEN;
- regularly reviewing and updating the policy and development plans;
- explaining the element of provision for children with SEN but without statements that the LEA normally expects to be met from the budget share of mainstream schools and that normally to be met from central funding.

LEA planning should provide for the inclusion of children with SEN in mainstream schools. The LEA should:

- monitor and review the role and quality of central SEN support services and parent partnership services;
- take account of current and predicted pupil numbers;
- monitor the kinds of needs identified and where children are placed; and
- develop SEN policies in consultation with schools and others and keep them under review.

(Department for Education and Skills 2001, para. 1.15)

Reference
Department for Education and Skills (2001) *Special Educational Needs Code of Practice.* London: DfES.

Looked after children

In England, within the wider group of up to 400,000 **children 'in need'**, are two slightly overlapping groups of 32,000 children on the child protection register and 53,000 children who are 'looked after' by a local authority (Department of Health/Department for Education and Employment/Home Office 2000).

Under the Children Act 1989, a Care Order may be made placing a child in the care of a local authority. Care proceedings are brought through a Family Court by a local authority or by the National Society for the Prevention of Cruelty to Children. While a Care Order is current, the local authority has rights and duties in relation to the child. These normally include the right to decide where the child is placed. In making the Order, the court must be satisfied that:

- the child is out of parental control; and
- the child is suffering harm (or is likely to suffer harm) from the care currently being given (or likely to be given).

Harm is defined as either: impairment of physical or mental health; impairment of physical, intellectual, emotional, social or behavioural development; ill-treatment (including sexual abuse and non-physical forms of ill-treatment).

A Care Order puts the child under the 'care' of the local authority, giving the local authority parental responsibility for the child.

A child who is 'looked after' by a local authority may be the subject of a Care Order or may be voluntarily accommodated. Day-to-day responsibility may rest with foster parents, guardians or residential social workers.

If a child is voluntarily accommodated, that is accommodated by the local authority under voluntary arrangement with the child's parents, the child's parents retain parental responsibility and act in partnership with the local authority as far as possible.

When a looked-after child has SEN, the designated teacher for looked-after children should work closely with the SEN coordinator. Schools should make sure that the child's social worker and, where possible, the parents are involved in the child's education and in matters relating to SEN (Department for Education and Employment/Department of Health 2000).

The education of a looked-after child may be arranged by social services. If so, and if the LEA considers that in its role as the child's parent it has made suitable provision under the Education Act 1996, section 324 (5) (a), it may refrain from making the provision specified in the child's statement of SEN. The child may also be placed with:

- a community home with education on the premises;
- a children's home providing education; or
- an independent fostering agency providing education.

In these circumstances, the LEA may conclude that suitable arrangements have been made and that it is relieved of its duty to arrange the provision specified in the child's statement of SEN (Department for Education and Skills 2001, sections 8.98 to 8.104).

Where a child is the subject of a Care Order, an Education Supervision Order or accommodated by the local authority, the social services department must include information on the child's education in the Child Care Plan. The social services department must review the Child Care Plan, involving the child in the process. The Child Care Plan incorporates a Personal Education Plan setting out the educational arrangements made for the child. This should include information from the child's statement of SEN, Individual Education Plans and any annual review of the statement. LEAs and social service departments may link the review of the Child Care Plan with the annual review of the statement of SEN.

The Children (Leaving Care) Act 2002 provides that every eligible person looked after by a local authority on their sixteenth birthday (including those with SEN) has a pathway plan. This builds into the Care Plans and Personal Educational Plans and seeks to set a direction towards independence. The local authority appoints an adviser who will normally act as the Connexions personal adviser for the young person, devising with them and others the pathway plan and ensuring that it is implemented. The pathway plan may be the same document as the Transition Plan and the Connexions personal action plan to avoid duplication (Department for Education and Employment 2001, section 9.68).

References

Department for Education and Employment/Department of Health (2000) *Guidance on the Education of Children and Young People in Public Care.* London: DfEE/DoH.

Department for Education and Skills (2001) *Special Educational Needs Code of Practice.* London: DfES.

Department of Health/Department for Education and Employment/Home Office (2000) *Framework for the Assessment of Children in Need and their Families.* London: The Stationery Office.

Mastery learning

Mastery learning is a form of individualised instruction with features similar to direct instruction. With mastery learning, the curriculum is broken up into small, manageable, sequential steps. Pupils are taught each step until they have achieved mastery of the skill (a previously agreed level of competence). Only then do they progress to the next step.

If children have difficulty achieving mastery, the focus is placed on the quality of the teaching rather than on any assumed shortcomings of the pupil. Different teaching approaches may be tried until progress is made. The individualised

instruction aspect of mastery learning has several implications that relate to special education:

- different pupils will take different lengths of time to master skills;
- if pupils work at the pace that is appropriate for them, this implies that not all pupils will master necessary skills in the usual period of compulsory schooling and may need to continue their progress into further education;
- mastery learning is demanding of teachers' time and is more feasible with small groups of pupils than with large classes.

Mathematics difficulties

Among mathematics difficulties are:

- acalculia – difficulties with number symbols and mathematical operations – the term is sometimes used when referring to damage to previously apparent mathematical abilities following brain damage; and
- dyscalculia – difficulties with mathematics generally but particularly with arithmetical operations.

In order to meet the difficulties experienced by some learners in mathematics, attention has been paid both to curriculum content and teaching methods. Within the context of the National Curriculum, it is possible for children with special educational needs to build on a curriculum of obvious relevance to the learner based on the mathematical skills needed at home and at work.

In the National Curriculum programmes of study, the common requirements on access enables material to be selected from earlier or later key stages where necessary to allow individual pupils to progress and achieve. The context in which this material is presented should be age-appropriate. Pupils should also be given opportunities to develop their information and communications technology capability in mathematics and to apply it.

Regarding teaching methods, practical activities are important. Language needs to be at the appropriate level and should be used to help the learner come to terms with the concepts and operations involved.

A potential weakness in mathematics teaching arises when classes are set by ability, and lower ability groups are taught with too great a dependence on individual work cards supported by a teacher who is not a mathematics specialist. Such an approach can offer insufficient room for discussion to develop understanding. It is important that pupils have the opportunity to explain their way of reaching a solution and that the teacher encourages the thinking and understanding of mathematics rather than over-emphasising rote learning.

(See also *Dyslexia, Numeracy hour*)

Further reading
El Naggar, O. (1996) *Specific Learning Difficulties in Mathematics: A Classroom Approach.* Stafford: National Association for Special Educational Needs.

Medical conditions

The medical aspects of special educational needs (SEN) exert a variable influence depending on the nature of the SEN. For example, medical screening is essential for cases of phenylketonuria (PKU) an inherited metabolic disorder caused by a recessive gene. Normally, an enzyme turns phenylalanine present in the body into harmless substances. In PKU, this vital enzyme is missing and severe learning difficulties may be caused if the condition goes untreated. A special diet started as early as possible prevents intellectual deterioration. Here we see a direct link between medical screening, diagnosis and treatment and the prevention of learning difficulties which would otherwise occur.

In other instances, medical advice, support and treatment are important. For example, in epilepsy, the effects of medication need to be monitored, and in other conditions careful monitoring of health is important. When a Statement of SEN is drawn up, a section of the Statement requires that medical evidence be documented.

Medical conditions are diverse and include sickle cell disease, cystic fibrosis, diabetes, epilepsy, haemophilia, kidney failure, spina bifida, leukaemia and muscular dystrophy to mention only a few. Medical conditions require differing responses but there are some general themes which emerge. Children with certain medical conditions (such as arthritis) may need to spend periods of time in hospital. This may require the class teacher or SEN coordinator to liaise with a hospital teacher. If there have been long periods of absence, the school will want to ensure that the pupil picks up friendships and settles successfully back into the routine when they return to school.

For each condition, teachers should be aware of the likely implications for education but this awareness will need to be informed by the actual effects on education in each individual case. For example, a child with Juvenile Chronic Arthritis (a progressive disease causing inflammation of the lining membranes of joints in children) may experience stiffness in the hands which is likely to make handwork painful and slow. Other forms of communication may need to be additionally used such as tape recorders. While this will be borne in mind as a general approach, the specific strategies that will be useful for a particular child will be determined individually and individually monitored.

Weakness, tiredness and fatigue may be brought about by some conditions and this may reduce the child's capacity to learn. Concentration may be difficult. In some cases, children with potentially life threatening conditions such as heart disease may experience emotional and behavioural difficulties related to the condition, to the restrictions it imposes and to the treatment which is necessary.

There are curricular implications for some conditions. For example, for a pupil with brittle bones (osteogenesis imperfecta), hard contact sports would be inappropriate but activities like swimming may be suitable.

Other conditions have dietary implications. Yet others such as asthma and diabetes may require medication to be administered. Some conditions may call for particular care and provision to be made for hygiene, for example where the child is incontinent or where dental treatment needs special priority.

The social implications of some conditions need to be recognised. Care should be taken that a child with a condition which creates physical differences or who has treatment which creates physical changes such as hair loss is not singled out on this account.

Further reading
Closs, A. (ed.) (1999) *The Education of Children with Medical Conditions.* London: David Fulton Publishers.

Address

Long Term Medical Conditions Alliance
Unit 212
16 Baldwin Gardens
London EC1N 7RJ

Tel: 020 7813 3637
Fax: 020 7813 3640
e-mail: alliance@lmca.demon.co.uk
www.lmca.demon.co.uk

Members of the Alliance are voluntary bodies meeting the needs of those with long-term illnesses.

Medication (drug treatment)

Drugs may be used to treat such conditions as epilepsy (anticonvulsant drugs, e.g. the barbiturate phenobarbitone), cerebral palsy (muscle relaxing drugs, e.g. diazepam), psychiatric illness (e.g. antidepressant drugs, antipsychotic drugs/major tranquillizers).

Antipsychotic drugs are used in the management of the problem behaviours of people with severe learning difficulties. Among drugs used are promazine and haloperidol. Where drugs are used to manage behaviour it is important that drug use and its effects are monitored, that the minimum effective dose is used and that alternative methods are tried and adopted as appropriate.

The possible side effects of drugs should be balanced against the necessity for treating the condition. For example, in controlling attacks of epilepsy, frequent drowsiness and occasional hyperactivity or irritability is caused by the use of phenobarbitone.

Medicine

Among medical professionals who may be invloved with children with special educational needs (SEN) are:

- General practitioner;
- Paediatrician (a doctor concerned with childhood development and the diagnosis, treatment and prevention of childhood diseases);
- Orthopedic surgeon (involved in surgery relating to disorders of the bones and joints and their muscles, tendons and ligaments);
- Orthoptitian (concerned with evaluating squint and with corrective techniques);
- **psychiatrist**.

Other medically related therapeutic professions include:

- physiotherapy;
- occupational therapy;
- speech and language therapy; and
- music therapy.

Medical research and treatment has enabled progress to be made in quality of life and quality of learning. For example, the medical treatment of epilepsy enables pupils to benefit more than they would otherwise from education, being less disabled than previously by the effects of their condition.

In the statementing procedure for a child with SEN, medical advice must be sought as part of the assessment. Aspects of a 'medical model' is evident in the medicalised terminology of such learning difficulties as dyslexia, where terms such as 'diagnosis', 'clinic' and 'treatment' are used with regard to a difficulty with reading, spelling and number.

Address

British Medical Association
BMA House
Tavistock Square
London WC1H 9JP

Tel: 020 7387 4499
Fax: 020 7383 4499
e-mail: info.web@bma.org.uk
www.bma.org.uk

Mentor for teachers

Using a model employed in industry and commerce, education has begun to develop mentoring. In initial teacher training, some learning models use the support of a university tutor, open learning materials and a school-based mentor to structure a course leading to qualified teacher status. Newly qualified teachers may be supported by a mentor to guide them through the crucial first year of teaching. A mentor may be a seasoned and experienced member of the school's staff and should be allocated non-teaching time to fulfil her or his obligations. Mentors may also support newly appointed first time head teachers.

Moderate learning difficulties (MLD)

For a child with MLD, the general level of academic attainment is significantly below that of peers, although not as far below as that for pupils with severe learning difficulties or profound and multiple learning difficulties. There may be difficulty acquiring basic literacy and numeracy skills, speech and language difficulties and poorly developed personal and social skills. Emotional and behavioural difficulties may be evident.

In the *Special Educational Needs Code of Practice* (Department for Education and Skills 2001), pupils who 'demonstrate features of...moderate learning difficulties' are considered to 'require specific programmes to aid progress in cognition and learning' (Code 7.58).

The educational needs of pupils with MLD are generally met through the flexibility allowed by the National Curriculum Orders. The subject areas of the National Curriculum are covered but at a slower pace and with greater emphasis on practical learning through doing. Where there are emotional/behavioural difficulties, care is needed to meet the emotional and behavioural needs of the pupils.

Reference

Department for Education and Skills (2001) *Special Educational Needs Code of Practice.* London: DfES.

Further reading

Robinson, C. and Cornwall, J. (2001) *IEPs – Learning Difficuties.* London: David Fulton Publishers.

Address

Equals
PO Box 107
North Shields
Tyne and Wear NE30 2YG

Tel: 0191 258 4914
Fax: 0191 272 8600
e-mail: admin@equals.co.uk
www.equals.co.uk

Equals is a national organisation for teachers of pupils with moderate, severe and profound and multiple learning difficulties.

Modern languages

The successful teaching of modern languages to pupils with special educational needs (SEN) involves, among other things, the training of teachers, careful planning for progression, the effective use of accreditation, the use of practical materials and methods in the classroom and a recognition of the importance of motivation. As well as reading and writing, such activities as music and movement can be used effectively. Suitable accreditation is important and a range of alternatives is available.

The Centre for Information on Language Teaching (CILT) project was established in 1991 and formed a national network for collating and sharing information and examples of best practice. At the outset, 20 local education authorities were involved. CILT is now an ongoing national network for information and good practice in the area of modern foreign languages and SEN.

The experiences of the initial CILT project indicated two things. Firstly, learning a foreign language is valuable to most pupils with SEN, helping them develop linguistic and social skills and widening cultural awareness. Secondly, it is possible within the framework of the National Curriculum to deliver a meaningful programme of language learning to pupils with SEN.

Further reading

McColl, H. (2000) *Modern Languages for All*. London: David Fulton Publishers.

Address

The Centre for Information on Language Teaching and Research (CILT)
20 Bedfordbury
London WC2N 4LB

Tel: 020 7379 5101
Fax: 020 7379 5082
e-mail: library@cilt.org.uk
www.cilt.org.uk
Electronic discussion forum:
www.mailbase.ac.uk/lists/mflsen-forum

The CILT is an independent charitable trust which serves all sectors of education, holds conferences, issues publications, including *CILT Direct Yearbook*, and provides information and resources.

Montessori method

Maria Montessori (1870–1952) founded a school for 'feeble minded' children in 1899 and later adapted her methods so that they could also be used with children who did not experience disabilities. The child's interests and stage of intellectual development are important. The educational process is not driven by curricular requirements alone, but also by an understanding of child psychology. Children are encouraged to learn from their surroundings and activities encourage pupils to use all the senses. Music and dance are important.

Address

Montessori Centre International	Tel: 020 7493 0165
18 Balderton Street	Fax: 020 7629 7808
London W1Y 1TG	e-mail: mci@montessori.ac.uk
	www.montessori.ac.uk

Motor impairment

An inability to perform motor skills appropriate to one's age, motor impairment is best understood by reference to motor development. Gross motor development includes skills such as walking and throwing, while fine motor development includes skills like tying a knot or cutting with scissors which require fine coordination. Normal motor development implies strength, coordination and tone. Tone concerns the amount of tension and firmness in muscles and helps a person maintain a particular position. It is controlled by the brain.

Dyspraxia is a motor impairment in which a person is unable to perform voluntary, purposive movements, although they are neither paralysed nor have a defect of muscle coordination.

Impaired motor development may be, in some cases, treated by **physiotherapy**. However, in other cases, it has more complex implications related to learning difficulties. Motor development may be delayed in children with severe or moderate learning difficulties. It may be permanently impaired in children with certain physical disabilities such as cerebral palsy. In such instances, neurological damage which causes the motor impairment may also cause learning difficulties. Language and other senses may also be affected.

Restricted movement may limit the opportunity to learn from touching various objects or from manipulating them and having spacial experiences. The direct importance of motor development and its more subtle influences on learning emphasise the importance of motor development to learning. Where motor development is impaired, remedial programmes may be used.

(See also *Conductive education*)

Further reading

Kirby, A. and Drew, S. (2002) *Guide to Dyspraxia and Developmental Coordination Disorders.* London: David Fulton Publishers.

Address

MOVE Europe	Tel: 020 7414 1493
The Disability Partnership	Fax: 020 7414 1495
Wooden Spoon House	e-mail: moveeurope@disabilitypartnership.co.uk
5 Dugard Way	www.disabilitypartnership.co.uk
London SE11 4TH	

The MOVE programme aims to provide mobility for people who have difficulty with sitting, standing or walking. It uses education to enable the acquisition of motor skills so that participants practise them while engaged in other educational or leisure activities. MOVE provides a sequence of age-appropriate motor skills based on needs which range from minimal self-management to independent self-management. It lays a foundation for the development of further skills in self-care, expressive language and work opportunities, bringing together therapy and education to meet the functional needs of students when they reach adulthood. MOVE International (Europe) office promotes information, training and research about the MOVE curriculum.

Movement therapy

In movement therapy, the emotions can be expressed and there can be a cathartic release of emotions. Increased physical skills can improve confidence and self-esteem. Pupils with physical and sensory difficuties may be introduced to movements to improve their body awareness and self-image. Creative dance is a form of movement therapy.

Address

Association for Dance Movement Therapy UK   e-mail: query@admt.org.uk
c/o The Quaker Meeting House   www.dmtuk.demon.co.uk/
Wedmore Vale
Bristol BS3 5HV

Multidisciplinary teamwork

There is, and has been for some time, much talk of closer working between professionals and others involved with children with special educational needs, in particular education, health, social and voluntary services. Difficulties arise when:

- local education authority (LEA), social services and health service geographical boundaries do not coincide;
- colleagues work on different sites;
- there is competition between services, high staff turnover and distrust;
- there are different professional perceptions and different practices regarding confidentiality;
- there are different line managers, different strands of funding and different priorities among groups of colleagues; and
- different professionals do not sufficiently appreciate the legal and professional framework that others work under.

Also, while education and social services are managed locally, health services have a more direct link to central government. Collaboration that does exist attempts to avoid the problems of fragmented approaches to provision for children. Examples are:

- local initiatives using joint funding;
- education and social services combining under one line manager;
- groups of professionals and voluntary services sharing the same building;
- joint committees and working groups;
- developing a common database (e.g attempting to dovetail a speech and language therapy list of clinical priority with a database of statements which give speech and language therapy as a special educational provision); and
- service level agreements.

In collaborative multidisciplinary teamwork, members of different services and disciplines take responsibility for their 'area' in the initial assessment of a child's difficulties (sometimes working together jointly assessing). Team members then contribute to a broad-based individual programme which is implemented by one or two members of the team who may call on other team members as consultants.

Further reading

Lacey, P. (1998) 'Multi-disciplinary work: challenges and possibilities', in Daniels, H. (ed.) *Special Education Reformed: Beyond Rhetoric?* London: Falmer Press.

Multisensory environments

One interpretation of a multisensory environment is the sensory stimulation room. This is often a feature of schools for pupils with severe learning difficulties (SLD) and profound and multiple learning difficulties (PMLD). Such rooms may include devices which respond to touch or sound by producing sounds or visual effects. This may encourage responses from pupils using a behavioural model. Therapeutically, it may be a relaxing environment for a child who is feeling frustrated or stressed. There may be a soft room and a ball pool. There may be an Optikinetics projector, bubble tubes, a glass fibre optics light tail and a transmitter of sound effects or music.

Approaches using multisensory stimuli have been adapted and expanded to merge into National Curriculum subjects in some schools for pupils with SLD.

Sensory stimulation rooms are sometimes called 'snoezelen' rooms. Snoezelen is a combination of two Dutch words meaning 'sniffing' and 'dozing' and the word was used by pioneers of the approach, Hulsegge and Verheul. Snoezelen is now a registered trademark of one company that produces multisensory environments and unless one is referring to that company, the term sensory stimulation room is generally used. More critical evaluation needs to be undertaken of the educational and therapeutic value of sensory stimulation rooms.

Further reading

Pagliano, P. (2001) *Using a Multisensory Environment: A Practical Guide for Teachers.* London: David Fulton Publishers.

Multisensory teaching methods

Multisensory approaches may be used in the teaching of reading, spelling, phonics and number. These approaches assume that learning through several senses is likely to be more efficient and effective than learning through one. Where a learner finds learning through one sensory mode more difficult than another, a multisensory approach, while exercising the 'weaker' senses, is likely to also involve the 'stronger' sensory mode and so enhance learning. Care is taken to identify the 'stronger' mode through testing. There is an implication that a reinforcement of the various senses by each other is likely to make learning more secure. Use may be made of the various perceptual systems: visual, auditory, tactile-kinaesthetic and oral-kinaesthetic. Activities may involve seeing, listening, touching, doing, reading, saying, writing and drawing.

An example of a multisensory approach is a VAKT method involving verbal, auditory, kinaesthetic and tactile modes. In reading, normally the visual aspect of the written word is reinforced by hearing the word and saying it. In a multidisciplinary approach, touch and movement are added by tracing the word perhaps in a sand tray. Also words may be divided into their constituent syllables before they are read.

Information and communications technology, including computers using compact disks with read only memory (CD-ROM), is used to interactively present the visual and sound aspects of a multisensory approach.

(See also *Dyslexia*)

Music therapist

A music therapist may work in a hospital, special school, day centre or private centre and may be employed by health, education or social services.

Address
Association of Professional Music Therapists (APMT)
26 Hamlyn Road   Tel: 01458 834919
Glastonbury   e-mail: APMToffice@aol.com
Somerset BA6 8HT   www.apmt.org/theapmt-whatis.htm

The APMT supports and develops the profession. The association's members are qualified music therapists who have undertaken a recognised postgraduate training course in music therapy. The association aims to maintain high standards of practice through administering and monitoring a range of professional development schemes.

Music therapy

A fundamental aspect of music therapy is the development of a relationship between the client and the therapist. Music making is the basis of communication within this relationship. Sessions may be for an individual or group and generally, therapist and client(s) actively participate in sessions by playing, singing and listening. The aim of the therapy is to help the client achieve positive changes in behaviour and emotional wellbeing, increase self-awareness and self-esteem and improve quality of life. For those who find verbal communication an inadequate form of expression, music therapy provides the opportunity to express and release feelings. Clients may experience learning difficulties, physical or emotional difficulties or sensory impairments.

Further reading
Bunt, L. (1994) *Music Therapy: An Art Beyond Words*. London: Routledge.

Address
British Society for Music Therapy (BSMT)   Tel/Fax: 020 8368 8879
25 Rosslyn Avenue   e-mail: denize@bsmt.demon.co.uk
East Barnet   www.bsmt.org
Herts EN4 8DH

The Society organises conferences, workshops and meetings on music therapy which are open to all. The BSMT information booklet giving details of music therapy, training courses, books and meetings is sent to all enquirers. The BSMT has its own publications and sells music therapy books. Members receive the *British Journal of Music Therapy* and the *BSMT Bulletin.*

Named local education authority officer

An officer of a local education authority who is involved when the LEA consider making a statutory assessment of special educational needs. The LEA must give parents the name of a member of staff (the named officer) who provides parents with information and explains the procedure if the LEA decide to go ahead with a statutory assessment.

Need

Need implies values so it is not always possible to agree that a particular need should be satisfied. Deciding children's needs is not an objective process and to assess needs it is necessary to establish what is required for a particular end. For example, if you 'know' that you need medicine, then you assume that it is valuable to be healthy. You have to know or believe that the medicine will improve your health. You also have to recognise that you are sick.

In the case of special educational need, there is usually consensus as to what the 'need' is and that it is appropriate to satisfy it. The implication is that everyone has a right to equal access to learning and if there is an impairment to this then the child 'needs' help to overcome it. Need is not always so easily agreed. For example, in the case of delinquency, it is not always easy to establish whether the delinquency is an aspect of emotional and behaviour disturbance or a calculated disregard for the rule of the law. Depending on the interpretation of the behaviour, people's views about what the child committing the delinquency 'needs' are likely to differ. Certainly the term 'need' introduces value judgements of which one should be aware.

Neurologist

A neurologist is a medical practitioner who has undergone additional training in the diagnosis and treatment of diseases of the nervous system. A child neurologist may contribute to the assessment of children with certain conditions such as epilepsy which bring about special educational needs.

Neurology

Neurology is a branch of medical science and practice dealing with the nervous system (brain, spinal cord and nerves) and its diseases.

Address

Institute of Neurology
University College London
Queen Square
London WC1N 3BG

Tel: 020 7837 3611
Fax: 020 7278 5069
e-mail: support@ion.ucl.ac.uk
www.ion.ucl.ac.uk

Together with the National Hospital for Neorology and Neurosurgery, the Institute of Neurology provides a national resource for postgraduate teaching, professional training and research in neurology and related disciplines.

Non-maintained special school

In the case of special schools, it is possible to have schools which are non-maintained but not independent. Under the Education Act 1996, section 342, the Secretary of State approves these special schools. Generally schools are run by voluntary bodies concerned with specific disabilities (e.g. the special schools run by I-CAN for pupils with severe speech and language difficulties). One specification of the above regulations is that non-maintained special schools cannot be run for profit (unlike independent schools). Non-maintained special schools charge fees.

Address

National Association of Independent and Non-Maintained Special Schools

15 Downs Court	Tel: 020 8985 1459
Amhurst Road	Fax: 020 8985 0337
London E8 1AT	www.nasschools.org.uk

Aims to promote and maintain high standards.

Note in lieu

If, after carrying out a statutory assessment, the local education authority decides not to issue a statement of special educational needs (SEN), they may issue to the child's parents and to the child's school a note in lieu of the statement. It describes the child's SEN, explains why the LEA thinks it should not issue a statement and makes recommendations about appropriate provision for the child. The advice received during the statutory assessment is attached to the note in lieu sent to the parents. If the parents agree, this information may also be attached to the note sent to the school.

Numeracy hour

The National Numeracy Strategy definition of numeracy adopted by the Numeracy Task Force in 1997 includes the ability and inclination to solve numerical problems including those involving money and measures, and requires familiarity with the ways in which numerical information is gathered by counting and measuring and the way in which this information is presented. Primary schools provide a daily session lasting 45 to 60 minutes devoted to mathematics and between three and five of these lessons concentrate on numeracy. The whole-class teaching which is a major part of these sessions requires teachers to be particularly skilled in differentiating questions and other work for pupils with special educational needs. The role of the learning support assistant when the teacher is teaching the whole class should be clear.

Further reading

Berger, A., Morris, D. and Portman, J. (2000) *Implementing the National Numeracy Strategy for Pupils with Learning Difficulties: Access to the Daily Mathematics Lesson*. London: David Fulton Publishers.

Address

National Numeracy Strategy	Tel: 0118 902 1001
Centre for School Standards	Fax: 0118 902 1417/1418/1426
60 Queens Road	e-mail: l&n@cfbt-hq.org.uk
Reading RG1 4BS	www.standards.dfes.gov.uk

Object of reference

Objects of reference are objects which are given a special meaning. They are used to assist memory, to communicate and to aid understanding. The objects may be signs that are part of the event or object for which they stand, for example a coat for 'going out'. They may relate to the things for which they stand by physical resemblance, for example a cup for 'drinking'. Objects of reference may relate to what they stand for by some agreed arbitrary link such as a three-dimensional shape for 'begin'. Learners who cannot read and write, those with visual disabilities and deafblind children may benefit from the use of objects of reference.

Occupational therapist

Occupational therapists (OTs) are trained through degree or diploma courses and most are employed by the health service. Paediatric OTs specialise in the assessment and management of childhood disabilities in order to help children and young people achieve the skills they need for activities related to everyday life. OTs may carry out therapy and/or recommend specialist equipment and (if necessary) building adaptations. OTs also work with children who have emotional difficulties, helping them develop confidence in coping with everyday needs.

Occupational therapy

Occupational therapy (OT) involves assessing needs which arise from physical disability or psychological difficulties and recommending therapy, aids and adaptations. It may include the provision of training programmes for self-help, work and leisure skills.

Occupational therapy with children and young people also involves working with families and teachers to enhance such abilities in the home and classroom environments. In addition to the role of OT in helping children with emotional or physical disabilities, it has been observed that some children with difficulties in sensory awareness, perceptual skills and motor coordination, given OT, improve in academic performance.

Occupational therapists use a number of approaches in treating these perceptuo-motor or motor learning disorders. Where assessment indicates the presence of particular learning difficulties thought to be associated with inadequate sensory integration, the OT may recommend treatment which includes specific movement exercises to stimulate more efficient sensory responses.

Programmes are designed to help a child or young person progress towards independence in personal, self-help or leisure skills. These may include the development of specific abilities, for example, the hand/eye coordination and visual perception required for skills such as handwriting. OTs may also advise on aids to assist communication and mobility.

Further reading
Swee Hong, C. and Howard, L. (2002) *Occupational Therapy in Childhood.* London: Whurr.
Jenkinson, J., Hyde, T. and Ahmad, S. (2002) *Occupational Therapy: Approaches for Secondary Special Needs.* London: Whurr.

Address

College of Occupational Therapists (COT)	Tel: 0207 357 6480
106–14 Borough High Street	Fax: 0207 450 2299
London SE1 1LB	www.cot.co.uk

The College of Occupational Therapists is the professional body representing occupational therapists in the United Kingdom. It is responsible for setting standards of entry to the profession, setting standards of practice, and representing the profession with the Government, other professional bodies, statutory and voluntary organisations. The college provides advice to members on educational, professional and ethical matters. It also has a library and databases to assist members in study and research, and publishes a monthly professional journal and a monthly house magazine for members.

Office for Standards in Education (Ofsted)

Ofsted is a non-ministerial government department established under the Education (Schools) Act 1992 and is responsible for the inspection of schools in England. Her Majesty's Inspectors are members of its professional staff. In inspecting schools, with reference to special educational needs, inspection teams consider, among other things, the effectiveness of schools' policies and practices and the degree to which schools have regard to the *Special Educational Needs Code of Practice* (DfES 2001).

Reference
Department for Education and Skills (2001) *Special Educational Needs Code of Practice.* London: DfES.

Address

Office for Standards in Education	Tel: 020 7925 6800
Alexandra House	Fax: 020 7421 6707
33 Kingsway	e-mail: info@ofsted.gov.uk
London WC2B 6SE	www.ofsted.gov.uk

Parent

In the SEN Green Paper (DfEE 1997), the government saw the parents of children with SEN as facing 'exceptional pressures'. The aspiration was to help parents cope with these pressures and provide the opportunity for them to contribute to their child's education, working in 'partnership' with others. Parents would be able to express a preference for a special school place for their child, 'where they believe it necessary'. A person offering independent advice and support should be available to all parents whose child's needs are being formally assessed. Parent partnership schemes would be in place in every LEA in England. Improved arrangements for encouraging dialogue between parents and others should 'be reflected in' fewer appeals to the SEN tribunal.

The 'programme of action' (DfEE 1998) set out actions relating to these aspirations such as that from April 1998 standards funding for parent partnership schemes was reinstated (p. 40).

The *Special Educational Needs Code of Practice* (DfES 2001) devoted a chapter to, 'Working in Partnership with Parents'. This defined parental responsibility; set out key principles in communicating and working in partnership with parents; how schools and parents should work in partnership; supporting parents during statutory assessments; how local education authorities should work with parents; and working in partnership with the voluntary sector. The chapter also sets out minimum standards expected of LEAs for effective parent partnership services and effective disagreement resolution services.

A parent, under the Education Act 1996, section 576, includes any person who is not the parent of a child but who has parental responsibility for him or who cares for him. Parental responsibility under the Children Act 1989, section 3(1), means all the duties, rights, powers and responsibilities and authority that parents have regarding their child and his property.

Under the Children Act 1989, section 2, those having parental responsibility are:

• mothers and fathers who were married to each other when the child was born, whether or not they subsequently separated or divorced;
• mothers who were not married to the father when the child was born; and
• fathers who were not married to the mother when the child was born, but who have obtained parental responsibility by agreement with the child's mother or through a court order.

The Children Act 1989, section 12 provides for a court to make a 'residence order' in favour of any person who is not the parent or guardian of the child. That person then has parental responsibility for the child while the order is in force.

Under section 33(3) of the Act, a social services department designated by a care order in respect of a child has parental responsibility for the child. It has the power, subject to certain provisions, to determine to what extent the parent or guardian of the child may meet his or her parental responsibility for the child. The social service department only has parental responsibility for a child when there is a care order or when an emergency protection order is in force under section 44 of the Act.

References

Department for Education and Employment (1997) *Excellence for All Children: Meeting Special Educational Needs.* London: DfEE.

Department for Education and Employment (1998) *Meeting Special Educational Need: A programme of action.* London: DfEE.

Department for Education and Skills (2001) *Special Educational Needs Code of Practice.* London: DfES.

Further reading

Greenwood, C. (2002) *Understanding the Needs of Parents: Guidelines for Effective Collaboration with Parents of Children with Special Educational Needs.* London: David Fulton Publishers.

Address

Independent Panel for Special Education Advice (IPSEA)   Tel: 01394 380518
6 Carlow Mews   www.ipsea.org.uk
Woodbridge
Suffolk IP12 1DH

Offers free, independent advice; free advice on appealing to the Special Educational Needs and Disability Tribunal; and free second professional opinions.

Parent partnership services

This service provides advice and information to the parents of children who have special educational needs. Providing neutral and factual support regarding the SEN framework they help parents take an active and informed role in their child's education. Funded by the LEA, they are run at 'arm's length' from the LEA or by a voluntary organisation to help ensure impartiality.

Peer tutoring

Peer tutoring may involve a tutor and learner of the same age, an older tutor teaching a younger child (cross-age tutoring), a less able child teaching a younger child, a more able child teaching a less able child (of the same age or younger), the use of untrained adults including parents as tutors and many other approaches. Mathematics, science and reading are areas of the curriculum which have been often chosen for research into peer tutoring. Indeed 'paired reading' is a form of peer tutoring.

It has often been observed that to teach something is to understand it better oneself so it is not surprising that peer tutoring generally appears to benefit both tutors and learners. However, the different approaches advantage each to different degrees, making it important that the teacher considers carefully the aims for both the tutor and the learner and chooses the approach to be used accordingly. Among other advantages of the approach is that it allows the teacher more time to give support to individuals and groups himself.

Further reading

Hornby, G., Atkinson, M. and Howard, J. (1997) *Controversial Issues in Special Education.* London: David Fulton Publishers.

Perceptual disorder

A perceptual disorder is one where individuals have difficulty in interpreting sensory information. Among forms of perceptual disorder are the following:

- visual agnosia: an inability to recognise what is seen although vision is unimpaired;
- auditory agnosia: an inability to interpret sounds (non-verbal) or an inability to understand the meaning of spoken words even though hearing is unimpaired;
- tactile agnosia: an inability to recognise familiar items by touch.

Gerstmann syndrome, associated with damage to the brain's left parietal lobe, is characterised by:

- finger agnosia: an inability to determine which finger has been touched by another person
- right/left confusion
- writing difficulties
- arithmetical difficulties.

Perceptual disorders can hinder learning, e.g. visual agnosia hampers learning to read. Attempts to compensate for perceptual disorder have included training programmes aiming to improve visual perceptual and perceptuo-motor skills. An example of a perceptual disorder test is the Developmental Test of Visual Perception (Frostig Test). This measures the skills of: eye-motor coordination, figure ground perception, form constancy, position in space, and spacial relationships.

It is intended for the age range 4–8 years. It was thought that impaired visual perception is responsible for some learning difficulties in children, although this view has been questioned. A training programme in perceptual skills is available which assumes that, if the relevant perceptual skills are improved, related learning difficulties will be eased.

Performance indicators (P-Scales)

An example of performance indicators, the 'P-scales' (also known as P-levels or differentiated performance criteria), forms an important tool in target setting and may be later used in benchmarking and in developing value added approaches. Schools that previously set zero-rated targets were required to set their first measurable pupil performance targets by December 2001 (for 2003), at the relevant key stage, using the P-scales or other performance criteria.

Criteria were published in 2001 providing descriptions of attainment leading to Level 1 and within Levels 1 and 2 of the National Curriculum for English and mathematics, and descriptions leading to Level 1 in science (Department for Education and Employment 2001a). An earlier document had included scales for personal and social development (Department for Education and Employment 1998). A series of documents concerned with pupils with 'learning difficulties' (e.g. Department for Education and Employment 2001b) contained subject materials on planning, teaching and assessing each National Curriculum subject, religious education and personal, social and health education and citizenship. These included descriptions of pupil's attainment indicating progress up to Level 1 of the National Curriculum.

It is a weakness of Individual Education Plan targets that it is difficult to establish whether the targets are sufficiently challenging. Performance indicators offer the opportunity of developing target setting, benchmarking and value added approaches for pupils with SEN that will go some way to overcoming that weakness.

References

Department for Education and Employment (1998) *Supporting the Target Setting Process: Guidance for effective target setting for pupils with special educational needs.* London: DfEE.

Department for Education and Employment (2001a) *Supporting the Target Setting Process: Guidance for effective target setting for pupils with special educational needs.* London: DfEE.

Department for Education and Employment (2001b) *Planing, Teaching and Assessing the Curriculum for Pupils with Learning Difficulties: General Guidelines*. London: DfEE.

Further reading
Buck, D. and Davis, V. (edited by Berger, A.) (2001) *Assessing Pupils' Performance Using the P Levels*. London: David Fulton Publishers.

Peripatetic teacher

Moving from school to school to help individual children or groups, the peripatetic teacher works with children with or without Statements.

Under arrangements for the Local Management of Schools and the Local Management of Special Schools, schools may purchase the services of a peripatetic teacher to support particular children who may not have Statements. (S)he might teach reading, giving specialist tuition such as music, help other teachers with particular skills, or support other special needs.

A peripatetic teacher may provide home tuition for children who are unable to attend school because of disability, accident or other reasons.

(See also *Support teacher*)

Personal adviser

As part of the **Connexions Service**, personal advisers fulfil a central role in providing guidance and support to help young people take advantage of vocational and educational development opportunities.

Further reading
Department for Education and Employment (1999) *ConneXions – The Best Start in Life for Every Young Person*. London: DfEE.

Address
The National Association of Careers and Guidance Teachers (NACGT)
9 Lawrence Leys   Tel: 01295 720 809
Bloxham   Fax: 01295 720 809
Banbury   e-mail: nacgt@freeuk.com
OX15 4NU   www.nacgt.org.uk

The NACGT is a professional organisation for teachers and others practitioners involved in careers education and guidance (CEG). It aims to promote the highest professional standards by supporting professional development, lobbying nationally to raise standards in CEG, providing information and disseminating details of initiatives, and providing publications and other services for members.

Personal and social development

The contexts through which schools infuence pupils' personal and social development include ethos, relationships within the school and through the curriculum, routines and procedures. The social context in which teaching occurs is central for all pupils, including those with special educational needs (McLaughlin and Byers 2001). Individual Education Plans and other forms of record-keeping and evaluation, managing transition such as that from school to work or further and higher education, and support for individual pupils can all focus on and enhance personal and social education.

Reference

McLaughlin, C. and Byers, R. (2001) *Personal and Social Development for All*. London: David Fulton Publishers.

Personality

Personality, so far as aspects which can be assessed are concerned, includes such features as temperament and interests. Personality tests may be constructed using factor analysis. A test is devised which aims to measure particular traits and it is given to a trial population. The results are factor analysed and items which do not fit the traits being measured are omitted as the test is refined. Another test construction approach is to use criterion groups. Two groups are given the test; one has a known personality characteristic (e.g. neurosis) while the other group has not. Items which distinguish between the two populations are kept while items which do not are discarded. Such tests are less objective than tests constructed using factor analysis and involve clinical judgement and subjective interpretation.

Another way of classifying tests is according to the response necessary and its interpretation. For example, projective techniques and tests are used to reveal personality characteristics by encouraging the respondent to 'project' his personality (perhaps unconscious) feelings, concerns and attitudes into the relatively unstructured task. Responses can be analysed according to the frequency or usualness of the response or by comparing responses with those of known respondents (e.g. emotionally disturbed respondents). Such techniques are often underpinned by psychoanalytic theory. The validity of such techniques is questionable and their reliability is low compared with standardised tests. An example of a projective technique is an association test in which the respondent is shown a picture or given a word and is asked to express the first idea that comes to mind.

Apperception tests are projective tests in which a person is shown pictures and is encouraged to make up stories concerning them. These are interpreted to gain an insight into the personality of the respondent.

The Thematic Apperception Test (TAT) is used for adults and adolescents. The Children's Apperception Test (CAT) is used for children from 3–10 years old. The interpretation is used to contribute to an assessment of a child's emotional difficulties.

Addresses

(test suppliers)

NFER-Nelson
The Chiswick Centre
414 Chiswick High Road
London W4 5TF

Tel: 020 8996 8444
Fax: 020 8996 5358
e-mail: edu&hsc@nfer-Nelson.co.uk
www.nfer-nelson.co.uk

The Psychological Corporation
Foots Cray High Street
Sidcup
Kent DA14 5HP

Tel: 020 8308 5750
Fax: 020 8308 5702
e-mail: tpc@harcourt.com
www.tpc-international.com

Philosophy

Philosophy is a skill or activity, which, while it can be informed by study, it is improved by being practised. There is no coherent philosophy of special education although there is a good deal of theorising, mainly along sociological lines. However, aspects of philosophy can be related to special education: definitions, logic, epistemology, ethics and metaphysics.

An important issue in the philosophy of special education is that of clarifying the meanings of terms particular to special education. Many words taken as comparatively objective are in fact value laden. Even a word such as 'special' can be understood in many ways. Other such terms include, 'disability', 'impairment', 'normalisation', 'integration' and 'development'. In a more general sense, a carefulness with terminology can help us distinguish between more objective language and evaluative or emotive language.

Linked to this, is a concern with logic which has to do with the validity and invalidity of arguments. Logic and an examination of word meanings can help us to examine the ideas, theories, arguments, issues and problems associated with special education.

Epistemology is concerned with the theory of knowledge. This includes, for example, debate about what should constitute the study and practice of special education.

Ethics includes questions such as the moral justifications or otherwise of certain interventions with people having special needs such as the use of behaviour modification techniques. Other difficult moral questions include the pros and cons of the use of plastic surgery to supposedly aid the normalisation of someone with Down's syndrome or the sexual freedom appropriate for someone who may experience difficulties in understanding or forming meaningful relationships. Such issues relate to the whole moral and value structure on which we base our actions and beliefs.

Metaphysical issues are to do with, among other things, trying to establish first principles as a foundation for other knowledge. First principles in special education might include the encouragement of autonomy in all human beings however limited their movement towards such autonomy might be assumed to be.

Philosophising about special education makes it more difficult to maintain uncritical views. It helps us move towards having a clear set of coherent concepts which we can debate and assess and modify as necessary.

In a more general sense, one sometimes speaks of one's own philosophy of special education, meaning a principled basis for our actions. The activity of philosophy can clarify our own approach and may uncover inconsistencies and views which have remained uncritically held. While philosophy is principally an activity, it can be informed by drawing on the philosophising of others. The study of ideologies in special education and the thoughts of influential philosophers of special education can be helpful in shaping our own thoughts and beliefs.

Further reading

Reinders, H. S. (2000) *The Future of the Disabled in Liberal Society: An Ethical Analysis.* Notre Dame, IN: University of Notre Dame Press.

Physical disability

Physical disability refers to disabilities which limit mobility. Among the causes are: congenital (e.g. cerebral palsy), accident or injury. Some pupils with physical disability may have sensory impairments, neurological difficulties and learning difficulties.

The inclusion of pupils with physical disabilities in an ordinary school may involve:

- building adaptations (e.g. ramps for wheelchair access, wide lifts between floors);
- aids to mobility (e.g. wheelchairs);
- **adaptive equipment**;
- other equipment (e.g. larger size computer keyboards);
- providing a classroom assistant.

Conditions associated with physical disability include **cerebral palsy**, heart diseases, spina bifida and hydrocephalus. Cerebral palsy is associated with interference to the normal development of the brain caused by injury, disease or a failure to develop normally. It can occur before, during or soon after birth and is characterised by difficulty in controlling the limbs and/or difficulties with speech, balance, hearing and sight. Spina bifida is often associated with hydrocephalus but hydrocephalus can occur independently. Spina bifida is a congenital condition in which part of the spinal column is improperly closed. In hydrocephalus more cerebrospinal fluid is produced in the skull than can be absorbed, the resulting pressure if untreated, can lead to an enlarged head and other physical symptoms and to learning difficulties.

Further reading

Cornwall, J. (1995) *Choice, Opportunity and Learning: Educating Children and Young People who are Physically Disabled.* London: David Fulton Publishers.

Kenward, H. (1996) *Physical Disabilities.* Stafford: National Association of Special Educational Needs.

Addresses

Association for Spina Bifida and Hydrocephalus (ASBAH)

ASBAH House	Tel: 01733 555988
42 Park Road	Fax: 01733 555985
Peterborough PE1 2UQ	e-mail: postmaster@asbah.org
	www.asbah.org

ASBAH offers information and advice for parents, students, teachers and other professionals regarding mobility, continence management, medical problems and education through their advisers and specialist advisers working throughout England and Northern Ireland.

Royal Association for Disability and Rehabilitation (RADAR)

12 City Forum	Tel: 020 7250 3222
250 City Road	Fax: 020 7250 0212
London EC1V 8AF	e-mail: radar@radar.org.uk
	www.radar.org.uk

RADAR is a national disability organisation campaigning for disabled people's rights and full inclusion in society. It has an information and advisory service and is active in the fields of employment, mobility, housing, holidays, social service provision, social security, education and civil rights. Publications include the *RADAR* bulletin (monthly), factsheets and books. RADAR administers the National Key Scheme for accessible toilets.

SCOPE	Tel: 020 7619 7100
6 Market Road	Fax: 020 7619 7399
London N7 9PW	www.scope.org.uk

SCOPE promotes and provides facilities for treating, educating and caring for people with cerebral palsy.

Physical education

Sport and recreation for children and young people with special educational needs has been enhanced by the increase in opportunities in these areas for adults. Successful practice includes effectively assessing the movement skills of the learner; ensuring that tasks and activities match the learner's needs; and breaking down skills into small steps to make them accessible.

Issues relating to care and health and safety may arise with regard to particular conditions such as asthma and cardiac conditions and appropriate medical advice should be sought.

Further reading
Wright, H. and Sugden, D. (1999) *Physical Education for All: Developing Physical Education in the Curriculum for Pupils with Special Educational Needs.* London: David Fulton Publishers.

Address
United Kingdom Sports Association for People with Learning Disability

Ground Floor	Tel: 0870 770 2464
Leroy House	Fax: 0870 770 2466
436 Essex Road	e-mail: office@uksapld.freeserve.co.uk
London N1 3PQ	

Promotes and coordinates sport and recreation for people with learning disability. Organises conferences, seminars and workshops.

Physiotherapist

A health service professional, the physiotherapist gives treatment to improve a client's physical condition, in particular mobility and posture. Physiotherapists may be based in a hospital or in the community and may visit homes and schools. Like **speech therapists** they work increasingly as advisers alongside parents and teachers. A physiotherapist undergoes a three-year training and must pass qualifying examinations.

Physiotherapy

Physiotherapy encompasses treatments which aim to improve posture and movement and particular functions relating to them. Methods involve, for example, movement, exercises, positioning, physical aids and hydrotherapy and the use of warmth and vibration. Among areas of specialisation within physiotherapy are developmental physiotherapy with children with special needs, orthopaedic physiotherapy, respiratory and chest physiotherapy and rehabilitative physiotherapy. A developmental physiotherapist begins by conducting a thorough assessment of the person's level of functioning and physical abilities. A treatment plan is developed which may involve others. For example, those caring for the child will work closely with the physiotherapist using his/her advice on positioning, exercises and the use of aids and appliances. The aids and appliances may be provided in consultation with medical personnel.

Further reading
Porter, A. (2003) *Tidy's Physiotherapy*. London: Butterworth/Heinemann.

Address

The Chartered Society of Physiotherapy
14 Bedford Row
London WC1R 4ED

Tel: 020 7306 6666
Fax: 020 7306 6611
e-mail: csp@csphysio.org
www.csp.org.uk

The Chartered Society of Physiotherapy represents Britain's 31,000 chartered physiotherapists, physiotherapy students and physiotherapy assistants. It combines the role of professional and educational body, and independent trade union. It has over 20 special interest groups, one of which is the Association of Paediatric Chartered Physiotherapists (APCP), whose members are willing to provide advice and information on all aspects of physiotherapy and children. This group can be contacted via the Chartered Society of Physiotherapy.

Play

Play is an activity followed for its own enjoyment and which normally has no serious aim: being pursued predominantly for pleasure. As a key aspect of learning and as an indication of a child's development, it is important for children with special educational needs.

For children with behavioural and social difficulties, play can indicate those difficulties and can be used by the teacher to encourage and develop social skills such as turn taking, negotiating the rules of a game and complying with the rules once they are agreed. Children who have experienced only a limited language environment can be helped by social play which encourages and develops language. Imaginative games and role play can be indicators of emotional difficulties and can be a way of expressing such difficulties. In general, play helps children to explore and make sense of their physical, emotional and social world.

Further reading
Macintyre, C. (2002) *Play for Children with Special Needs*. London: David Fulton Publishers.

Address

Action for Leisure
c/o Warwickshire College
Moreton Morrell Centre
Moreton Morrell
Warwickshire CV35 9BL

Tel: 01926 650 195
Fax: 01926 650 104
e-mail: enquiries@actionforleisure.org.uk
www.actionforleisure.org.uk

Play areas (including safety)

The provision in any playground should be informed by the needs of the children, including special educational needs. For example, in the case of pupils with emotional and behavioural difficulties (EBD) particular attention could be given to the layout of equipment to improve safety. Children with EBD tend to have difficulty in sustaining social play and even parallel play close to other children may prove difficult. Therefore, a playground could have some comparatively isolated play areas along with more social areas. This would offer a temporary respite for youngsters who feel unable to join their peers and would tend to reduce the number of playground conflicts which add to safety dangers with pupils with EBD. Vigilant supervision is very important.

By far the most single dangerous feature of a school playground is likely to be hard surfacing, most serious injuries being caused by head impact with the surface. A popular alternative is loose fill material such as pea shingle or crushed bark to a depth of 9–12 inches under climbing equipment and some moving equipment like swings. The area should be kept well drained, of even depth and clean.

Equipment design faults also contribute to accidents. Among examples of poorly designed equipment are high, steep slides with low sides and equipment that can trap fingers. Plank swings can strike passing youngsters. Some rocking horses and similar constructions can trap limbs. Climbing frames which exceed a height of two metres form an unnecessary risk. For a child who is poorly coordinated, a piece of equipment such as a 'witches hat' or 'ocean wave' should be avoided because of the equipment's unpredictable motion. Equipment maintenance is important. Fixed equipment should be properly installed, treated and checked. This will help ensure that dangers such as corrosion below ground level are avoided.

Address

Kids Active   Tel: 020 7736 4443; National Information
Bishops Park   Service 020 7731 1435; Minicom 020 7384 2596
Pryor's Bank   Fax: 020 7731 4426
London SW6 3LA   e-mail: office@kidsactive.org.uk
                                       www.kidsactive.org.uk

Promotes and provides play for disabled children

Play therapy

> Play therapy is the dynamic process between child and play therapist, in which the child explores, at his or her own pace and with his or her agenda, those issues past and current, conscious and unconscious, that are affecting the child's life in the present. The child's inner resources are enabled by the therapeutic alliance to bring about growth and change. Play therapy is child centred, in which play is the primary medium and speech is the secondary medium. Play therapy encompasses many approaches but the foundation of all approaches is child centred.
>
> (Association of Play Therapists, Code of Ethics, January 1996)

Play therapy may take place in a play room, perhaps within a child guidance centre or in a hospital. The child is encouraged to play freely with materials which aid imagination and expression such as miniature objects, puppets and paints.

(S)he expresses feelings and fantasies in play and certain themes may recur indicating to the therapist the child's concerns.

Where non-directive approaches are used, this implies that the child has the capability to resolve his own problems. Such approaches use the technique of reflective listening in which the therapist refers back to the child the feelings which are being expressed in play. Directive approaches on the other hand involve the therapist in structuring the play situation and impinging upon the child's unconsciousness in a purposeful way. The aim of directive approaches is to help the child deal with current feelings rather than explore early difficult experiences.

Address

The Association of Play Therapists
PO Box 98
Amersham
Buckinghamshire
HP6 5BL

The Association provides a support network for play therapists and information on training courses.

Politics

Politics may be understood as an activity depending on the expression of diverse opinions about proposed aims and how they should be achieved. Consequently, politics works through debate and compromise to resolve conflicting views and differing aspirations and to arrive at solutions to economic and social problems. Therefore, debate and persuasion is a crucial part of the political process. It assumes that any state will contain many ways of life and that the responsive political order must make it possible for people to follow their own ways within the rule of law. It is ruling by the consent of those who are governed.

While the study of politics may assume that politics is a system or a mechanism drawing on data to produce theories, in fact much of the study of politics is historical and descriptive. If the causes of what happens in politics is to be found in economics, social processes and culture, then politics loses its autonomy. But politics is autonomous and assumes that people act rationally.

When considering political aspects of SEN, it is important to distinguish between political debate where different views may be held, but which are amenable to argument and contrary evidence, and ideology which is less amenable to contrary evidence. Ideology may be signalled by the presence of a tripartite structure of theory. First, past history is regarded as the oppression of some abstract class of person and particular grievances are gathered into the 'symptomatology' of the structurally determined oppression. Secondly, supporters of the ideology must mobilise the oppressed class into a struggle against the oppressive system. Thirdly, the aim of the struggle is to attain a fully just society in a process of liberation (Minogue 1995: 17).

If this is taken as an indicator of ideology, the ideal might be that society is to be managed so that where anyone is not fully accepted, political action should be taken and attitudes changed so that harmony prevails. Politics becomes the authoritative allocation of values so that the purpose of society is to tell individuals what their views should be. Those in power will be the managers of equality, building increasingly greater detail of the rules of life.

To take only one example, elements of ideology are evident in the views of some supporters of that aspect of inclusion concerned with the balance of special schools and mainstream schools. Ideological supporters of inclusion in the mainstream may wish to see all pupils educated in mainstream schools and the closure of special schools which are seen as segregating and oppressive.

In considering ideology, it was indicated that past history is regarded as the oppression of some abstract class of person and that particular discontents are drawn into the symptomatology of the structurally determined oppression. In such a view, the past history of provision for pupils with SEN is presented as the oppression of these pupils. Instead of seeking to tackle any particular dissatisfactions with special schools in the real world, specific discontents are gathered into a vision of structurally determined oppression.

The second aspect of ideology was that supporters must mobilise the oppressed class into a struggle against the oppressive system. Accordingly, supporters of this aspect of inclusion ideology seek to mobilise adults who have experienced SEN into a struggle against the oppressive system. This may relate to the view that disabled adults must participate much more actively in the education of disabled children for it is only people with direct experience who know just how disabling it can be. It is not always specified how a disabled person, say with a physical disability, could have any more insight into the SEN of a child with profound and multiple learning difficulties than that child's parents. The grouping together of such disparate physical disabilities and learning difficulties under the umbrella term of 'disabilities' seems to ignore these differences. Neither is it realistic to think in terms of disabled people speaking for other disabled people simply because they are also disabled. To take only one example, some disabled people support the approach of inclusion of pupils with SEN in mainstream schools while others, including many deaf people, prefer special school education.

The third aspect of ideology was that the aim of the struggle is to attain a fully just society in a process of liberation. In SEN, this liberation will be achieved when all pupils attend mainstream schools.

If ideological views are held, it is less likely that they are responsive to political debate. The same holds true to anyone, for example, supporting the continued development of special schools on ideological grounds only because they represent 'diversity' in schooling.

Reference
Minogue, K. (1995) *Politics: A Very Short Introduction*. Oxford: Oxford University Press.

Portage scheme

A home-based scheme which aims to assist the development of preschool children with special educational needs (SEN), particularly children with moderate learning difficulties but also children with severe learning difficulties. The project was developed in Portage, Wisconsin. It is a teaching package which encourages partnership between parent and professional, to enable the parent to work systematically with the child using behavioural principles.

A Portage team member visits the family at home for about an hour each week. The parent is shown how to complete a developmental checklist and specify a teaching target. This is broken down into manageable steps using task analysis, and a series of teaching activities is agreed which it is estimated will take about a week to implement.

In the Portage pack are cards which relate to the developmental checklist and which set out suggested teaching activities. The visitor shows the parent how these can be carried out using behavioural techniques such as reinforcement and shaping.

The parent works with the child for short periods each day and systematically records progress. Each week, the visitor reviews progress and plans activities for the following week.

(See also *Behaviour modification*)

Address

National Portage Association (NPA) Tel/Fax: 01935 471641
127 Monks Dale   e-mail: npa@portageuk@uk.freeserve.co.uk
Yeovil   www.portage.org.uk
Somerset BA21 3JE

The NPA is a home visiting service for preschool children with SEN.

Post-sixteen provision

April 2001 saw the formation of an executive Non-Departmental Public Body, the Learning and Skills Council (LSC). The LSC carries responsibility for strategic development, planning, funding, management and quality assurance for post-16 education and training, except higher education, aiming to continue improvements in standards and bring more cohesiveness and responsiveness to the systems used. The remit of the LSC includes further education, community and adult learning, work-based training for young people and workforce development. Its main function is to meet the learning needs of businesses, communities and individuals through a coherent funding system.

The LSC assumed responsibility from various previously existing bodies for:

- funding colleges from the Further Education Funding Council for England;
- advising the government on the National Learning Targets from the National Advisory Council for Education and Training Targets;
- funding Modern Apprenticeships, National Traineeships (although these go on beyond the age of 19) and other government-funded training and workforce development from the Training and Enterprise Councils.

The LSC also assumed responsibility for:

- developing, together with local education authorities, arrangements for adult and community learning;
- providing information and advice and guidance to adults; and
- working with the pre-16 education sector to ensure coherence across 14–19 education.

Under the Learning and Skills Act 2000 (section 13), the LSC has a duty to consider funding places at residential specialist colleges for learners over the age of 16 who have learning difficulties and/or disabilities. The duties concern three age groups:

1. For those over compulsory school age but not 19. If the LSC is satisfied that it cannot secure the provision of facilities for education and training which are sufficient in quantity and adequate in quality, unless it also secures the provision of boarding education, the LSC *must* secure that boarding provision.

2. For those who have reached the age of 19 but who are not 25. If the LSC is satisfied that it cannot secure the provision of reasonable facilities for education and training, unless it also secures the provision of boarding education, the LSC *must* secure that boarding provision.

3. For those who have reached the age of 25. If the LSC is satisfied that it cannot secure the provision of reasonable facilities for education and training, unless it also secures the provision of boarding education, the LSC *may* secure that boarding provision.

    Where the learner wishes to attend a residential establishment but does not meet the residence criteria, the LSC will be willing to meet the costs of the programme and additional support. The learner would secure residential costs elsewhere, for example from social services.

Regional Development Agencies have an important role in the planning for learning skills with national and local links between the LSC and the Regional Development Agencies. The LSC operates through a network of local LSCs. Among the responsibilities of the local LSCs are that they set out proposals for widening access, particularly to those people who are disadvantaged in the labour market because of disability (or race, gender or age). The strategy **Connexions** concerns the education and training of young people.

Further reading

Department for Education and Employment (2000) *Learning to Succeed*. London: DfEE.
Learning and Skills Council (2002) *Circular 02/01. Specialist College Placements – Arrangements for Placements at Specialist Colleges: Learners with Learning Difficulties and/or Disabilites for 2002/2003*. Coventry: LSC.

Address

Learning and Skills Council   Tel: 024 7670 3241
101 Lockhurst Lane   Fax: 024 7649 3600
Foleshill   e-mail: info@lsc.gov.uk
Coventry CV6 5SF   www.lsc.gov.uk

Prader Willi syndrome

Prader Willi syndrome is a congenital condition named after the two Swiss paediatricians A. Prader and H. Willi who first identified it. It is characterised by moderate to severe learning difficulty, delay in speech and walking, underdeveloped genitals, excessive appetite, and other features. Diabetes mellitus often develops. Behavioural difficulties may occur in relation to the demand for food.

Further reading

Waters, J. (1999) *Prader Willi Syndrome: A Guide for Teachers and Other Professionals.* London: David Fulton Publishers.

Address

Prader Willi Syndrome Association (PWSA-UK)
125A London Road   Tel: 01332 365 676/668 790
Derby DE1 2QQ   Fax: 01332 360 401/668 790
                                    e-mail: Office@pwsa-uk.demon.co.uk
                                    www.pwsa-uk.demon.co.uk

Precision teaching

Precision teaching (PT), a behavioural teaching approach aimed at helping pupils with special educational needs, includes a detailed form of criterion-referenced testing. This aims to show whether the pupil has acquired a specific skill based on the teacher's judgement of what the pupil needs to know. The test is based on the teacher's own criterion. The criterion is the level of proficiency sufficient to demonstrate that the pupil has acquired a particular skill.

PT aims to evaluate accurately and quickly a pupil's progress. The teacher can then assess the conditions under which a pupil works best. If several pupils are tested, the teacher could evaluate a certain teaching method or scheme. The feedback involved in PT appears to motivate the pupils and enhance performance. If the teacher is using a curriculum-based scheme founded on stages of progress (e.g. a phonic-based reading programme), PT helps ensure that the step sizes are suitable. Using PT, the teacher identifies what a pupil can do and at what point he is failing. The teacher can identify what help a pupil needs and can assess the success of a particular intervention.

Testing used as part of PT relates to the curriculum and has direct teaching implications. The tests are usually constructed by the teacher and teaching goals are decided on the basis of an assessment of a pupil's strengths and weaknesses. The teacher makes a statement about how the pupil's behaviour will change. PT does not dictate any particular teaching method; it uses a precise criterion-referenced test. The entry to the materials is a 'probe' (a very short test). Targets may be organised into a graded hierarchical programme and it is important to break the task into manageable units. Techniques from **behaviour modification** may be used such as chaining, fading, shaping and prompting. Errorless discrimination can be effective. This involves decreasing the number of choices involved in a task so that the correct response is more likely.

Fitting PT into broad areas of work involves identifying priority areas, deciding on key skills within an area, writing the target objective, assessing the child on the target behaviour and, if necessary, doing a task analysis. A probe is an important feature of PT. It is a special test which must be repeated frequently and on which the 'rate' is important. A probe involves five factors:

1. presentation, e.g. a list of words;
2. instructions, e.g. 'Say these words aloud';
3. method of response, e.g. pupil says the words;
4. recording, e.g. tick for a correct word and cross for an incorrect word; and
5. length of task, e.g. 2 minutes.

Commonly, probes are written for reading, handwriting, spelling and simple addition. Probes are given daily at the same time and in the same place if possible. The rate of response is governed by the pupil. For example, in an orally administered test, the pupil says when (s)he is ready for the next item. The teacher notes the number of errors when testing. Daily recording is important. The daily record sheet gives the day, date, time, test length, number of correct responses, number of incorrect responses, the rate of correct responses per minute (divide total correct responses by number of minutes), and rate per minute of incorrect responses.

Further reading

Kessissoglou, S. and Farrell, P. (1995) 'Whatever happened to precision teaching?' *British Journal of Special Education*, 22(2), 60–3.

Prevalence and incidence

The prevalence of special educational needs (SEN) is defined as the number of children with SEN:

- in a specified population (usually the general population);
- over a specified period (e.g. 0–5 years old, school age etc.).

The extent to which a SEN is socially determined makes prevalence harder to estimate. For example, a general term such as emotional/behavioural difficulties is relative and to an extent socially determined. Consequently, its prevalence is more difficult to judge than a more clearly defined condition. Prevalence is affected by various factors:

- age (e.g. a child with SENs may leave school and cope in employment so as to be no longer known to the authorities);
- medical progress (e.g. the number of adults per 1,000 with Down's syndrome in Britain has decreased partly because of prevention and genetic counselling);
- race (e.g. West Indian children are disproportionately represented in some special schools);
- gender (e.g. more boys than girls experience language difficulties);
- socio-economic influences (e.g. mild learning difficulties without signs of neurological impairment are more prevalent in lower socio-economic groups);
- social structure and complexity (e.g. people with learning difficulties who might have managed in a simpler, rural society in the past may find it difficult to cope with the complexities of modern society).

Prevalence rates or ranges are important for planning services and to evaluate the effects of social and other changes on the prevalence conditions. However, to some extent, services may also influence what are regarded as prevalence rates particularly in the case of special education needs such as emotional and behavioural disturbance which are defined in a comparative way and where definitions do not always agree. Also, it is not always clear that the number of people known to appropriate agencies reflects the true prevalence of a condition.

Incidence is the number of new cases of a condition:

- in a specified population (often a rate per 1,000 of the population);
- over a specified period (e.g. at birth, in the first year of life etc.).

Incidence is usually expressed as the number of cases per 1,000 live births in a given year. Prevalence is related to incidence in that prevalence is determined by the incidence of a condition and its duration.

Further reading

Department for Education and Skills (annually) *Statistics of Education: Special Educational Needs in England*. London: DfES.

Primary education

In England, Wales and Northern Ireland, primary education is the stage of statutory full-time education for children between 5–11 years old. In Scotland the corresponding ages are 5–12 years. The school structure associated with primary education appears to lend itself more readily to consistently identifying pupils with special educational needs (SEN) than that of secondary education. Pupils tend to spend most of the day with one teacher who can observe and record the response of pupils to different activities. This can help the teacher gain a broad assessment. In secondary schools where pupils change teachers as well as change lessons throughout the day, the broader picture of an individual pupil can be more difficult to put together.

However, other issues arise. Because primary school teachers may not teach classes other than their own, they may not always be able to make judgements influenced by the whole school population about the relative needs of their own pupils. For example, decisions relating to the assessment and provision for children in the framework of the *Special Educational Needs Code of Practice* (DfES 2001) can be difficult. The SEN coordinator has an important role in encouraging consistency in the identification of pupils thought to have SEN.

A whole-school approach is important, as is clarity about the respective roles of governors, teaching and non-teaching staff. When identifying and assessing children with SEN, there again needs to be clarity about how this is organised, and about work with parents, drawing on support services and staff development. Systems of providing for pupils and maintaining and fully using records need to be manageable in the long term as well as in the short term when intensive work may take place in developing them.

Reference

Department for Education and Skills (2001) *Special Educational Needs Code of Practice*. London: DfES.

Further reading

Croll, P. and Moses, D. (2000) *Special Needs in the Primary School: One in Five?* London: Cassell.

Profound and multiple learning difficulties (PMLD)

Among pupils with PMLD are those functioning at a level comparable with the earliest levels of development and who have physical and sensory impairments. Some may exhibit **challenging behaviour** and/or communication difficulties. Some may not be ambulant. The range and complexity of these difficulties require the involvement of various professionals such as teachers and therapists and close working relationships with parents. Planning a curriculum for pupils with PMLD involves ensuring that:

- planning begins with the pupil's needs, interests, aptitudes and achievements;
- pupils are entitled to a broad and balanced curriculum (including the National Curriculum) which provides progression and continuity;
- pupils have access to programmes of study enabling them to progress and demonstrate achievement;
- teachers distinguish clearly between achievement in planning, assessing, teaching, recording and reporting;
- planning takes account of issues such as communication which permeate the whole curriculum;
- while planning is subject-focused, it recognises links between subjects.

Among the issues which offer a challenge when teaching pupils with PMLDs is providing a rich and varied curriculum which meets pupils needs. The development of communication and of personal and social skills are particularly important.

Access to a broad and balanced curriculum can be helped by the use of aids or adapting materials to assist learning; treating aspects of the curriculum in depth or in outline as appropriate, drawing on material from various key stages to create meaningful learning opportunities for the pupil.

Further reading
Dorchester Curriculum Group (2002) *Towards a Curriculum for All: A Practical Guide for Developing an Inclusive Curriculum for Pupils Attaining Significantly Below Age Related Expectations.* London: David Fulton Publishers.

Address
Equals	Tel: 0191 258 4914
PO Box 107	Fax: 0191 272 8600
North Shields	e-mail: admin@equals.co.uk
Tyne and Wear NE30 2YG	www.equals.co.uk

Equals is a national organisation for teachers of pupils with moderate, severe and profound and multiple learning difficulties.

Protective appliances and clothing

The aims of using protective appliances (including clothing) (PA) are to protect people with self-injurious behaviour and/or emotional/behavioural disturbance. PAs should be used as part of a behavioural programme which aims to decrease inappropriate behaviour and replace it with alternative behaviour. PAs can prevent tissue damage, are usually preferable to human restraint (which can reinforce the unacceptable behaviour) and can be helpful if staffing levels are low. On the other hand, PAs restrict activities, can reinforce the unacceptable behaviour and can make the disabled person dependent on the appliance. PAs may be used not for their intended purpose but predominantly to allay staff anxiety. This can be avoided if PAs are reserved for emergency use, there are clear instructions about use and records are kept of the frequency of use, the circumstances and the duration of use of PAs.

PAs should be chosen after a functional analysis has been made of the behaviour and the environment. Behaviour should be monitored before and after the PA is used. Staff should aim for minimal use of PAs to avoid hindering motor development. The PA should cause minimal restriction and as far as possible, should allow participation in activities.

If the PA is easily and quickly put on, it is less likely to involve giving adult attention to the inappropriate behaviour which could reinforce the behaviour. Clear plans should be formed for gradually dispensing with the use of the PA. The fitting of the PA should only be done when the unacceptable behaviour occurs. The PA should look attractive. Protective environments include cot padding (usually to prevent damage from head banging), padded chairs and plastizote cushions.

Minimum physical restraints can take various forms. Muffs are used particularly where the person uses their own clothes as a form of self-restraint. Mittens prevent biting of hands, fingers and wrists and stop probing with the fingers into the nose, mouth or anus. It can be difficult to keep mittens on and they restrict manual activities. Elbow splints are used where the person may damage their head, face or eyes with fists or fingers or where they pick slow healing scars. They allow full use of the hands and may be made of plastizote, canvas or foam. Variable hinged arm splints can allow elbow flexion for feeding. Palm splints prevent hand biting, wrist biting and hair pulling. Capes prevent using the fists to hit the head and the striking of the head on the shoulders. The user can use the hands to eat using long handed cutlery but cannot reach the face. A mouth guard or lip splint prevents lip biting.

Protective helmets protect against head banging and hitting the head or face. Chin protection can be added. An orthotic helmet is made and fitted by an orthotist (a specialist appliance maker) and is expensive and for longer-term use. Commercial helmets are not as secure as orthotic ones.

Psychiatric disorders

Psychiatric disorders in general have an establishable time of onset, are usually temporary and can often be alleviated or cured. Two main groups of psychiatric disorders are neuroses and psychoses. Neuroses include anxiety disorder and obsessive compulsive behaviour. The less common and more serious psychoses include schizophrenia and dementia.

When people experience both psychiatric disorders and learning difficulties they are said to be 'dually diagnosed'. There are difficulties in diagnosing psychiatric disorders in people with learning difficulties. However, some people with learning difficulties exhibit behaviours and symptoms related to psychiatric disorders. **Challenging behaviour** may also be a feature of people who are dually diagnosed. The diagnosis of psychiatric disorders among people with severe learning difficulties is important for the following reasons:

● psychiatric disorders may determine residential placement (e.g. in a hospital unit);
● they may be a potential source of stress to patient/family;
● they may involve major problems of management;
● disorders are often treatable;
● they may occasionally be preventable.

There are several reasons for the higher vulnerability of people with learning difficulties to psychiatric illness. Structural brain abnormality/dysfunction is found in most people with **profound and multiple learning difficulties (PMLD)** and in some people with **moderate learning difficulties**. The cause of the dysfunction may be genetic (e.g. tuberous sclerosis), infective (e.g. rubella), toxic (e.g. foetal alcohol syndrome) or trauma (e.g. child abuse). Brain injury may affect behaviour, personality and emotions. It depends on the site of the damage, the stage of development at which damage occurred and the nature of the processes concerned. Brain injury may predispose a person to disturbances in level of activity, to irritability, noisiness or defects in social and emotional control.

Another factor is **epilepsy**. Brain injury predisposes a person to epilepsy. The prevalence rate of epilepsy is higher among people with severe learning difficulties and higher still among people with PMLD. Also there appears to be an overall relationship between neurological dysfunction, learning difficulty, epilepsy and psychiatric disorder.

A further consideration is the potential effects of severe learning difficulties and moderate learning difficulties on social relationships. People with learning difficulties are vulnerable to the negative social consequences of educational failure and social rejection. Also they may feel isolated as children and not have other children with whom to play. As adults they may feel a lack of status, tending to have poorer prospects and being less likely to form lasting relationships.

General problems exist in diagnosing psychiatric disorder in people with severe learning difficulties or moderate learning difficulties. Diagnosis and symptomatology are largely language based while the language of people with severe learning difficulties or PMLD is an area of difficulty. Symptoms such as thought disorder, hallucinations and delusions, are all language based. Obsessional conditions include feelings of subjective compulsion, resistance to it and retention of insight. This can only be properly conveyed through nuances of meaning in language.

A further problem of diagnosis relates to development. Behaviours which might indicate psychiatric disorder in someone not having learning difficulties may in the case of a person with SLD be related to earlier developmental stages (e.g. repetitive, stereotyped behaviours).

Psychiatrist

A psychiatrist is a medical doctor who has undertaken further training to qualify in psychiatry. Because of their training in physical medicine, the training of psychiatrists includes the study of mental disorders caused by physical disorders (especially of brain function) and the related physical treatments. Training also includes social and psychological treatments. Most psychiatrists draw on a number of different types of treatment according to the perceived needs of the individual patient. All psychiatrists are able to prescribe medication if necessary. They tend to treat the more serious mental illnesses such as schizophrenia and manic depression.

Address
Royal College of Psychiatrists
17 Belgrave Square
London SW1X 8PG

Tel: 020 7235 2351
Fax: 020 7245 1231
e-mail: rcpsych@rcpsych.ac.uk
www.rcpsych.ac.uk

Psychiatry

Psychiatry is a branch of medicine concerned with emotional and behaviour disorders and psychiatric illness. It covers the study and research, diagnosis, treatment and prevention of these conditions.

Psychoanalysis and psychotherapy

1. Psychoanalysis and Freudian theory

Psychoanalysis is a body of knowledge and a method of treating emotional difficulties based on the personality theories of Sigmund Freud and others. In Freudian theory, most emotional difficulties originate in the repression of infantile sexuality. Freud developed a theory of psychosexual development characterised by the following sequential stages.

   a) oral-erotic phase (0–2 yrs)
       – the infant gains pleasure from sucking and biting.
   b) anal-erotic phase (2–4 yrs)
       – pleasure, achievement or possibly guilt are related to the retention and expulsion of faeces.
   c) phallic stage (completion of toilet training to start of latency period)
       – the child shows sexual curiosity and interest in his/her genitalia. Boys work through the Oedipus complex in which the child feels jealousy and anger towards his father for sharing mother's affection. Girls work through the Electra complex, experiencing feelings of rivalry with their mother for their father's affections.
   d) latency phase
       – sexual conflicts are subdued.
   e) genital phase (begins at puberty)
       – adult sexual feelings begin to be established.

Freud hypothesised that emotional difficulties would develop if any of the above stages were not passed through appropriately. Later adult problems were related to childhood psychosexual stages. For example, an adult who showed 'anal retentive' traits such as obstinacy and miserliness may have been inappropriately toilet trained at the close of the anal-erotic phase.

The treatment for emotional difficulties involved working through the feeling linked with early parent–child relationships. This may lead to abreaction, a release from emotionally charged memories and repressed fears. Abreaction is brought about by drawing the original unconscious experience into consciousness and living through it once more in the imagination. Methods for making contact with these early memories and feelings, include:

● free association (an interview in which the person is encouraged to say whatever enters the mind)
● hypnosis
● dream analysis.

2. Psychotherapy

Developments from and modifications of Freud's theories have evolved into different approaches to analysis. The wider use of some psychoanalytical approaches without the therapist necessarily subscribing to all aspects of the related theory has led to various psychotherapeutic approaches. Psychotherapy concerns the treatment of emotional difficulties by a variety of methods, each of which relate to its own theoretical framework.

Psychotherapy is offered individually in some residential schools for emotionally and behaviourally disturbed children. Sometimes a whole-school approach draws on psychotherapeutic principles and individual psychotherapy or psycho-therapeutic counselling may be offered within this regime.

Individual psychotherapy may be offered in a clinic which the child (and perhaps parents) attends regularly.

3. Psychodrama

Among methods of group psychotherapy is psychodrama or drama therapy. This uses drama to treat emotional and interpersonal difficulties. Situations are acted out and directed by the therapist. The drama may depict a personal problem of one of the participants who assists other players to depict the people represented as convincingly as possible. The director may use various techniques to determine emotional 'blocks' in the main character's life. These techniques include reversal of roles and changing the situation or characters. As the emotional blocks are identified, an attempt is made to resolve them through the drama. This approach is sometimes used in schools for pupils with EBD to help with relationship difficulties.

4. Family group therapy

Family group therapy is a form of group psychotherapy which was originally based on psychoanalytic techniques but now may include other psychotherapeutic approaches. It takes the view that some emotional and behavioural difficulties are aspects of the relationships between members of the family. This may apply to behaviours which are expressed in school or elsewhere outside the family group. The child expressing EBD is not seen as the sole cause or the sole 'location' of the difficulty. Accordingly, treatment involves members of the child's family. The venue for family therapy may be a child guidance clinic although some residential schools for children with EBD have facilities for family group therapy. A single therapist usually works with the family. In conjoint family therapy, two therapists manage the treatment jointly.

5. Psychotherapy and learning difficulties

Some psychotherapeutic work is being carried out with people with learning difficulties. Among the concepts emerging from this work are the following:

- a distinction between cognitive intelligence and emotional intelligence. This recognises that clients may score low on a cognitive intelligence test yet still demonstrate emotional depth and a preparedness to recognise painful emotions;
- a distinction between the damaged and less damaged parts of the same personality. The less damaged part of the personality may, because of organic, psychological, social and other external factors, be submerged for long periods. The disability may be exaggerated as a defence;
- learning difficulty has been interpreted as a defence against trauma. For example, in some cases learning difficulty seemed to give a screen against acknowledging experience of sexual abuse;
- mild secondary disability. This involves the person exacerbating their original disability to keep others in the outside world happy with them;

- opportunist disability. Here a severe personality mal-development which is linked with the original disability is added to that disability. The disability is used to express hostility and envy.

(See also *Child psychotherapist*, *Play therapy*)

Further reading
Bonoc, V. A. (1999) *Communicative Psychoanalysis with Children*. London: Whurr.

Addresses
The British Association of Psychotherapists

37 Mapesbury Road	Tel: 020 8452 9823
London NW2 4HJ	Fax: 020 8452 5182
	e-mail: mail@bap-psychotherapy.org
	www.bap-psychotherapy.org

Brings together psychotherpists with different theoretical traditions, offering clinical work and professional training in Jungian analytic and psychoanalytic psychotherapy.

The British Psychoanalytic Society	Tel: 020 7563 5000
112a Shirland Road	Fax: 020 7563 5001
London W9 2EQ	e-mail: editors@psychoanalysis.org.uk
	www.psychoanalysis.org.uk

Psychology

Psychology is a biological/social science concerned with mental processes and behaviour and its origin and development. A psychologist is a person trained in the methods of psychology. Specialist applied psychologists include **educational psychologists** and **clinical psychologists**. Psychological advice is required in the process of drawing up a Statement in the case of a child with special educational needs.

Further reading
Leadbetter, J., Morris, S., Timmins, P., Knight, G., and Traxon, D. (1999) *Applying Psychology in the Classroom*. London: David Fulton Publishers.

Psychometric tests and testing

Assessment and testing including National Curriculum tests and tasks are an important part of the teaching and learning cycle. Psychometric tests enable the tester to report, compare and gather objective information to inform teaching. Assessment is used for various purposes among which are to:

- evaluate the effectiveness of a teaching strategy;
- lead to a record of information about a child suitable for passing to an employer or another school;
- monitor the progress of a particular pupil;
- identify pupils who need help or special provision;
- check a child's understanding of specified topics.

A NFER–Nelson survey indicated that teachers value tests which have certain characteristics. They should be:

Fit for their purpose – relate to children's experience, engage their attention, be purposive but not too strenuous.

Valid and relevant – do what they say they do and provide suitable information – use current and up-to-date language.

Reliable – be dependable, consistent and fair.

Manageable – be as brief, lucid and simple as the situation requires.

Teacher-friendly – be easy to administer and mark, and require little or no subjective judgement.

Tests may be of intelligence, ability and aptitude. Some may be administered to individuals or groups or both. Some are diagnostic while others provide global assessments.

When considering ordering a test from a commercial source it is advisable to consider the following:

- is testing necessary? Will it give any substantial information which is not already apparent from one's own knowledge of a particular child?
- when was the test last standardised?
- was it standardised in the country of its intended use?
- is the cost in money and time justified?

Addresses

NFER-Nelson
The Chiswick Centre
414 Chiswick High Road
London W4 5TF

Tel: 020 8996 8444
Fax: 020 8996 5358
e-mail: edu&hsc@nfer-Nelson.co.uk
www.nfer-nelson.co.uk

The Psychological Corporation
Foots Cray High Street
Sidcup
Kent DA14 5HP

Tel: 020 8308 5750
Fax: 020 8308 5702
e-mail: tpc@harcourt.com
www.tpc-international.com

Pupil (participation)

The *Special Educational Needs Code of Practice* (DfES 2001) (especially Chapter 3) encourages pupil participation. Pupils, 'where possible', should participate in all the decision-making process occurring in education, 'including the setting of learning targets and contributing to IEPs, discussion about choice of schools, contributing to the assessment of their needs and to the annual review and transition process' (Code 3.2). A balance should be found between encouraging pupils to participate and over-burdening them when they lack insufficient experience and knowledge to make judgements without support.

Reference

Department for Education and Skills (2001) *Special Educational Needs Code of Practice*. London: DfES.

Pupil referral unit (PRU)

Under the Education Act 1993, local education authorities had to make educational provision for children out of school. This led to the creation of pupil referral units intended to provide relatively short-term support for pupils, many of whom were expected to be re-integrated into mainstream schools. PRUs do not have a governing body but are administered by a mangement committee. The head teacher normally reports directly to the LEA. While PRUs are expected to provide a broad and balanced curriculum, they do not have to follow the National Curriculum. Most have between 10 and 30 pupils, including some with statements of special educational need.

A review based on inspections of about half of the PRUs in England (Office for Standards in Education 1999) found that the standards of attainment of most pupils was below national expectations often because of previous poor attendance at schools. Progress of pupils was judged satisfactory with many gaining nationally recognised accreditation. Among the factors making it difficult to judge progress was the general absence of effective baseline assessment on entry. The majority of pupils behaved well and developed good attitudes to work. Most PRUs were effectively led and well-staffed. While overall attendance was poor, many pupils attended regularly, which few had done before. The range of subjects provided was often restricted and the assessment and recording of pupils' progress was weak.

The *Special Educational Needs Code of Practice* (DfES 2001) perpetuates the confusion about the role of the PRU, describing it in its glossary as a 'school', then referring to it in chapter 8 of the Code under 'Education otherwise than at school' (8.92).

References

Department for Education and Skills (2001) *Special Educational Needs Code of Practice.* London: DfES.

Office for Standards in Education (1999) *Special Education 1994–98: A Review of Special Schools, Secure Units and Pupil Referral Units in England.* London: The Stationery Office.

Further reading

Fisher, D. (1996) *Pupil Referral Units.* Windsor: National Foundation for Educational Research.

Pyramid clubs

The National Pyramid Trust, an independent registered charity, was established in 1992. It offers a method of preventative work with potentially vulnerable primary age children. The Pyramid System comprises a package of three procedures:

1. screening
2. multi-agency consultation for teachers
3. short-term therapeutic activity groups, run as after school 'clubs', for selected children.

The Pyramid System contributes to a school's response to the requirements of the *Code of Practice*. The aim of the Trust is to 'help all children achieve self-esteem, cope with school and succeed in life'.

Further reading

Makins, V. (1997) *The Invisible Children: Nipping Failure in the Bud.* London: David Fulton Publishers.

Address

The National Pyramid Trust for Children
84 Uxbridge Road
London W13 8RA

Tel/Fax: 020 8579 5108
e-mail: enquiries@nptrust.org.uk
www.nptrust.org.uk

The National Pyramid Trust for Children helps primary school children to fulfil their potential by building their skills, confidence and self-esteem. The approach is based on needs assessment, multidisciplinary meetings and therapeutic group work (the pyramid club). The project is run by a locally managed pyramid scheme which employs a local pyramid coordinator who works with local primary schools.

Raising achievement

A theme of increasing importance in the field of special educational needs (and in education generally) is that of raising the achievement of pupils. Related issues are the early identification of difficulties, high expectations, both academic and behavioural, of pupils and the judicious use of value added measures to inform teaching and provision generally. A whole-school review of policies, practices and procedures which asks at each stage, what is being contributed to the raising of achievement, is also valuable.

Further reading

Farrell, M. (2001) *Standards and Special Educational Needs: The Importance of Standards of Pupil Achievement.* London: Continuum.

Reading Recovery

An approach to the teaching of reading developed in New Zealand, Reading Recovery has been used in Australia, the United States of America, Canada and Britain. Most pupils taken into the Reading Recovery programme achieve faster rates of progress and tend to achieve a level which is average for their class group in 12–20 weeks. The programme provides half an hour of one-to-one tutoring by certificated teachers who have successfully completed a programme of professional development.

Pupils are screened at six years old and it is recommended that the bottom 20 per cent of readers in the age band be offered the programme. The scheme uses contextual approaches and concentrates on learning to read through the activity of reading rather than through exercises. It aims to correct early inadequate strategies used by children so that they will become independent readers. Children are taught to use all the skills and strategies they have. They are encouraged to monitor their own reading, detect and correct their errors through checking responses against all the possible strategies.

Further reading

Sylva, K. and Hurry, J. (1995) *Early Intervention in Children with Reading Difficulties: An Evaluation of Reading Recovery and a Phonological Training.* London: Schools Curriculum and Assessment Authority.

Regional planning

In the Green Paper, *Excellence for All Children* (Department for Education and Employment 1997), the Government proposes to encourage regional cooperation so that specialist facilities are available as needed. Government wishes to see the development of regional planning arrangements 'for some aspects of SEN provision' (GP 5.4). Social services departments, health authorities, the voluntary sector and the independent sector would be partners in the arrangements. Voluntary regional cooperation would be encouraged 'between LEAs and between LEAs and other statutory, voluntary and private sector providers, including non-maintained special schools and independent schools catering for SEN, and institutions providing teacher training' (GP 5.5). Such arrangements might include: planning for places for low incidence disabilities; encouraging cooperation in SEN support services; developing provision for specialised in-service teacher training; and gathering and comparing data on SEN provision.

Regional coordination in relation to pupils with sensory impairment was considered by a National Institute for the Blind working party (1998). This reported on the feasibility and desirability of coordinating some specialist services on a regional basis. It recommended that the then Department for Education and Employment, consulting with others, progress plans for developing regional coordination and consider the implications of the report for other low incidence areas of SEN.

References

Department for Education and Employment (1997) *Excellence for All Children: Meeting Special Educational Needs*. London: DfEE.

National Institute for the Blind (1998) *Regional Coordination of Provision for Pupils with Sensory Impairment: Achieving Equality of Access*. London: RNIB.

Research

A researcher in the area of special educational needs (SEN) may be involved in gathering, collating and analysing data on such matters as policy or teaching approaches. Research provides helpful information on the success or otherwise of policies and the extent to which the policy is having the intended effect.

Among the institutions involved in research including research into SEN is the National Foundation for Educational Research, and universities. Research into the causes and treatment of conditions which give rise to SEN is carried out in teaching hospitals and medical research units. Other focuses for research include the psychological, sociological, psychiatric, communication, motor and other aspects of SEN.

A common issue is that there is insufficient interaction between research and practice in special education. Of course, some research appropriately focuses on areas with no immediate practical application. Even so, research does not always sufficiently emerge from practice issues. Neither are the results of research always effectively conveyed to practitioners. Important in this are good review articles which draw together previous research in circumscribed areas and synthesise it. Links can be further developed between researchers and practitioners. Also, practitioners themselves may pursue research, perhaps in the course of studying for a research based degree.

Further reading

Rose, R. and Grosvenor, I. (2001) *Doing Research in Special Education – Ideas into Practice*. London: David Fulton Publishers.

Address

National Foundation for Education Research
The Mere
Upton Park
Slough
Berkshire SL1 2DQ

Tel: 01753 574123
Fax: 01753 691632
e-mail: enquiries@nfer.ac.uk
www.nfer.ac.uk

Residential therapy

A planned approach to therapy is adopted in some residential settings for children (and young people) with **emotional and behavioural difficulties**. Such settings are sometimes known as therapeutic communities. Among the influences contributing to such residential work are psychoanalysis and psychotherapy, theories of social groups and group dynamics and the sociology of organisations.

Residential therapy may involve various features including: planning the environment to be therapeutic, attempting to bring the ethos and organisation of the setting into a theoretical discipline so that they can be assessed, and therapeutic work involving the conscious and current interaction of residents. Conscious use is made of everyday living experiences and these are shared by a team of professionals and the children (or young people). The aim is to achieve jointly a solution to children's difficulties and to develop in the child insight and increasing self-control.

Respite care

Respite care offers a break for parents of children with particularly demanding special needs. Such care is offered by: local authority social service departments, voluntary groups and parents' self-help schemes.

The Children Act 1989 provides that local authorities have a duty to support children in need and their families. This can include help to allow the family and the child to have a holiday. The types of respite care are:

● care in the child's family home provided by a care worker;
● family based care, often with a vetted respite foster family;
● school holiday schemes offering playgroup facilities;
● residential care in, for example, a boarding school or a hospital.

The local social services department should be able to advise on schemes available and on the necessary safeguards such as insurance. Respite tends to be more successful when it is:

● planned;
● explained, so far as it is possible to the child;
● accepted by parents as necessary and without feelings of guilt or failure;
● seen as a strategy by which a child can often be looked after in the family home for longer than might otherwise be the case.

Where parents have other children who do not have special needs, respite can give them a rare opportunity to spend time with those children and perhaps enjoy activities which would be difficult otherwise. It also helps alleviate the isolation that some families experience and enables easier contact with friends, neighbours and community organisations.

Responsible person

When the LEA conclude that a pupil has special educational needs (SEN), it must inform a designated 'responsible person' who ensures that all those who will teach the child know about the child's SEN. This person may be the head teacher or an appropriate governor. This appropriate governor is the chairperson, unless the governing body have delegated another governor for the role. In a nursery school the responsible person is always the head teacher.

Rett syndrome

A rare condition, Rett syndrome affects girls only. First described in the 1960s by Austrian Andreas Rett, the syndrome was medically recognised in the 1980s. Affecting about one in 15,000 baby girls it is thought to be caused by a genetic disorder. Symptoms usually occur when the child is 12 to 18 months old. Skills such as walking and talking that had been acquired gradually decline. Other characteristics are odd, repeated hand movements and unexplained outbursts of laughter. There is presently no cure for the condition which is associated with severe learning difficulties and requires constant care and attention.

Further reading

Lewis, J. and Wilson, D. (1998) *Pathways to Learning in Rett Syndrome*. London: David Fulton Publishers.

Address

Rett Syndrome Association   Tel: 020 8361 5161
113 Friern Barnett Road   Fax: 020 8368 6123
London N11 3EU   e-mail: info@rettsyndrome.org.uk
                                   www.rettsyndrome.org.uk

School action and school action plus

'School action' and 'school action plus' are aspects of the graduated response to SEN set out in the *Special Educational Needs Code of Practice* (DfES 2001).

In school action, a class teacher or a subject teacher and the SEN coordinator identify that a pupil has SEN. They then provide interventions that are additional to or different from those provided as part of the school's usual differentiated curriculum and strategies.

In school action plus, the class teacher and the SENCO are provided with advice or support from outside specialists. This is to provide alternative interventions and strategies that are additional to or different from those provided for the pupil under 'school action'. The SENCO usually takes the lead but day-to-day provision remains the responsibility of the class or subject teacher.

Reference

Department for Education and Skills (2001) *Special Educational Needs Code of Practice*. London: DfES.

School effectiveness

In considering school effectiveness in relation to special educational needs (SEN), it is necessary to be precise about what is meant by the term 'effective'. This may refer to a school that responds to a diverse range of pupil needs suggesting that, in providing effectively for minorities, the school provides well for all. Another view is that the effective school responds well to most pupils. The question arises whether an effective school for most pupils can also be an inclusive school for pupils in minorities, such as those with SEN, both as regards participation and optimal attainment.

School 'league tables', as a reflection of an effective school, relate to the attainment of most pupils, for example aiming for an increasingly higher percentage of pupils reaching Level 4 of the National Curriculum at the end of Key Stage 2. There is less reflection of value that might be added to the attainments of those pupils with SEN who might progress well from a low starting point but still not cross the Level 4 threshold. An alternative to this is to set standards in the form of targets for different sub-groups, such as pupils with learning difficulties, and pupils without learning difficulties with the aim of reducing the difference between the two (Norwich 1998). Taking seriously raising standards for pupils with SEN as well as those for pupils who do not have SEN can also be seen as a form of equality. Raising the standards of pupils without SEN and only 'meeting the needs' of pupils with SEN could be seen as offering the latter second best.

Reference
Norwich, B. (1998) 'Inclusion in Education', in Daniels, H. (ed.) *Special Education Reformed: Beyond Rhetoric?* London: Falmer.

Further reading
Farrell, M. (2002) *Standards and Special Educational Needs.* London: Continuum.

School nurse

Every school has a named school nurse as part of the school health team comprising a nurse and a doctor. The team helps promote the health of schoolchildren, enabling each child to get the best from their education. In the term after a child's fifth birthday, the school nurse carries out a health and developmental assessment which includes hearing, vision and growth. Parents are invited to attend. The expertise of the school nurse includes: the management of allergies and asthma in school; enuresis; behaviour management; and bullying.

Address
Royal College of Nursing (RCN)   Tel: 0845 772 6100 (headquarters);
20 Cavendish Square   020 7647 3749 (school nursing)
London W1G 0RN   e-mail: carol.bannister@rcn.org.uk
                                   www.rcn.org.uk

The RCN council's priorities include: responding to the developing needs of members; promoting the evidence base of nursing by identifying and working on issues that impact on the quality of health care; promoting recognition and understanding of all talents and skills and the elimination of discrimination in nursing and healthcare provision; and positioning nursing and nurses' roles in a reformed healthcare delivery system so that nurses' contribution to healthcare is understood and valued.

School phobia

Phobia is an irrational fear of a situation, person or object. School phobia is an ambiguous term. It may be seen as evidence of a neurotic disorder expressed as a resistance to leaving home. The psychoanalytical view is that phobias arise when distressing internal conflicts are externalised and projected onto the initially neutral object. This object is then avoided. School refusal is a more useful term because it can encompass refusal to go to school which is more rational and conscious.

Return to school can be approached by working with the child to agree a planned return. Therapy, medication and home education are also used.

Science

Science activities have characteristics which can help pupils with special educational needs achieve success. These characteristics include that science involves first-hand experience and that concentration can be aided by the use of practical activities which develop knowledge and skills. Also, some aspects of science can be related to everyday life, for example, the study of light and shadow. Using such links can help pupils to better understand their surroundings. Particular care is needed with safety so that pupils can experiment and work independently within their capabilities but within safe limits.

Further reading

Marvin, C. and Stokoe, C. (2003) *Access to Science: Curriculum Planning and Practical Activities for Pupils with Learning Difficulties*. London: David Fulton Publishers.

Secondary education

An important issue in the secondary education of pupils with special educational needs is that effective links have been forged between the primary feeder school and the secondary school. Effective communication and the transfer of records help ensure that provision is continued. Time is saved if the secondary school does not have to spend too much time assessing and deciding provision all over again. Balanced against this however, is the possibility that some learning difficulties may have a strong contextual element. For example, in a particular case, a behaviour difficulty at a primary school may be less prominent at a secondary school where aspects of the primary school provision contributed to the difficulty.

Another important point in secondary education, where a pupil has a Statement, is the drawing up of an effective transition plan to make the move from secondary school smoother. The transition may be to work, further or higher education, or further special provision or elsewhere.

Further reading

Farrell, M. (2001) *Key Issues in Secondary Schools*. London: Routledge.

Section 11 teacher

Under section 11 of the Local Government Act 1966, teachers are funded by a Home Office grant. They work in geographical areas having: 'substantial numbers of immigrants from the Commonwealth whose language or customs differ from those of the rest of the community' (section 11).

Local education authorities (LEAs) and appropriate community groups bid for the grant which is to support equality of opportunity. This is pursued by providing members of ethnic minority communities opportunities, help and encouragement which they require to take their full part in the wider community.

Many teachers of English as a Second Language, are funded by section 11 grants. LEAs employ section 11 teachers to support individual pupils in schools and to advise staff. Grant qualification requires that the work is school based and whenever possible, takes place in the mainstream classroom.

Further reading

Home Office Circular *78/90 Section 11 of the Local Government Act*. London: Home Office.

Secure unit

Social service departments of local authorities manage secure units and there is also a Home Office secure training centre. The young people in these units, normally of secondary school age, require secure accommodation for various reasons and may have severe emotional and behavioural difficulties. Their stay can range from a day to several years depending on their remand order or sentence and the age at which they were admitted.

A review of provision between 1994 and 1998 found that several factors were inhibiting educational provision developing satisfactorily (Office for Standards in Education 1999). These were: not enough liaison between education and care staff; frequent interruptions and withdrawals of pupils from lessons; and insufficiently clear staff roles and responsibilities. Pupil progress and the quality of teaching were judged satisfactory or better in three-quarters of units. Most pupils showed interest in lessons and generally they concentrated and behaved well. Some succeeded in externally accredited courses.

Where a young person is detained under a court order in secure accommodation, the LEA is no longer responsible for them and under no duty to maintain the statement. However, LEAs may provide these young people with educational facilities and should make sure that the institutions receive information about the inmates' SEN. The institutions should try to make the appropriate educational provision. The LEA should be involved in the young person's 'exit plan'.

Reference

Office for Standards in Education (1999) *Special Education 1994–98: A Review of Special Schools, Secure Units and Pupil Referral Units in England*. London: The Stationery Office.

Addresses

The Secure Accommodation Network (SANE)
c/o Sutton Place Safe Centre
347 Salthouse Road
Hull HU8 9HR

Tel: 01482 374 186
Fax: 01482 712 173
e-mail: roy.walker@hullcc.gov.uk

The support network has no offices of its own but the chairperson's role rotates between secure unit managers who use their unit address. The address above is that of the current incumbent.

Home Office
Queen Anne's Gate
London SW1H 9AT

Tel: 020 7273 4000
Fax: 020 7273 4517
e-mail: public.enquiries@homeoffice.gsi.gov.uk
www.homeoffice.gov.uk

Self-injurious behaviour (SIB)

SIB is stereotyped, repetitive behaviour which causes physical harm. Examples are: self-biting, eye gouging, head banging and hair pulling. It is prevalent among people with severe learning difficulties, among schizophrenics, and among those dually diagnosed as having severe learning difficulties and mental illness.

In Lesch-Nyhan syndrome, self-injury often takes the form of biting the lips and fingers. In this clinical condition the cause is a metabolic disorder which is inherited.

Among other possible causes or occurrence of SIB are the following:

- positive reinforcement (e.g. attention seeking)
- negative reinforcement (e.g. avoidance)
- self-stimulation in the absence of insufficient stimulation.

A systematic approach to SIB is necessary involving observation, an assessment of the likely cause(s), intervention and monitoring. The intervention may involve behaviour modification techniques. Aversion therapy, where a noxious stimulus is linked with the behaviour to discourage it, may be considered where the injury or likely injury is sufficiently serious.

Self-management

In a behavioural approach to self-management a child with special educational needs is involved in implementing strategies which may help his/her behaviour change. A 'target behaviour' is identified. The self-management strategies may then be applied to the antecedents or the consequences of the target behaviour. The technique has been used by people with moderate and severe learning difficulties. In applying the technique to behavioural consequences, the person may use self-observation, evaluation, recording and reinforcement. Applying self-management techniques to antecedent procedures allows the person to make choices and to use self-instruction (e.g. self-talk, printed instructions). Self-management involves, ideally, the following:

- the person recognises their own problem;
- the person recasts the problem in terms of behaviours which need to be changed;
- the person finds naturally occurring events (contingencies) which will support change; alternatively, they would need to create such contingencies;
- the person arranges the contingencies so that change will occur.

Some people may achieve only partial participation in their own behaviour change and will need teaching and support to progress. Self-management is important for learning new skills, for learning to manage time effectively, for addressing problems and for achieving goals. All these are aspects of moving towards autonomy.

Semantic and pragmatic disorders

Semantics refers to the meaning of words or phrases. Semantic disorders may be considered as disorders of receptive language and of higher level language. Difficulties for children with such problems tend to relate to working out what a sentence is about, for although they may understand the possible meanings of a word, their difficulty lies with working out how the word is being used on a specific occasion. One particular difficulty is with metaphorically used words or phrases such as 'give me a hand'.

Pragmatics concerns knowing what to say, when to say it and how to say it. Children with pragmatic difficulties find it hard to use language in a social context. They tend to have problems with social conventions like taking turns in conversation or indicating to the speaker signs of interest in what is being said. Others often feel that the conversation of such children is irrelevant or inappropriate.

Children with semantic and pragmatic disorders have unusual characteristics of language. They find the understanding of certain words and sentences difficult, and use others inappropriately or oddly. Their social development and play may be limited. Appropriate educational provision includes effective assessment and close working partnerships between teachers, parents, speech and language therapists and educational psychologists.

Further reading
Leinonen, E., Letts, C. and Smith, B. R. (2000) *Children's Pragmatic Communication Difficulties*. London: Whurr.
MacKay, G. and Anderson, C. (2000) *Teaching Children with Pragmatic Difficulties of Communication: Classroom Approaches*. London: David Fulton Publishers.

Address
AFASIC – Overcoming Speech Impairments
50–52 Great Sutton Street   Tel: 020 7490 9410; 0845 355 5577 (helpline)
London EC1V 0DJ   Fax: 020 7251 2834
    e-mail: info@afasic.org.uk
    www.afasic.org

AFASIC works for improved services for children and young people with speech and language difficulties and provides information and advice for parents and professionals.

Severe learning difficulties (SLD)

Factors associated with, or causing, severe (and moderate) learning difficulties are varied. Chromosome abnormalities such as translocation or genetic disorders such as Duchenne muscular dystrophy may be implicated. Prenatal factors include infections such as maternal Asian influenza, chemicals like alcohol or prenatal malnutrition. Perinatal factors include **birth difficulties** such as injury and anoxia, a state in which the body lacks oxygen. Postnatal factors may be related to infection such as meningitis, malnutrition, poisoning (e.g. lead) or cerebral trauma. Subcultural factors include social deprivation.

The whole curriculum for children with SLD is underpinned by the National Curriculum. It is primarily developmental. A major aim is developing knowledge, skills and attitudes which will enable the pupil in later life to be as autonomous as possible and to live in the community to a degree which is appropriate and safe.

Among pupils with SLD, an important yet sometimes neglected area is that of the pupils expressing preferences and making choices. This may involve choice in decision-making and choice as an expression of autonomy. Pupils may communicate preference and choice by body movements, smiles or grimaces, and lip and mouth movements. Verbal expressions and signing may be less used. Staff responsiveness to child initiated non-symbolic behaviour is important in helping the child develop social and communication skills. Attention to a child's expressions of preference by teachers and others are important to encourage such skills – especially pre-symbolic skills.

Further reading
Aird, R. (2001) *The Education and Care of Children with Severe, Profound and Multiple Learning Difficulties*. London: David Fulton Publishers.

Address
Equals   Tel: 0191 258 4914
PO Box 107   Fax: 0191 272 8600
North Shields   e-mail: admin@equals.co.uk
Tyne and Wear NE30 2YG   www.equals.co.uk

Equals is a national organisation for teachers of pupils with moderate, severe and profound and multiple learning difficulties.

Sex education

In the case of people with severe learning difficulties (SLD) in particular, sex education has been a controversial subject. On the one hand, such people may need extensive care and support. On the other hand, they have physical needs and emotional needs just as do people without SLD. Sex education should be set within the context of loving relationships in just the same way as when teaching all pupils.

Further reading
Drury, J., Hutchinson, L. and Wright, J. (2000) *Holding on, Letting Go: Sex, Sexuality and People with Learning Disabilities*. London: Souvenir Press.

Sick children

Circular 12/94: The Education of Sick Children gives guidance to local education authorities (LEAs) who have a duty to provide education otherwise than at school where this is necessary to meet a pupil's needs. Taking into account the health of a sick or injured child, continuity in education is important whether education takes place at home or in a hospital.

Hospital schools should have policies to ensure continuity of provision, teaching arrangements and the ability to reflect the National Curriculum. The annual report should include information on the implementation of the hospital school's special educational needs policy. Long stay pupils need planned provision to help them return to an ordinary school once they are better.

Liaison between education, medical and administrative staff in the hospital is essential. Hospital teachers and named home school teachers need to liaise if the educational programme is to be effective. The hospital teacher should aim to provide a broad and balanced curriculum which is complementary to and comparable with the curriculum in an ordinary school.

Recording academic progress is important to the exchange of information with the ordinary school teacher. Sufficient classroom accommodation should be provided and it should be near to the children's wards. The home school should help provide or lend resources including books. Certain groups have specific requirements. These include children on adult wards, recurrent admissions, those requiring psychiatric care and children with head injuries.

Turning to home tuition, LEAs should consider the individual circumstance of sick children. Children should not be without tuition for more than four weeks. LEAs should take into account how the absence is likely to affect the pupil's return to education. Home schools should normally provide work as appropriate in the case of short absences (less than four weeks). Effective links between the hospital and the home tuition service are vital. LEAs should have a written policy on home tuition concerning organisation and staffing, timing of provision and giving a named contact.

Among observations made in a report on the education of sick children (National Association for the Education of Sick Children 1996) are that teaching should start as soon as the medical condition allows. Also, because educating sick children requires the skills of mainstream teachers as well as expertise in the impact of illness on learning, specialist teachers of sick children are needed.

References

Department for Education, Department of Health and National Health Service Executive (1994) *Circular 12/94: The Education of Sick Children.* London: HMSO.

National Association for the Education of Sick Children (1996) *Education for Sick Children: A Directory of Provision in England and Wales with a Commentary on the Problems and Issues.* London: NAESC.

Address

National Association for the Education of Sick Children (NAESC)

Regus House	Tel: 01332 638 5861
Herald Way	Fax: 01332 638 206
Pegasus Business Park	e-mail: naesc1@aol.org.uk
Castle Donnington DE74 2TZ	www.sickchildren.org.uk

The National Association for the Education of Sick Children is a charity working towards equal access and entitlement to a good education for all children temporarily unable to attend school because of illness or injury.

Sign language

A sign language is any system of communication that uses bodily signs; hand and finger movements, facial expression and body movements. Among sign languages are the following:

1. British Sign Language (BSL)

The most widely used sign language in the United Kingdom for people with hearing impairment.

2. Makaton or BSL (M)

Makaton is a nine stage vocabulary of about 350 manual signs taken from British Sign Language. It is used with children and adults who experience:

- severe learning difficulties
- hearing impairment and learning difficulties
- severe language impairment.

3.   Signalong

Based on BSL, Signalong is a sign supporting system adapted for people with learning difficulties. It is used in environments where English is the main language with: people with learning difficulties who find BSL too complex, children whose language is delayed and who may use the signs as a visual prompt to help develop word selection and comprehension, and others who have communication difficulties. Signalong is used in various settings including nurseries, schools, clinics and the homes of people with learning difficulties. The basic vocabulary comprises over 1,600 signs and is taught in four phases. In phase 1 the vocabulary corresponds to everyday objects and actions. Concept formation is aided by using real objects when teaching the first two stages and re-teaching the signs when pictures are introduced. Augmentative communication resources (including pictorial symbols) are available through Widget software on the Rebus 2000 collection. The Signalong Group (a registered charity) also produce printed photocopiable symbols.

4.   Signed (Exact) English (SEE)

SEE is a system which uses signs from the deaf which are used in the same order as in spoken English. Further signs and finger spelling indicate such features as tense. SEE can be used alongside spoken English to give a parallel representation of speech and to complement lip reading.

5.   Paget–Gorman Sign System (PGSS)

Like Signed (Exact) English, the PGSS is designed to parallel as exactly as possible the grammar, morphology and syntax of spoken English. It is meant both to complement speech and enhance ability to write in a grammatically correct way.

6.   Signs Supporting English (SSE)

Unlike Signed (Exact) English, SSE uses signs for only some aspects of spoken English. It gives an extra aid to understanding spoken English.

7.   Cued speech

This is a system of shapes made with one hand around the lips. It aids lip reading by providing information about sounds which are not conveyed by lip reading alone. Cued speech is used where children have some understanding of speech. It also opens up the possibility of learning to read using phonetic approaches.

The decision about whether to use a signing system and, if so, which one is informed by the aim of enabling the child to communicate with as many people as possible. For children with profound hearing impairment, both a signing system and spoken English should be learned. It is widely agreed that signing should be accompanied by speech when communicating with a child no matter how severe his or her hearing loss.

(See also *Total communication*)

Address

The Signalong Group   Tel: 01634 819915 (enquiries/administration);
Communication and Language Centre   01634 832469 (training/development)
North Pondside   Fax: 01634 814417
Historic Dockyard   e-mail: mkennard@signalong.org.uk
Chatham   www.signalong.org.uk
Kent ME4 4TY

The Signalong Group provide research and training and publish (priced) manuals and other resources.

Social skills

Skills involved in social contacts may need to be explicitly taught to some pupils, for example pupils with severe learning difficulties (SLD) or with emotional and behavioural difficulties (EBD). In the case of pupils with SLD it is important that the reason behind the behaviour is explained where appropriate so that skills are not just learned almost as superstitious rituals. Where pupils with EBD are concerned, the main issue is often that of expressing social skills in the context of mutual respect for others. The earlier experience and current behaviour of such pupils may make such an approach difficult for them to accept. Social skills training in a more limited respect may apply to behaviour modification techniques applied to challenging behaviours.

Further reading

Kelly, A. (1998) 'Social skills training for adolescents with a learning disability', in Fawcus, M. (ed.) *Children with Learning Difficulties: A Collaborative Approach to Their Education and Management.* London: Whurr.

Social worker/social services department

A social worker has a wide range of responsibilities. Among these is supporting people with disabilities and emotional, social and economic difficulties. Some social workers focus on children with special needs and their families. Social workers' former qualifications have been replaced by a single qualification, the Diploma in Social Work.

Working with others is a theme of the *Special Educational Needs Code of Practice* (Department for Education and Skills 2001). For example, the effective implementation of school-based stages of assessment will be feasible only if schools forge good working relationships with others including the social services department. The Children Act 1989 and the Education Act 1996 place duties on school, local education authorities, health services and the social services departments to help each other in taking action on behalf of children with special educational needs.

Reference

Department for Education and Skills (2001) *Special Educational Needs Code of Practice.* London: DfES.

Address

British Association of Social Workers (England) Tel: 0121 622 3911
16 Kent Street Fax: 0121 622 4860
Birmingham B5 6RD e-mail: info@basw.co.uk
www.basw.co.uk/england/

The largest association representing social work and social workers in Britain. It offers help, support and advice to, and campaigns on behalf of, social workers. Publications include *The British Journal of Social Work*.

Sociology

The sociology of special education seeks to challenge what are seen as the 'recipe' approaches of such disciplines as psychology, medicine and unreflective pedagogy. It brings its perspectives to bear on the social structures, social processes, policies and practices that constitute special education. It describes, analyses, explains and theorises about social interactions and relationships. Applying the general principles and findings of sociology to the administration and processes of special education, the sociology of special education does three things. First, it deals with concepts such as society, culture, social class, community, status and role. Secondly, it compares the contexts in which special education takes place both within a particular society and between one society and another. Thirdly, it analyses sociological processes within educational institutions.

Its concerns include the effect of the economy on the sort of special education provided by the state. It is interested in the social institutions (such as the family) involved in the process of special education. Another focus is the school as a formal organisation and social change in relation to special education. The sociology of special education seeks to understand special education as a social process in a social context.

A functionalist view seeks to explain why social structures exist in relation to their role in society as a whole. It starts with an analysis of society rather than of the individual, recognising the importance of the interrelationships of inter-dependent parts. Also pertinent is the way in which the functioning of the parts is vital for the wellbeing of the whole. Values are the key determinants of behaviour. In special education a functionalist approach includes the use of methods like the social survey aiming to determine such 'facts' as the number of people with SEN. It may also see SEN as a 'social problem' and focus on organisation, management, provision and direction. The functionalist perspective rests on the assumption that consensus in society is a normal state. While conflict arises from time to time, it is explained as an evolutionary phenomenon. A criticism is that this perspective takes insufficient account of disorder and conflict, such as that arising from time to time between those involved with SEN, who may take different views, children, local education authority officers, parents, teacher unions and so on.

The structural-functionalist rubric is a form of functionalism concerned with order and equilibrium in society. Structures in society interact with each other to perform positive roles for society as a whole. Everything in society has some positive function. A criticism is that some structures such as organised crime appear to lack any positive function. Those with SEN are not regarded as 'normal' because of the definition of normality applied by the rest of society. This approach is concerned with fitting those with SEN into society including finding suitable employment for school leavers with SEN.

Conflict theorists emphasise the struggle in societies between different groups. These struggles were thought to centre around access to limited economic resources or power. Marxist emphases concentrate on class conflict about economic resources. Neo-Marxist conflict approaches in education see a given educational structure as the result of social class struggles. Class interests lie behind any pattern of educational organisation. Economics is seen as a key determinant of behaviour. Disability theory (e.g. Barnes *et al.* 1999) has elements of neo-Marxist theory. Approaches relating to the work of Max Weber concentrated more on the struggle between different groups over power and status as well as resources. One group's dominance over another can arise in various ways and authority is seen as an important aspect of dominance. In this view, group interests permeated education and dominant interest groups could reform educational structures for their own ends. Regarding special education, approaches include considering the nature of historical development and economic, political and social climates in which SEN developed. There is also an interest in the way such developments help maintain a particular order in society.

An interpretative perspective starts its analysis from the level of the individual and works 'up' to the level of society as a whole. Research tends to be focused upon small-scale interactions in everyday life. Interpretative views developed from phenomenological perspectives. Phenomenological approaches relate to the social construction of the 'world' and its maintenance, and the interactions of participants. Phenomenology views social reality as the creation of the participants in it. Communication and interaction between people produce social categories and social knowledge. Reality is 'socially constructed'.

The social constructionist perspective attributes the causes of disability to environmental factors, including teaching methods and the attitudes of those who interact with the child. It discourages labelling and categorisation which is seen as a problem of the individual model. There is a fine line to be drawn between the identification of difficulties and labelling and there is a danger that this perspective could make invisible those who may need support.

While the social constructionist view sees the problem as being in the minds of able-bodied people, manifested in prejudice or social policies reflecting a 'tragic' view of disability, the social creationist perspective sees the problem as being in the institutionalist practices of society. Disability is seen as oppression. Difference is to be not just tolerated but also celebrated. One aim is pressing for changes in state and welfare provision to improve the material circumstances of disabled people. Disabled people no longer have needs, they have 'wants'. The perspective has informed studies of knowledge and the curriculum, the classroom and teacher interactions. It is difficult (Baylis 1998: 71) to see how this view can apply to some children with autism, or who have profound and multiple learning difficulties or are deafblind. Where such children interact with others very little, it is hard to see how their difficulties could be socially constructed or socially created.

Clark *et al.* (1998) seek to identify common elements of what they call the post-positivist paradigm, which is essentially a social view. First, they suggest that SEN is seen as a product of social processes. These processes encompass the social use of 'discourses' out of which concepts and categories of need are constructed. They embrace the functioning of social institutions which generate failure and develop special needs provision as a means of managing it. They include the structural social and socio-economic processes through which certain groups are systematically disadvantaged and marginalised. Secondly, special education is seen as non-rational. This stems from the view that SENs are socially produced; for if they are, then special education may be seen as part of the process of social production. It helps to sustain the social arrangements out of which the processes emerge and sustains the power of those who benefit (such as professionals with vested interests). The rational façade of special education is false. Thirdly, liberal, humane values are important. If special education is seen as oppressive, then it requires a response based on an ethical stance. Oppression should be revealed and oppressed people should be made better able to resist it. This requires a stand on issues such as rights and inclusion.

References

Barnes, C. Mercer, G. and Shakespeare, T. (1999) *Exploring Disability: A Sociological Introduction*. Cambridge: Polity Press.

Baylis, P. (1998) 'Models of complexity: theory driven intervention practices', in Clark, C., Dyson, A. and Milward, A. (eds) *Theorising Special Education*. London: Routledge.

Clarke, C., Dyson, A. and Millward, A. (1998) 'Theorising special education: time to move on?', in Clarke, C., Dyson, A. and Millward, A. (eds) (1998) *Theorising Special Education*. London: Routledge.

Special class

A special class is a class which provides for pupils with special educational needs (SEN) within an ordinary school. The class size is usually small. Pupils may have varying SENs but often the class comprises pupils with similar needs (e.g. moderate learning difficulties). Where the special class is part of a large school and where it provides for varying SEN, the pupils tend to be from the surrounding neighbourhood. If the special class is part of a smaller school and provides for pupils with similar needs, pupils tend to be from a wider area. Among the advantages of a special class are that it can draw on resources (staff, equipment and materials) from the school in which it is based. Among the disadvantages is the potential for class members to be predominantly with one teacher which may restrict access to a broad and balanced curriculum.

Special education

In legal terms, special education is education provided for a child with SEN. A child is defined in the Education Act 1996, section 312(5), as a person under the age of 19 who is registered at a school. However, for a child under the age of two, special educational provision is defined as 'educational provision of any kind'. Therefore, special education may be taken to mean special educational provision for a child under the age of 19.

A child does not have to be of compulsory school age to be considered as having SEN. The *Special Educational Needs Code of Practice* sets out the arrangement for the statutory assessment of children under statutory school age (4.39–4.40) and special educational provision for them (4.51–4.53). It covers the criteria for the statutory assessment of children under compulsory school age and over the age of two (4.41–4.46) and guidance on statements for children in the same age range. It also sets out guidance on statutory assessments and of statements for children under two (4.47–4.50).

A young person of 19 may be considered to have SEN. The Connexions service, for example, helps ensure the 'participation and progression of young people aged 13–19' (Code 9.56). Where the Connexions service is involved with a person over 19, the terminology is normally 'learning difficulty' and 'disability'. For example, referring to the Connexions service, the Code (10.16) states, 'Exceptionally, a person with complex learning difficulties or disabilities may need continued enhanced guidance beyond the age of 19.'

As a body of knowledge and skills, special education draws on several disciplines including: psychology, sociology, philosophy, politics, economics and history. Medicine and related disciplines are important because aspects of a medical approach inform areas of psychology and because some children with SEN also have medical needs.

Special Educational Needs (SEN)

In terms of the Education Act 1996, section 312, children have special educational needs (SEN) if they have a learning difficulty which calls for special educational provision to be made for them. Children have a learning difficulty if they:

(a) have a significantly greater difficulty in learning than the majority of children of the same age;

(b) have a disability which either prevents or hinders them from making use of educational facilities of a kind generally provided for children of the same age in schools within the area of the local education authority; or

(c) are under the compulsory school age and fall within the definition at paragraph (a) and (b) above or would do so if special educational provision were not made for them.

A child must not be regarded as having a learning difficulty solely because the language or form of language of the home is different from the language in which he or she is or will be taught.

Special educational provision means:

(a) for children of two or over, educational provision which is additional to, or otherwise different from, the educational provision made generally for children of their age in schools maintained by the LEA (other than special schools) in the area; and

(b) for children under two, educational provision of any kind.

A child is a person who is under the age of 19 and is a registered pupil at a school.

It will be seen from the legal definition that a child may have a 'disability' that does not constitute a 'learning difficulty' because the disability is not such that it prevents or hinders the child from using the educational facilities of the kind 'generally provided', as defined in the Act. Similarly, a child may have a 'difficulty in learning' that does not constitute a 'learning difficulty' because it is not significantly greater than that of the majorty of children of the same age. Even when a 'disability' or a 'difficulty in learning' does constitute a 'learning difficulty' the learning difficulty may not be considered an SEN unless the learning difficulty calls for 'special educational provision' to be made. This special educational provision is that which is additional to or different from that generally provided, or education provided in a special school.

Areas of SEN are set out in the *Special Educational Needs Code of Practice* (Department for Education and Skills 2001) which states that, 'Although needs and requirements can usefully be organised into areas, individual pupils may well have needs which span two or more areas' (7.53). The 'areas', with examples of what they may include, are:

1. Communication and interaction (7.55–7.57)
    –   speech and language difficulty;
    –   specific learning difficlties such as dyslexia or dyspraxia;
    –   hearing impairment;
    –   autistic spectrum disorders;
    –   moderate learning difficulty, severe learning difficulty, profound and multiple learning difficulty.

2. Cognition and learning (7.58–7.59)
    –   moderate learning difficulty, severe learning difficulty, profound and multiple learning difficulty;
    –   specific learning difficulties such as dyslexia or dyspraxia;
    –   autistic spectrum disorders.

3. Behaviour, emotional and social development (7.60–7.61)
    –   emotional and behavioural difficulty;
    –   withdrawn, isolated;
    –   challenging behaviour;
    –   disruptive, disturbing;
    –   hyperactive, lacking concentration;
    –   immature social skills.

4. Sensory and/or physical (7.62–7.63)
    –   hearing impairment;
    –   visual impairment.

The Code also notes that there are 'specific needs that usually relate directly to particular types of impairment' (7.52).

References
Department for Education and Employment (1996) *Education Act 1996.* London: Her Majesty's Stationery Office.
Department for Education and Skills (2001) *Special Educational Needs Code of Practice.* London: DfES.

Address
The National Association for Special Educational Needs (NASEN)
NASEN House
4/5 Amber Business Village   Tel: 01827 311500
Amber Close   Fax: 01827 313005
Amington   e-mail: nasen@bbcnc.org.uk
Tamworth   www.nasen.org.uk
Staffordshire B77 4RP

NASEN aims to promote the development of children and young people with SEN and supports those who work with them.

Special Educational Needs Coordinator (SENCO)
The SENCO is a teacher having responsibilities for coordinating special education

under the *Special Education Needs Code of Practice*. The head teacher or deputy head teacher may be the SENCO in a small school. A team of teachers may coordinate special education in a large school and may be known as the SEN coordination team or the learning support team. In early education settings, the SENCO is responsible for:

- ensuring liaison with the parents and other professionals regarding children with SEN;
- advising and supporting other practitioners in the setting;
- ensuring that appropriate Individual Education Plans are in place; and
- ensuring that relevant background information about children with SEN is collected, recorded and updated.

In a mainstream primary school, the duties of the SENCO may include:

- overseeing the day-to-day operation of the school's SEN policy;
- liaising with and advising teacher colleagues;
- coordinating provision for children with SEN;
- overseeing the records on all pupils with SEN;
- liaising with the parents of children with SEN;
- contributing to staff in-service training;
- liaising with external agencies (e.g. educational psychological services, medical services, social services, voluntary bodies and other support agencies);
- managing learning support assistants.

In a mainstream secondary school, the duties of the SENCO are the same as those of the SENCO in primary school except for the last two responsibilities listed above which, in secondary, are better expressed as:

- liaising with external agencies (e.g. educational psychological services, the Connexions personal assistant, medical services, social services, voluntary bodies and other support agencies); and
- managing the SEN team of teachers and learning support assitants.

The timetable of the SENCO needs careful thought if teaching responsibilities are to be balanced appropriately with other responsibilities. The particular circumstances of the school and resources will need to be taken into account.

Further reading
Jones, F., Jones, K. and Szwed, C. (2001) *The SENCO as Teacher and Manager: A Guide for Practitioners and Trainers*. London: David Fulton Publishers.

Special Educational Needs policy (Schools)

Certain educational settings and schools must have a written SEN policy. These are:

- settings receiving government funding for early education;
- maintained nursery schools;
- community, foundation and voluntary schools;
- community and foundation special schools;
- City Academies;
- City Technology Colleges;
- City Colleges for Technology of the Arts.

The SEN policy must contain the information laid out in the Education (Special Educational Needs) (Information) Regulations 1999. These regulations are appended to the *Special Educational Needs Code of Practice* (Department for Education and Skills 2001). SEN policies in early education settings and City Academies must contain information as set out in the conditions of the grant. LEAs must ensure that pupil referral units have suitable SEN policies.

Governing bodies of all maintained mainstream schools must publish information about (and report on) the schools SEN policy. The governing body must at least annually 'consider and report on' their school policies and on the effectiveness of the school's work on behalf of children with SEN. The governing body's annual report must include information on the implementation of the governing body's policy on pupils with SEN and any changes to the policy in the previous year.

Reference
Department for Education and Skills (2001) *Special Educational Needs Code of Practice.* London: DfES.

Further reading
Tarr, J., Thomas, G. and Davies, J. D. (2003) *Reviewing Your Special Educational Needs Policy: Development Through Action Planning.* London: David Fulton Publishers.

Special Educational Needs and Disability Tribunal

Parents may appeal against a decision made by the Local Education Authority (LEA) concerning statutory assessments or Statements. The appeal is made to an independent body, the Special Educational Needs and Disability Tribunal.

The Tribunal is intended to be easily accessible and to resolve disputes fairly and quickly. Parents are able to put their case in person. Hearings take place within reasonable travelling distance of the parents' home. Most appeals in London and the South-East, for example, are heard at the Tribunal's London headquarters. Parents are able to bring a friend or relative to speak for them if they prefer.

The Tribunal has published a guide explaining what it does, how to lodge an appeal, and what will happen at the hearing. The guide is available from LEAs, libraries, voluntary organisations and the Citizens' Advice Bureau. It also explains how long the appeal procedure is likely to take.

Each appeal is heard by three Tribunal members: a legally qualified chairman, and two lay members with experience in special educational needs and/or local government. The chairman gives a decision in writing and explains the reasons behind it. The Tribunal has jurisdiction over LEAs but not over individual schools. Its decision is binding on both parties to the appeal.

Address
Special Educational Needs and Disability Tribunal
71 Victoria Street   Tel: 01325 392 555 (helpline)
London SW1H 0HW   Fax: 020 7925 6926
                                  e-mail: tribunalqueries@sent.gsi.gov
                                  www.sentribunal.gov.uk

Special school

A special school is specially organised to provide for pupils with SEN. It may be maintained by a local education authority (LEA) as a community or foundation special school, or may be non-maintained or independent. In an LEA-maintained school, governors are responsible for most of the school's budget. A **non-maintained special school** is often provided by a voluntary body and is non-profit-making, but is eligible for grants from public funds for certain things. An independent special school may be profit-making.

A report by Her Majesty's Inspectors (Office for Standards in Education 1999) reviewed the findings of inspections of maintained special schools and of independent and other non-maintained special schools in England between 1994 and 1998. In the first three years of the four-year review, it was found that standards of pupil achievement were rising slowly but that in the final year standards rose more quickly so that in nine out of ten schools pupils made satisfactory progress or better. Standards improved in most subjects but not in information and communications technology where progress was satisfactory in only a half of the schools. The quality of teaching improved until it was satisfactory or better in nine out of ten schools. It was lowest in schools for pupils with emotional and behavioural difficulties. Fewer than half of the schools had satisfactory practice in assessing and recording pupil progress. However, the general picture was one of improved and improving special school provision.

A report on the impact of the National Literacy Strategy on special schools (Office for Standards in Education 2000) indicated the need for more suitable materials for pupils in special schools, especially for pupils with severe learning difficulties.

The Government Programme of Action (Department for Education and Employment 1998) envisaged a continuing and developing dual role for special schools in providing for pupils with the most severe and complex special educational needs (SEN) and at the same time supporting the inclusion of some pupils with SEN in mainstream schools.

References

Department for Education and Employment (1998) *Meeting Special Educational Needs: A Programme of Action.* London: DfEE.

Office for Standards in Education (1999) *Special Education: A Review of Special Schools, Secure Units and Pupil Referral Units in England 1994–98.* London: The Stationary Office.

Office for Standards in Education (2000) *The National Literacy Strategy in Special Schools 1998–2000.* London: Ofsted.

Further reading

Office for Standards in Education (1999) *Handbook for Inspectors: Special Schools and Pupil Referral Units.* London: Ofsted.

Specialist college

As well as provision in such a venue as a **college of further education**, a person with a disability or a learning difficulty may obtain a place in a specialist college. Such colleges provide specially for disabilities and learning difficulties and have specialist staff and resources. They can create a more adult pattern of living than school and their programmes can include experience in the local community. The college may be residential which may be valuable to young people who have previously remained at home, giving them opportunities for independence. However, if the setting is rural, this may make it more difficult to encourage many of the skills relevant to someone who will ultimately return to an urban setting.

The Learning and Skills Council considers funding for a placement in a specialist college under the Learning and Skills Act 2000 and sets out criteria for considering requests (Learning and Skills Council 2002).

Reference
Learning and Skills Council (2002) *Circular 02/01. Specialist College Placements – Arrangements for Placements at Specialist Colleges: Learners with Learning Difficulties and/or Disabilites for 2002/2003.* Coventry: LSC.

Address

Learning and Skills Council	Tel: 024 7670 3241
101 Lockhurst Lane	Fax: 024 7649 3600
Foleshill	e-mail: info@lsc.gov.uk
Coventry CV6 5SF	www.lsc.gov.uk

Specialist teacher

The Teacher Training Agency has developed national standards for specialist teachers (Teacher Training Agency 1999) and a framework for their training taking in current qualifications (Teacher Training Agency 1998). These relate to those in schools or in local education authority services who work with pupils with severe and complex forms of SEN and other teachers considering specialising in the teaching of pupils with complex SEN.

The Core standards set out the professional knowledge and understanding, skills and attributes needed by effective specialist SEN teachers. Specialist standards set out the additional skills needed in each of the following areas of specialist work: autism; emotional and behavioural difficulties; deafness; blindness; deafblindness; physical disabilities; severe and profound learning difficulties; specific learning difficulties; speech, language and communication difficulties; and visual impairment. A set of standards concern the additional roles and responsibilities assumed by some SEN specialist teachers, such as that of an LEA adviser. The standards required will be applied according to the exact nature of a teacher's role. Using the standards, specialist teachers should be enabled to plan and monitor their professional development, their training and performance. This should enable them to set targets for improving their effectiveness.

The TTA states that training should cover needs assessment and target setting. It will be flexible and concentrate on practical professional training, building on the existing skills of teachers.

References
Teacher Training Agency (1998) *Options for the Delivery of Training for Special Educational Needs Specialists.* London: TTA.
Teacher Training Agency (1999) *National Standards for Special Educational Needs (SEN) Teachers.* London: TTA.

Specific learning difficulties (SpLD)

Specific learning difficulty may refer to a particular difficulty in reading or mathematics for a child who otherwise performs adequately in other areas of the curriculum.

Among specific learning difficulties are:

- acalculia: difficulties with number symbols and mathematical operations. The term is sometimes used when referring to damage to previously apparent mathematical abilities following brain damage;
- dyscalculia: difficulties with mathematics generally but particularly with arithmetical operations;
- dyslexia: difficulties with reading, writing and spelling
- dyspraxia: difficulties with the planning and organisation of physical movement.

With all these, the important issues are identifying the areas of difficulty and providing educational programmes to address them, monitoring progress and adjusting the programme as necessary.

There are a range of strategies helpful when teaching pupils with specific learning difficulties. Preventative approaches with younger pupils involve trying to prevent difficulties growing. Helping with difficulties with orientating letters might include making sure that the child has an appropriate pencil grip. Problems with phonological development may be aleviated by approaches such as teaching literacy skills using **multisensory teaching methods**. Difficulties may emerge from poor listening skills and poor memory of auditory sequences and these may be reduced by such means as checking that instructions have been heard properly by asking pupils who have difficulties to repeat what has been said. To aleviate difficulties in classroom organisation, one approach is to ensure that a pupil knows where resources are kept. Learning difficulties can be reduced by, for example, using variety in presenting information such as pictorial aids and artefacts instead of just spoken presentations. Motivational difficulties can be met by such strategies as anticipating frustration and avoiding disapproval if a child's difficulty hinders his performance.

As well as trying to prevent or at least diminish difficulties, the teacher can recognise the difficulties. This might include ensuring subject text books are within the reading capability of a pupil. Also, it could involve being careful before asking a pupil to read aloud in front of peers – perhaps giving the pupil the opportunity to prepare first.

Particularly for older pupils, direct work to remedy difficulties could include developing word banks for different subjects and teaching study skills such as note taking. Compensating for difficulties can include the use of a word processor with a spell checker and emphasising assessment by oral means or by multiple choice questions.

Speech and language difficulties

Language may involve verbal and non-verbal communications and symbols. It enables a person to make sense of experiences and to communicate. A central role in education is played by language because education centres around communication. Also, language use is an important factor in the poor school performance of disadvantaged children. Language development involves various aspects of language. The development of receptive language (e.g. listening or reading) interacts with the development of expressive language (e.g. speaking or writing). The study of development of phonology (the ability to recognise and produce sound contrasts), vocabulary and grammatical structure indicate that these features develop in a sequence and at typical average ages. However, there are sometimes wide variations in the age ranges at which such features normally develop. The impairment of normal language functioning affects a person's cognitive, emotional or social skills. Causes of language impairment may be predominantly biological or environmental.

Among biological causes are hearing impairment, neurological impairments and coordination difficulties. Hearing impairment hinders the reception of speech which leads to difficulties with speech expression. Certain neurological impairments can lead to communication difficulties even if the necessary mechanisms (auditory, visual, speech) are intact. Coordination problems can lead to writing difficulties.

Environmental causes of language impairment include an environment in which language does not play an important part; or a child may experience the inadequate use of language from those with whom (s)he is in close contact. It is also detrimental if a child is not encouraged to use and comprehend gradually more complex language.

To assess language development, to determine any difficulties and to resolve them, it is necessary to have a model of language structure. Language disorders can be grouped according to the mode of transmission, that is, speech, print or gesture (including sign languages). An example of a speech disorder would be stuttering; a disorder involving print would be reading difficulties, while dyspraxia (apraxia) is an example of a disorder involving gesture. Dyspraxia is the inability to carry out a pattern of movements, despite the person understanding what is required and being physically able to comply. It is caused by damage to/abnormality of certain parts of the brain. An aspect of dyspraxia may be deficits in speech coordination. Sounds can be made but not under conscious control to form words.

Another way of grouping language disorders is according to receptive or expressive activity. Receptive language includes reading and hearing and an example of a receptive disorder is **hearing impairment**. Expressive language includes writing and speaking and an example of an expressive disorder would be articulation difficulties. Difficulties with articulation can be associated with such factors as **cerebral palsy**, physical impairments to the palate and, indeed, hearing impairment. Articulation disorders may be substitutions (wead for read), distortions (a lisp), omissions (ca for cat), or additions (carn for car).

Another classification of language disorders is organic and functional. Organic disorders have an explicit medical cause; for example, receptive aphasia. Aphasia (dysphasia) is an absence or loss of language skills caused by damage to, or an abnormality of, the cerebral cortex. Expressive aphasia involves the loss of the ability to form ideas into words. Receptive aphasia is an inability to understand language. Functional disorders have no clear medical pathology and include such conditions as **dyslexia**.

Another distinction is between language delay and language deviance. Delay refers to a normal language pattern which is slow in developing. Deviance is an abnormal language feature which occurs with development which is otherwise normal.

The detailed assessment of language impairment may include the contributions of a **speech and language therapist** or a psychologist and, perhaps, a **neurologist**. A programme may be developed by a speech and language therapist working with a teacher. The programme may be delivered by a teacher and by others including the speech and language therapist. Depending on the impairment, provision may include individual sessions of structured language teaching and continuing assessments of progress.

Sometimes a distinction is made between 'speech difficulties' and 'language difficulties'. Language is taken to include such aspects as grammar, while speech is taken to be the physical utterances a person makes. If such a distinction is made, it is possible to have no language difficulties but speech difficulties and vice versa.

However, speech and language develop together and speech and language difficulties often coexist. Also there is a social and psychological context for communication.

While the prevalence of speech and language difficulties is not easy to determine because the concept of difficulty is relative, about 10 per cent of the school population is estimated to experience speech and language difficulties. Articulation difficulties account for about half of all speech and language difficulties. In the special school population the prevalence of speech and language difficulties is higher.

Speech and language therapy is an important provision for pupils with speech and language difficulties as part of an overall strategy involving related classroom work. In the classroom, a pupil with receptive difficulties may be helped by various strategies. The teacher may need to simplify or repeat instructions or may need to demonstrate what is required while accompanying this with the appropriate language. The social dimension of language is encouraged in the classroom and teachers seek to extend the pupil's language into new curriculum areas. As such, a social and educational dimension is not always available to a speech and language therapist who may see children individually. It is important that the perspectives of speech and language therapist and teacher are shared and understood. Joint professional working with small groups can be a helpful bridge to mutual professional understanding.

Further reading

Martin, D. (2000) *Teaching Children with Speech and Language Difficulties.* London: David Fulton Publishers.

Ripley, K., Barratt, J. and Fleming, P. (2001) *Inclusion for Children with Speech and Language Impairments: Accessing the Curriculum and Promoting Personal and Social Development.* London: David Fulton Publishers.

Addresses

AFASIC – Overcoming Speech Impairments
50–52 Great Sutton Street
London EC1V 0DJ

Tel: 020 7490 9410; 0845 355 5577 (helpline)
Fax: 020 7251 2834
e-mail: info@afasic.org.uk
www.afasic.org

AFASIC works for improved services for children and young people with speech and language difficulties and provides information and advice for parents and professionals.

I-CAN   Tel: 0870 010 4066
4 Dyer's Buildings   Fax: 0870 010 4067
London EC1N 2PQ   e-mail: ican@ican.org.uk
                                         www.ican.org.uk

A national educational charity for children with speech and language difficulties.

Speech and language therapist

Speech and language therapists (SALT) qualify through a three-year diploma course or a four-year degree course. Employed by the National Health Service, they work with adults and children assessing and treating communication difficulties through therapy and teaching.

It is important that SALT and teachers work closely together and understand each other's roles. Increasingly, SALT are working as consultants to teachers and parents who share the responsibility for delivering the activities designed to improve the child's communication. Also, SALT are working in multiprofessional teams where their expertise can be shared with colleagues including teachers.

Further reading
McCartny, E. (1999) (ed.) *Speech and Language Therpists and Teachers Working Together: A Systems Approach to Collaboration.* London: Whurr.

Speech and language therapy

The aim of speech and language therapy is to enable those with speech and langauge and communication difficulties, and associate difficulties with eating and swallowing, to communicate as well as possible and to achieve independence. A report of a working group on speech and language therapy (Department of Health and Department for Education and Employment 2000) made various recommendations. These included that:

- provision for speech and language impairment should normally be recorded as educational provision;
- government, the National Health Service and local education authorities should make a long-term commitment to supporting children with communication difficulties;
- support for specialised joint in-service training for teachers, speech and language therapists and teaching assistants should be provided to all English LEAs through the DfEE Standards Fund programme;
- LEAs and health bodies should use partnership arrangements introduced under the Health Act 1999 as a practical way of enhancing speech and language therapy provision for children with SEN.

The *Special Educational Needs Code of Practice* (Department for Education and Skills 2001) states that addressing speech and language impairment in statements of SEN should 'normally be recorded as educational provision unless there are exceptional reasons for not doing so' (Code 8.49). Where the National Health

Service does not provide speech and language therapy for a child whose statement specifies speech and language therapy as an educational provision, 'ultimate' responsibilty for that provision rests with the LEA unless the child's parents have made alternative appropriate arrangements (Code 8.51).

Reference

Department of Health and Department of Education and Employment (2000) *Provision of Speech and Language Therapy Services to Children with Special Educational Needs (England)*, November 2000.

Further reading

Kersner, M. and Wright, J. (2001) *Speech and Language Therapy: The Decision Making Process when Working with Children*. London: David Fulton Publishers.

Address

The Royal College of Speech and Language Therapists (RCSLT)
2 White Hart Yard   Tel: 020 7378 1200
London SE1 1NX   Fax:020 7403 7254
                         e-mail: postmaser@rcslt.org
                         www.rcslt.org

The RCSLT is the professional body for speech and language therapists in the UK, maintaining high standards in ethical conduct, clinical practice and education of therapists.

Statement of Special Educational Needs

A 'Statement' is a document prepared by a local education authority (LEA) under the Education Act 1996 section 324. A Statement is normally made when an LEA decides that the special educational provision necessary to meet the child's needs cannot reasonably be provided within resources normally available to the ordinary schools in the area.

Those who may request a statutory assessment of special educational needs (SEN) are: the child's parents; the school or setting in which the child is educated; or another agency such as the health services or social services. If the LEA decides not to assess the child's needs, it must give notice in writing of that decision to the child's parents. Parents then have the right of appeal to the Special Educational Needs and Disability Tribunal against the decision not to make a statutory assessment.

Should an LEA have carried out a statutory assessment of a child and decided not to make a Statement it must, within specified time limits, write to the child's parents. The LEA must tell parents of the decision and of the parents' rights to appeal against the decision to the Special Educational Needs and Disability Tribunal.

Where an LEA has made a statutory assessment of a child and has decided to make a Statement, they must serve a copy of a proposed Statement and a written notice on the child's parents. This must be done within specified time limits. The Statement comprises six parts:

1. introduction
2. special educational needs
3. special educational provision
4. placement

5. non-educational needs
6. non-educational provision.

Before an LEA makes a Statement it must issue to the parents:

- a copy of the proposed Statement;
- a notice setting out the arrangements for the choice of schools, the parents' right to make representations about the Statement's content, and their right to appeal against the contents of the final Statement to the Tribunal.

Normally, a period of no more than eight weeks should pass between:

1. the service of a proposed Statement and written notice, and
2. the service of a copy of a Statement.

Where an LEA makes a Statement they must serve a copy on the child's parents and give notice in writing of certain rights to appeal to the Tribunal. Appeals can be made:

- against the description in the Statement of the child's SEN;
- against the special educational provision specified in the Statement;
- against the school named;
- where no school was named, against that fact.

Regarding annual reviews of Statements a LEA must review a Statement of SEN at least once a year and can review the Statement more frequently if necessary. The review considers the child's progress towards targets set by the school after the Statement was made, and agrees new targets for the following year. The review meeting is usually held at the child's school. The head teacher must invite to the review meeting: the child's parents, the relevant teachers, a representative of the placing LEA, any person whom the LEA considers appropriate and specify in a notice, and any other person the head teacher considers appropriate. The LEA decides whether it is necessary to change the child's Statement. The first annual review after the child becomes 14 years old involves the development of a **transition plan**.

Statutory Assessment

A detailed assessment of a child's special educational needs undertaken by a local education authority and which may lead to the issuing of a **statement of special educational needs**. This may be requested by the child's school or setting; the child's parent or another agency such as the health service of social services.

Steiner School

Rudolph Steiner Schools seek to put into educational practice some of the ideas of Rudolph Steiner. Some independent schools cater for children with special educational needs. Steiner teachers do not follow the usual course of teacher education but study curative education, an approach associated with Rudolph Steiner's philosophy of anthroposophy. Particular attention is given to special therapeutic approaches to music and movement (eurhythmy), painting and mythology.

Further reading

Clouder, C. and Rawson, M. (1998) *Waldorf Education: Rudolph Steiner's Ideas in Practice*. Trowbridge: Floris Books.

Address

Committee for Steiner Special Education
c/o Peredur Trust
Altarnun
Launceston
Cornwall PL15 7RF

Tel: 01566 865 75
Fax: 01566 869 75
www.compulink.co.uk/~waldorf

Stereotyped behaviour

Stereotyped behaviour comprises persistent, repetitive but apparently meaningless movements. Their very persistence suggests that they serve some purpose for the person performing them. Some stereotyped behaviours can be harmful, such as eye gouging and excessive masturbation and relate to self-injurious aspects of **challenging behaviour**. Other stereotyped behaviours are less obviously harmful but their persistence hinders learning. Examples are rocking and hand flapping.

Stereotyped behaviours appear to sustain themselves. They may shut out varying aspects of what a child perceives as a threatening environment. They may be pleasurable in themselves.

Such behaviours are sometimes seen as more intense and persistent forms of natural developmental behaviour. Stereotyped behaviour is noticeable in children with autism, severe learning difficulties, profound and multiple learning difficulties or sensory disabilities.

Support services (LEA)

Among the essential functions of a local education authority, is to make effective arrangements for SEN by ensuring that 'high quality support is provided for schools and early education settings including through arrangements for educational psychology and other support services...' (Department for Education and Skills 2002, section 1.11). LEAs should monitor and review the role and quality of central SEN support services.

In early year action, LEA support services may be called on for occassional advice on strategies, equipment or staff training without the need for regular or ongoing input from external agencies. For early years action plus, typically there is involvement of external support services. LEAs have the power under section 318(3) of the Education Act 1996 to supply goods and services to assist early education settings outside the maintained sector in supporting children eligible for government funding who have SEN but not a statement. Support may be provided for school action and is typically provided at school action plus.

It is important for the local education authority that the services are coherent and are perceived by schools and others as such. Cooperation and clear communications between services should facilitate this. It should be clear to schools and others which personnel offer which services.

SEN support services can give a continuity of provision to schools, working with pupils from preschool, nursery and onwards. When SEN support services work with a cluster of schools they can gain a broader view of provision than, say, an

SEN coordinator based in a particular school can develop. The parents of pupils with SEN should be provided with information by the school, LEA or parent partnership service about the support services of the voluntary sector.

Reference
Department for Education and Skills (2001) *Special Educational Needs Code of Practice*. London: DfES.

Support teacher

The role of the support teacher involves close liaison with the class or subject teacher and either joint planning of the contribution in lessons or a clear understanding of the respective resposibilities. The support teacher will work with the pupil towards clear learning outcomes but the more individual approach or small-group setting may allow more flexibility in how these are achieved.

Support teaching

Support teaching is an approach which encourages the inclusion of pupils in mainstream classes and involves a support teacher (or teaching assistant). Usually, the support is provided in class although occasionally the child may be withdrawn from the classroom for individual or small-group teaching. Support may be given mainly to a particular pupil according to a requirement on a Statement of special educational needs or may be more flexible involving several pupils. In secondary schools and in upper primary schools, the support teacher should have subject expertise. Skill and sensitivity is needed on the part of the class or subject teacher and the support teacher to ensure that the child being supported is not so obviously singled out as to feel excluded from the work of peers. Lessons must be carefully planned so that the work of the class teacher and support teacher complement one another. Their respective roles should be clear and explicit. Particular care is needed about the role and contribution of the support teacher when the class or subject teacher is teaching the whole class so that the best use is being made of the support teacher's time and expertise.

Further reading
Lovey, J. (2002) *Supporting Special Needs in Secondary Classrooms* (2nd edn). London: David Fulton Publishers.

Symbols

Symbols are used as a form of graphical communication and as such should be considered as part of a broad definition of literacy. A well-known example of a symbol system is Blissymbolics.

Blissymbolics (the Bliss symbol system or semantography) was developed by Canadian, Charles Bliss. It comprises a series of signs or symbols originally designed to aid international communication. However, it has been adopted as a visual-graphic system to help people with severe language difficulties to communicate. Users with physical disabilities and speech impairment can indicate a symbol perhaps by pointing. People with severe learning difficulties may also use the system. Each symbol signifies a concept and symbols can be combined to represent complex ideas. A symbol board or display is necessary. If two people using Blissymbolics wish to communicate, they require access to both boards.

Further reading
Detheridge, T. and Detheridge, M. (2002) *Literacy Through Symbols: Improving Access for Children and Adults* (2nd edn). London: David Fulton Publishers.

Syndrome

In a syndrome, a group of signs and/or symptoms occur together with sufficient regularity and predictability to be considered as a pattern to which an identifying name is given. It is part of a system of classifying features allowing some predictions to be made about the likely outcomes for anyone who is correctly identified as having that syndrome. Information about syndromes might include their alternative names, their incidence, their defining characteristics, their prognosis and their implications for education, care and management.

Syndromes are often named after the person or people who originally identified them. Down's syndrome was first described by John Langdon Down. Asperger syndrome is named after Hans Asperger who, working in Vienna, published an account of the disorder he called 'autism' in 1944. Coincidentally, Leo Kanner, in Baltimore, published an account of the condition in 1943 leading to it also being referred to as Kanner syndrome. Tourette syndrome gets its name from Gilles de la Tourette, the French neurologist, who described it in 1885.

Other syndromes derive their names from prominent or noticeable physical features associated with them. Among the characteristics of Menkes Kinky Hair syndrome is that of normal hair becoming sparse and twisting. Cat-eye syndrome is associated with the self-explanatory characteristic giving it its name.

Yet other syndromes get their names from a feature which is descriptive of some typical behaviour. Pathological Demand Avoidance syndrome is recognised by, among other conduct, resistance to and avoidance of the regular demands of daily life through the person with the syndrome adopting strategies such as distracting adults, violence, excuses and appearing to become incapacitated.

The name of some syndromes indicates its cause. Foetal Dilatin syndrome is so-called because of the effects of the anticonvulsant drug Phenytoin (Dilatin), taken by the mother on the unborn foetus leading to such features as growth deficiency, heart defects and learning difficulties. Fragile X syndrome is brought about by the breaking off of the bottom tip of an X chromosome.

In diagnosing, it is important to remember that a minor abnormality occurring on its own does not constitute a syndrome. For example, skin tags in front of the ear when taken with a range of other features, such as one side of the face being under developed, abnormalities of the vertebrae, possibly hearing loss, eye lesions, limb abnormalities and heart and lung defects, may indicate Goldenhar syndrome. Such skin tags of themselves could have many other causes and on their own would not indicate Goldenhar syndrome.

A particular abnormality can occur in several syndromes, for instance microencephaly (an abnormally small cranium) is an aspect of Smith-Lemli-Opitz syndrome, Williams syndrome and others. A squint is one of the range of characteristics of several syndromes including Freema-Sheldon syndrome and Cri du Chat syndrome.

Every feature defining the syndrome is not always present in every individual who is diagnosed as having the condition. In some syndromes the likelihood in general of a feature being present is sometimes specified. For example, in Congenital Syphilis syndrome, deafness or seizures occur in some cases but not all. In Coffin-Lowry syndrome, severe learning difficulty is present in all affected males but in only a small proportion of affected females.

Also the number and severity of the characteristics may differ across different individuals with the same syndrome. In Maroteaux-Lamy Pyknodysostosis syndrome, mild learning difficulty may occur or, as in most cases, there may be no discernible effect on cognition.

Gilbert (2000) selects 100 syndromes using the criteria that they result in lifelong mental and physical difficulties and that help can be provided to improve the quality of life of those with the syndrome. These are a sample of the thousands of syndromes and inherited disorders that have so far been identified. Among the main issues for educators concerning syndromes is to focus on the educational needs which may be similar in different syndromes. At the same time, the teacher would respond to individual features that influence learning. Consideration of the possible educational implications of particular syndromes might lead to interventions based on modifying these provisional assumptions in the light of the early assessments and interventions involving the individual child.

(See also *Down's syndrome, Tourette syndrome*)

Reference
Gilbert, P. (2000) *A to Z of Syndromes and Inherited Disorders*. London: Stanley Thornes.

Address
Contact-a-Family   Tel: 020 7608 8700; 0207 608 8702 (minicom);
209–11 City Road   0808 808 3555 (helpline for parents and
London EC1V 1JV   families 10 am–4 pm Mon.–Fri.)
                                    Fax: 020 7608 8701
                                    e-mail: info@cafamily.org.uk
                                    www.cafamily.org.uk

A charity providing support and advice to parents whatever the medical condition of their child. Has a directory of rare and specific disorders.

Targets (individual)

Where possible, targets for learning should involve the pupil. Such involvement helps ensure the pupil's commitment to reaching the target and can increase pupil motivation. If strategies for reaching the target involve rewards for the pupil, it is important that (s)he has the opportunity to express what those rewards might be.

The target should be specific. For example, for a pupil who has difficulty reading, it could be, 'John will learn to read the following ten words by <date>'. The ten key words would then be specified. The strategy for reaching the target would be specified. It might be through a specified time of practice each day or it could involve writing the words, finger tracing them, speaking them into a tape recorder, recognising and reading the key word in a sentence of otherwise already known words and so on. The Individual Education Plan (IEP) should state who does what and when.

Effective targets are behavioural, that is, they describe behaviour which is observable and which when observed will indicate that the target has been reached. An IEP normally includes no more than three or four targets. The targets should be time limited. One target might take two or three weeks, others may take a little longer and should be reviewed at the completion dates by the teacher and renewed as necessary.

Some prioritising will be necessary if there is a range of special educational needs. Also there will often be an implied or explicit hierarchy in targets so that when one is reached the next one is apparent. For example, a target might aim to reduce from 20 to 15 the number of times a pupil gets out of his seat without permission in a specified lesson. If that target is reached in the specified time, the next target might reasonably be to reduce the number of times to ten.

Further reading

Department for Education and Skills (2001) *SEN Toolkit Section 5: Managing Individual Education Plans.* London: DfES.

Target setting (cohort)

Target setting is a way of encouraging higher standards by agreeing and aiming for whole-school targets which can include targets relating to cohorts of pupils with special educational needs. Where a school is broadly comparable with another in terms of such features as the social background of the children, it is possible to compare the achievement of pupils in the similar schools and draw on this and other information to inform realistic target setting.

In special schools, there are difficulties if one wishes to try to compare one special school with another for the purposes of setting challenging targets. One reason for this difficulty is that different local education authorities have different policies which lead to different populations of children being in special schools. One way of addressing this is to ensure so far as is practicable that cohorts that are being compared have similar baseline attainment from which to judge progress. Targets relating to English or literacy and to mathematics or at least numeracy are particularly important. Other areas of provision such as attendance, personal and social education, problem solving and behaviour can also provide equally important targets. It should be possible to establish targets for the whole school and for broad groups of pupils. For example, in a school for pupils with severe learning difficulties it may be helpful to consider targets relating to pupils with profound and multiple learning difficulties, pupils at higher levels of attainment for the school, and a group of pupils in between these two.

Further reading

Department for Education and Employment (2001) *Supporting the Target Setting Process: Guidance for Effective Target Setting for Pupils with Special Educational Needs.* London: DfEE.

Teacher

The classroom teacher and the subject teacher have a responsibility under the *Special Educational Needs Code of Practice* to identify pupils with special educational needs (SEN). This requires an understanding of learning difficulties and an assessment of the level at which a pupil needs to be recognised as having SEN. The teacher needs to be able to cooperate with the **special educational needs coordinator** in the school and to use skills such as the ability to use suitable teaching strategies to meet varying needs. As this expectation to identify pupils with SEN applies to all teachers, it has implications for the initial training of teachers and for the support of newly qualified teachers.

Address

General Teaching Council for England   Tel: 0870 001 0308
344–54 Grays Inn Road   Fax: 020 7841 2909
London WC1X 8PB   e-mail: info@gtce.org.uk
                                              www.gtce.org.uk

Teaching assistant

A teaching assistant may not work exclusively with pupils with special educational needs (SEN) but will need an understanding of children with SEN just as does a teacher. It is particularly important when a teaching assistant does work with pupils with SEN that she works closely with the teacher. Joint planning is the ideal, but failing this the teacher should convey to the teaching assistant the learning objectives of the lesson and the learning outcomes expected of the pupil(s) being supported. Assessments of what the pupil has done should be recorded and should inform subsequent teaching. The teacher should ensure that she does not lose the skill of working with pupils with SEN because their needs are met too readily by the involvement of a teaching assistant.

A special support assistant or a special needs assistant works with pupils with SEN in nurseries, special schools and mainstream schools. Presently, they undergo no formal training but work with trained staff carrying out such duties as general care (e.g. dressing), and educational duties requested by the teacher (e.g. working on agreed, preplanned tasks such as hearing children read).

Further reading

Balshaw, M. and Farrell, P. (2002) *Teaching Assistants: Practical Strategies for Effective Classroom Support*. London: David Fulton Publishers.

Teaching strategies

The *Special Educational Needs Code of Practice* (Department for Education and Skills 2001) refers to the nature of interventions used at different phases of education. These involve 'more effective strategies' at Early Years Action (4.26), and at School Action in both primary school (5.49) and secondary school (6.57). It involves LEA support services offering advice on 'new or specialist' strategies at Early Years Action Plus (4.29) and at School Action Plus in primary (5.55) and secondary school (6.63).

Different teaching strategies may be used to help in the teaching of pupils with various characteristics each according to his or her characteristics in a group setting. This implies an understanding of the individual differences between children and their entitlement and access to the National Curriculum. Individual differences include prior attainment and aptitudes and the pupil's learning strategies. The teacher encourages pupils' progress through the curriculum, adopting appropriate teaching approaches. In the case of a pupil with special educational needs (SEN), this implies the inclusion of the pupil with others in the classroom. However, this does not preclude the grouping of pupils in the classroom according to prior attainment.

Developing suitable strategies involves planning curriculum objectives, teaching and assessment approaches, learning activities and resources. Approaches include focusing on the following:

1. Outcome

   Pupils may be given the same task and content but the teacher assesses the outcome accordingly to each pupil's level. This is often seen as occuring almost automatically. In order for this not to become a 'strategy' by default or accident, the element of planning is particularly important. The expected outcome should be clear from the outset and it should be sufficiently challenging while still allowing some experience of success for the pupil. For example, where children are engaged in creative writing, one may be expected to write at greater length and with greater fluency than another. The teacher needs to take care that his or her expectations are realistic and challenging. Expectations which are too low will tend to inhibit a child's progress and lower his or her self-esteem.

2. Delivery or task

   The learning outcomes are the same but the delivery is different. For instance, in reading, one child may be working with a predominantly phonic approach while another may be using a predominantly 'look and say' approach.

3. Pace or extension

   This involves pupils being engaged in similar activities but allowing for individuals working at different speeds. Supplementary and extension work is required for the pupils who work faster. Importantly, the teacher needs to make it clear at the beginning of a session the expectation that specified pupils will finish the extension work in the same session. Otherwise extension tasks become optional extras and pace may not vary.

4. Level of work

   This usually occurs within a set scheme; for example in mathematics or reading. Individual children may be at different levels on the same scheme according to the level of previous learning.

5. Recording

   This strategy responds to the way in which a pupil records his or her response; allows for written responses, verbal responses or pictorial representation.

6. Resources

   The content of the lesson is the same but resources are used to allow access to learning or to aid learning. A pencil grip may be used for a pupil with coordination difficulties. Materials such as unifix blocks may be used to aid calculations in mathematics. Visual aids such as photographs or objects may be used to aid understanding for some pupils.

7. Organisation
   This may involve a teacher grouping children within a classroom according to criteria such as prior attainment in the particular lesson or task. This could help the allocation of resources to support learning. For example, pupils who require practical aids, such as a 'number line' for a mathematics task, might be grouped together so that the necessary materials could be shared by them.

8. Support
   This involves a pupil or group of pupils receiving planned support from the teacher or another adult working with the teacher in the classroom. This can be linked to varying the organisation so that the teacher can give support to groups who find a particular task or area of knowledge acquisition more difficult than others. If support is to be planned predominantly for one of several groups in a lesson, then, if there is one teacher for the class, it is important that other groups have comparatively self-sustaining tasks. This does not imply that the activities and the learning should not be challenging, rather that the work is structured and resourced in such a way as to need less teacher support.

9. Specialist techniques
   This includes using specialist methods of teaching suitable for the particular learning needs of a specific child. An example is multisensory methods using didactic approaches and encouraging the use of several senses.

The above list is not exhaustive, and there are other labels that could be used for some of the approaches and indeed other ways of demarcating the approaches themselves.

Reference

Department for Education and Skills (2001) *Special Educational Needs Code of Practice*. London: DfES.

Testing concepts

a) Age equivalent
An age equivalent is an age for which a raw score on a standardised test is the average performance. If children aged 10 years 0 months achieve on average a raw score of 75 on a given test, then 10 years is the age equivalent of a score of 75.

Using the age equivalent, comparisons can be made between a child's performance on the skills tested and his or her chronological age. Age equivalent scores should be interpreted with care for the differences between two consecutive age equivalents and another two consecutive age equivalents may not be similar. They can also carry a general implication of immaturity if the results are not conveyed properly.

b) Norm-referenced tests
Norm-referenced tests allow a child's performance to be compared with that of others. For example, a reading test might give its results as a 'reading age'. This allows the achievement to be compared with that of other age groups. A child with a reading age of, say seven years, has attained a reading level comparable with an

average seven-year-old in the sample of children on which the test was standardised. Attainment quotients are calculated as a ratio of reading age over chronological age expressed as a percentage:

$$\frac{RA}{CA} \times 100$$

This enables the tester to compare a child's attainment with that of others in his own age group. Deviation quotients allow more exact comparisons of a particular child's score with those of others in the same age group. Tests are often designed to have a mean score of 100 and a standard deviation of 15 points.

c)   Criterion-referenced test

The best-known example of a criterion-referenced test is probably the driving test. The examiner has criteria on which to judge the performance of the driver in various manoeuvres and the driver passes or fails on performance. Driving performance is not compared with that of other drivers (this would be norm-referenced testing).

Similarly in education, a criterion-referenced test is used to assess mastery to a specified level of knowledge or skills. The test is often based on previous teaching objectives to establish that learning has been effective before the teacher moves on to another topic or more complicated aspects of the same topic. It should form part of a cycle of learning involving teaching, assessment and further teaching as necessary depending on the assessment result.

d)   Curriculum-based assessment (CBA)

CBA is closely related to the objectives of the classroom teaching programme and the tests are usually constructed by teachers. A pupil's performance is then compared with peers; either others in the class or in the local area. CBA is usually a series of short parallel tests enabling regular assessment of progress.

Further reading

Reason, R., Farrell, P. and Mittler, P. (1990) 'Changes in assessment', in Entwistle, N. (ed.) *Handbook of Educational Ideas and Practices*. London: Routledge.

Addresses

NFER-Nelson	Tel: 020 8996 8444
The Chiswick Centre	Fax: 020 8996 5358
414 Chiswick High Road	e-mail: edu&hsc@nfer-Nelson.co.uk
London W4 5TF	www.nfer-nelson.co.uk
The Psychological Corporation	Tel: 020 8308 5750
Foots Cray High Street	Fax: 020 8308 5702
Sidcup	e-mail: tpc@harcourt.com
Kent DA14 5HP	www.tpc-international.com

Thinking skills

Developing thinking skills concerns thinking about thinking (metacognition) and may imply teaching children to reflect on the way they learn and tackle problems. Examples of teaching approaches which aim to assist metacognition include

Instrumental Enrichment (IE). A programme of cognitive intervention developed by Feuerstein and colleagues, instrumental enrichment aims to improve the learning effectiveness and problem solving abilities of children with learning difficulties. Emphasising the process rather than the content of learning, IE teaches essential thinking processes applicable across a range of curriculum subjects. The teacher provides a 'mediated learning experience' through selecting and organising stimuli in such a way as to affect the learner's cognitive structure. The learning potential of pupils is assessed through the use of a 'Learning Potential Assessment Device'.

Further reading

Wallace, B. (ed.) (2002) *Teaching Thinking Skills Across the Early Years: A Practical Approach for Children Aged 4 to 7*. London: NACE/David Fulton Publishers.
Wallace, B. (ed.) (2002) *Teaching Thinking Skills Across the Middle Years: A Practical Approach for Children Aged 9 to 14*. London: NACE/David Fulton Publishers.

Token economy

A regime in which tokens are used as an integral part of the ethos of the place of learning (e.g. a school) has a token economy. Tokens are a feature of behaviour modification. They are used as secondary reinforcers which can be traded in for different rewards. This enables the rewards to be varied (e.g. a trip to a place of interest, a privilege such as an extra play period).

Tokens may be, for example, points or plastic discs. The issuing of a token needs to be recorded and an accurate and up-to-date central record of tokens must be kept so pupils cannot forge tokens or carry out an illicit trade in them. Some special schools have successfully used a token economy. Chelfham Mill School in Devon, England is an example of a residential school for pupils with emotional and behavioural difficulties which uses such a system. Tokens may be used in a more limited and circumscribed way for a group of pupils within a school but a token economy helps ensure a wider approach to behaviour particularly in a residential setting.

Total communication

Total communication is a response to hearing impairment which aims to provide the fullest and richest language environment. This includes:

- normal speech
- lip reading
- a manual **sign language** and finger spelling
- writing and reading
- the best use of residual hearing
- **aids to hearing**.

Tourette syndrome

Gilles de la Tourette first diagnosed the syndrome that is named after him in 1885. An inherited neurological condition, more common in males, it is transmitted by an autosomnal dominant gene. In childhood, the condition is associated with repetitive tics and grimaces. As the disease progresses, involuntary noises may be emitted, and in about half the cases episodes of using obscene language appear. Antipsychotic drugs are sometimes used in treatment.

Among the educational implications is the management of the reactions of peers, their possible rejection of the person with Tourette syndrome and the management of the disruption that the condition can cause to learning.

Further reading
Carroll, A. and Robertson, M. (2000) *Tourette Syndrome: A Practical Guide for Teachers, Parents and Carers*. London: David Fulton Publishers.

Address
Tourette Syndrome (UK) Association
1st Floor Offices
Old Bank Chambers
London Road
Crowborough
East Sussex TN6 2TT

National helpline: 0845 4581 252 (24-hr voicemail)
Fax: 0845 4581 252
e-mail: enquiries@tsa.org.uk
www.tourettesyndrome.co.uk

Provides a helpline, membership forums, family networking, publications and advice.

Toy and leisure library

Toy libraries aim to benefit all children, including children with special educational needs. They offer a wide choice of good quality toys to borrow and can make expensive and specialist toys and equipment available to families. Socially, toy libraries provide opportunities for shared play for children and parents and an informal meeting place for parents, carers, professionals and volunteers.

Toy libraries can be found throughout the United Kingdom in community and family centres, nursery and primary schools, clinics and health centres, public libraries and hospitals. There are also toy libraries on mobile vans and play buses. Toy libraries are run by parents, voluntary organisations, local self-help groups and by the education, health, library and social services.

Leisure libraries offer leisure facilities and the loan of leisure equipment to young people and adults with learning difficulties. They also provide an informal meeting place for parents and carers, professionals and volunteers; information, advice and support; and contacts with other voluntary organisations and statutory services. Leisure libraries can be found in education centres, hospitals and resource centres. The first leisure libraries were joint ventures between the National Association of Toy and Leisure Libraries/Play Matters and social services and health departments. Some have evolved from existing toy libraries, expanding existing provision, while others are new projects run independently.

Further reading
National Association of Toy and Leisure Libraries (2001) *Getting Going: A Practical Guide to Setting Up and Running a Leisure Library*. London: NATLL.

Address
National Association of Toy and Leisure Libraries
68 Churchway
London NW1 1LT

Tel: 020 7387 9592
Fax: 020 7383 2714
e-mail: admin@natll.uk.net
www.natll.org.uk

The Association promotes play and recreation by providing: support for toy and leisure libraries; advice about appropriate equipment and resources; information about starting and running a toy or leisure library; a range of publications; and training for its members, for commercial organisations and for statutory bodies.

Transition plan

A transition plan is part of certain annual reviews of the progress of a pupil with a Statement of special educational needs. The first annual review after a young person's fourteenth birthday and any later reviews until the child leaves school should include a transition plan. The plan draws together information from various sources helping structure the young person's transition to adult life. At the annual reviews requiring a transition plan, the local education authority (LEA) must seek information from the social services department. This is to establish whether a child with a Statement under the Education Act 1996, part 4, is disabled and may require services from the local authority when (s)he leaves school. The LEA should consult others as appropriate, including the child health services, therapists, educational psychologists and occupational psychologists.

The issues which the transition plan should address are set out in the *Special Educational Needs Code of Practice* (DfES 2001) and concern the school, professions, the family and the young person concerned. Other matters relating to the transition plan are also set out in the Code (e.g. 3.16–3.17 and 10.17–10.18).

Reference
Department for Education and Skills (2001) *Special Educational Needs Code of Practice.* London: DfES.

Transport

Transport from home to school (or college) is a large proportion of the transport budget for many LEA. Transport is provided if it is specified on a statement of special educational needs (SEN). In a survey of LEAs (Clarke 2001), children with SEN in mainstream schools come under the same regulations as other children unless they had physical disabilities or communication difficulties or were wheelchair users. Some LEAs encourage pupils with SEN to travel on public transport with free passes. LEAs usually asked the parents of pupils with SEN to pay for transport if their preferred school was further away from home than the one recommended by the LEA. Some LEAs provided transport for students with a disability or difficulty in learning up to the age of 25.

Reference
Clarke, T. (2001) *Home to School and College Transport.* Slough: Education Management Information Exchange, National Foundation of Educational Research.

Value added

'Value added' is an aspect of school effectiveness concerned with adding value to pupils' education given pupil circumstances and school context. General issues about adding value apply to all pupils including those with special educational needs (SEN). Key factors are input-output measures. Input involves assessing prior achievement and may involve tests of cognitive ability or reading. Output measures may be examination results, such as General Certificate of Secondary Education as performance indicators. The use of such measures aims to ensure that progress is being considered rather than 'raw' achievement. Another factor is individual differences among pupils such as gender.

Also important are contextual factors that is socio-economic indicators such as the number of pupils having free school meals or the level of attendance at parents' meetings. The key question is, given adjustments for individual differences and socio-economic issues (that have a measurable effect on achievement), is the progress of pupils greater than that which would be predicted from statistical averages? Essentially, pupils' prior achievement and contextual variables are aggregated to establish characteristics. If after these have been taken into account there is greater progress than would be predicted, then this reflects the value which the school is adding.

In relation to public accountability, school league tables do not indicate the success that a school may have with pupils in its particular context. Considering value added addresses this anomaly. Another perspective of value added is the school's own self-evaluation and improvement.

Special schools face particular issues regarding value added. To address public accountability, schools for pupils with emotional/behavioural disturbance or/and moderate learning difficulties could in principle be compared regionally or nationally in the light of pupils' individual differences and socio-economic factors. Particular difficulties arise in relation to value added and the education of pupils with severe or profound and multiple learning difficulties because of the small steps generally made in progress.

The data arising from school inspections by the Office for Standards in Education (Ofsted) is likely to inform the national debate on value added.

Improvements in achievement, information from annual reviews, and, perhaps less reliably because of their subjective nature, reaching targets in Individual Education Plans are among indicators of the progress of pupils with SEN. The various focuses of added value can include the whole school, particular departments within a school and individual pupils.

Further reading
Farrell, M. (2001) *Standards and Special Educational Needs*. London: Continuum.

Very able children

Very able children are sometimes referred to as exceptionally able or gifted and talented. Very able children are judged to have outstanding potential in one or more of the following: intellectual ability, creative ability, particular academic ability, leadership, a performing art, or a visual art. There is an argument that very able children should be considered as having special educational needs (SEN) because, unless 'special' opportunities are provided, they may not develop their abilities to their full potential. However, very able children do not have SEN under the Education Act 1996.

Further reading
Clarke, C. and Callow, R. (2002) *Educating the Gifted and Talented* (2nd edn). London: David Fulton Publishers.

Address

National Association for Gifted Children (NAGC)

Suite 14   Tel: 0807 770 3217

Challenge House   Fax: 0807 770 3219

Sherwood Drive   e-mail: amazingchildren@nagcbritain.org.uk

Bletchley   www.nagcbritain.org.uk

Buckinghamshire MK3 6DP

A self-help support group for parents with gifted children.

Visual impairment

1. Visual acuity: the Snellen Chart and the Jaeger Chart

One method of assessing visual acuity is the Snellen Chart which comprises lines of letters in progressively smaller type face. The size of the letters on each line is designed so that it is known at what distance a person with normal acuity can read that line accurately. Visual acuity is represented as a fraction as follows:

$$\text{Visual acuity} = \frac{\text{distance from the chart}}{\text{letter size}}$$
(Snellen ratio)

If a child has visual acuity of 6:36, (s)he can only read letters at six metres which someone with normal acuity could read at 36 metres. The ratio of 6:36 is a guide to the level at which a child will probably need low vision aids if the ratio is found after correction in the better eye.

The Jaeger Chart assesses near vision using lines of print of different sizes and gives an indication of suitable reading material; normal print, large print books and so on.

2. Field of vision

Another aspect of visual impairment is limitations in the field of vision. When one looks directly forward with one eye at a time, the object which is in the focus of vision is seen most clearly. Objects some distance around are seen less clearly. The range of what can be seen without moving the eye is the field of vision.

3. Colour vision and the Ishihara Test

Defective colour vision, can affect education where colour is used in teaching and limits the choice of careers. Affecting about one person in fifty it is more common in males. Usually, difficulties lie in discriminating between reds and greens. The Ishihara Test of colour vision, comprises cards depicting numbers or patterns in spots of contrasting colours. The patterns which can be seen differ according to the person's degree of normal colour vision.

4. Conditions associated with visual impairment

Among the conditions associated with visual impairment are malformations of the cornea, the lens or the globe of the eye, retinitis pigmentosa, a hereditary degenerative disease of the retina and the effects of maternal rubella.

5. The range of visual impairment including blindness

Visual impairment covers a range of disability from minor impairment through to blindness. About four in 10,000 school pupils have special educational needs (SEN) due to visual impairment.

A person with visual acuity Snellen ratio of 3:60 in the better eye after correction, can legally register as being blind. Many people with a lower level of acuity, however, have some sight which can be used for various purposes including reading large or magnified print.

For educational purposes, a blind child is one who requires mainly non-sighted methods for learning; for example, **Braille** and hearing. About four infants per 10,000 under one year old are blind.

6. Educational implications of visual impairment

While assessments of visual acuity, field of vision and colour vision are important, as assessment of functional vision is necessary to determine the child's educational needs. This and other information, is used by a teacher or adviser of the visually impaired, in designing an appropriate educational programme. When a child's SEN are being assessed, and it is thought that the child may have a visual impairment, then educational advice must be sought in consultation with a qualified teacher of the blind.

Blind children and children with lesser visual impairment may be educated in residential or day special schools or in ordinary schools, either in an ordinary or special class.

Where a child with visual impairment is educated in an ordinary school, support is necessary for both teacher and pupil. This may be from a specialist support centre based in the ordinary school from which pupils with visual impairment could be included in mainstream classes, with support from the centre staff. Alternatively, a peripatetic service can support teachers and pupils. The support and advice that may be needed by a teacher in an ordinary class teaching a child with visual impairment includes the following:

- planned contacts with members of the advisory service to discuss issues and receive information;
- curriculum advice on suitable teaching materials;
- advice on aids such as low vision aids and on equipment;
- advice on the kind of illumination required;
- creating opportunities for the pupil to get to know the school, including its layout.

Further reading
Davis, P. (2003) *Including Children with Visual Impairment: A Practical Guide*. London: David Fulton Publishers.

Address
Royal National Institute for the Blind (RNIB)
105 Judd Street
London WC1 9NE

Tel: 020 7388 1266
Fax: 020 7388 2034 (general enquiries)
e-mail: rnib@rnib.org.uk
www.rnib.org

The RNIB provides information on the education of people with visual impairment, runs courses, offers individual advice and support and publishes a variety of leaflets.

Vocational opportunities

Regarding the employment of people with learning difficulties or disabilities, appropriate training and support may be necessary for successful employment. Training may focus on skills usable in 'real' work places. Flexibility and imagination can create productive work. Pairing a person with severe learning difficulties with a co-worker who does not have learning difficulties has been successful, for example, in Canada. The importance of work to people with a learning difficulty or disability can hardly be overestimated. As well as the skills directly applicable to work, it is important to develop and re-train skills and knowledge once the person is in employment. While ideally employment should be open and paid, failing this, such alternatives as community work or sheltered work should be available with reasonable remuneration.

Voluntary sector

The voluntary sector helps provide a safety framework for children with special educational needs (and, of course, others) and acts in varying degrees of partnership with government in decision-making and in the delivery of services. The main organisations in the sector are diverse but have in common the feature that they do not act for financial profit for themselves.

Voluntary organisations may be:

- self-help groups;
- service providers; or
- involved with research, advocacy or leisure.

Where voluntary organisations have charitable status, it precludes them from being politically motivated in the narrow sense. This sometimes creates a tension between non-charitable (and perhaps more politically active) organisations and charities who, while being less political, may have more formal influence with government.

Further reading
Miller, O. (1998) 'Inclusion and the role of the voluntary sector', in Daniels, H. (ed.) *Special Education* Re-*formed: Beyond Rhetoric*. London: Falmer Press.

Whole curriculum

The notion of the whole curriculum is important for all pupils including pupils with special educational needs. The National Curriculum and religious education (the basic curriculum) forms part of the whole curriculum. For pupils with moderate learning difficulties, the National Curriculum 'Orders' allow the flexibility to meet the curricular needs of such pupils in most cases. For pupils with severe learning difficulties the whole curriculum draws on the National Curriculum and is informed by a developmental perspective of such areas as motor, development, cognition, communication, social development and self-help.

Withdrawal of pupils

The withdrawal of pupils with special educational needs (SEN) from mainstream classes for individual or group work is appropriate in some cases. It may enable intensive work to take place and in the case of groups, may represent an economical use of the teacher's time. The alternative of in-class support is increasingly seen as generally appropriate because it can enable pupils with SEN to be educated with their peers. Where both approaches are used, a clear rationale should determine which approach is adopted for each pupil.

Youth clubs

Local authority clubs and voluntary organisation clubs (e.g. Gateway) offer youth services for people with special needs. The variety of activities in clubs and centres and the strong community links, encourages the inclusion of people with special needs. Such clubs also help develop social skills and interests. In these ways the youth service contributes to smoothing the transition from school to adult life.

Address

Gateway Clubs
MENCAP
Swan Courtyard
Yardley
Birmingham B26 1BU

Tel: 0121 707 7877
Fax: 0121 707 6305
e-mail: karen.nicol@mencap.org.uk
www.mencap.org.uk

MENCAP's Gateway Clubs help people with a learning disability to take part in a range of leisure, social and creative activities that provide opportunities for personal development.

Appendices 1 to 3: Introduction

- Appendix 1 concerns selected legislation and related reports and consultative documents from the Warnock Report to the present day.
- Appendix 2 deals with selected regulations from 1981 to the present.
- Appendix 3 concerns the guidance of selected circulars and circular letters from 1981 to the present and the special educational needs codes of practice 1994 and 2001.

These appendices relate to the usual divisions of the SEN framework comprising primary legislation, regulations and guidance. The statutory duties forming the core of the SEN framework in England is that of the Education Act 1996 as amended by the Special Educational Needs and Disability Act 2001. The remainder of the framework is provided mainly by: the Education (Special Educational Needs) (England) Regulations 2001, the Education (Special Educational Needs) (Information) (England) Regulations 2001 and related guidance such as the Special Educational Needs Code of Practice 2001. Regulations and guidance are provided separately for Wales by the National Assembly.

Legislation and Related Reports and Consultative Documents

Special Educational Needs: Report of the Committee of Enquiry into the Education of Handicapped Children and Young People 1978 (The Warnock Report)

The Warnock Committee was set up to:

> ...review educational provision in England, Scotland and Wales for children and young people handicapped by disabilities of body or mind, taking account of the medical aspects of their needs, together with arrangements to prepare them for entry into employment; to consider the most effective use of resources for these purposes...

The aims of education were seen as the same for all children. The report put forward the view that the term special education should be broadened. About one child in six at any one time, and about one child in five at some time in their school career will need some form of special education. Services should be considered accordingly. Most special education should take place in ordinary schools.

Parents should be more involved in the special education of their children. Priority areas for recommendations were:

- teacher education
- special education in the preschool
- special education for the 16–19 age group.

The concept of special educational need should replace categories of handicap. Recommendations were made for a structured system of assessment and the allocation of a 'named person'. The report recognised the continuing need for special schools for children with certain severe and complex disabilities.

Report of the Committee of Inquiry into Mental Handicap Nursing and Care 1979 (The Jay Report)

The Jay Report argued that all people with mental handicap should live in the community with support from the professional services. Its vision was of a new non-medical caring profession. It recommended the end of the dual system of hospital and local care, and a shift to local care. Staff in residential care units should receive social work training rather than nurse training. In the event, there was a transfer of some resources from the National Health Service to local authorities and the closure of large hospitals.

Education Act 1980

This Act made various provisions including the requirement that all schools should have parent and teacher representatives as members of the school governing body. Special schools were included. All parents were given some rights concerning the choice of school for their child. This did not include the parents of children attending special schools (or nursery schools).

West Indian Children in our Schools 1981 (The Rampton Report)

The Rampton Report was an interim report of a Committee of Enquiry on the educational needs and attainments of children from ethnic minorities. There was concern about the large number of pupils in special schools and classes for children with learning and behavioural difficulties who came from families with a West Indian cultural background. The Committee identified the main determinants of the underachievement of West Indian pupils which it argued were:

- difficult social conditions leading to inadequate preschool care
- parents' attitudes
- the unintentional racism, negative attitudes and low expectations of certain teachers.

Recommendations concerned:

- preschool provision
- school–community links
- the content of books and other teaching materials
- arrangements for special education (this included the ethnic mix of special schools for pupils with learning difficulties).

The aim was to develop a multicultural education system which would value the cultures of ethnic minorities and reduce racial bias.

After producing its interim report, the Committee was reconstituted under a new chairman, leading to the production of the report *Education for All* (The Swann Report) in 1985.

Education Act 1981

The Education Act 1981 received its commencement order on 1 April 1983. Under section 1, previous ten statutory and specific categories of handicap were replaced by a broad definition of special educational needs (SEN). A child has SENs if (s)he has learning difficulty which requires special educational provision.

A child has a 'learning difficulty' if he or she:

a) has a significantly greater difficulty in learning than the majority of children of his/her age; or

b) has a disability which either prevents or hinders him/her from making use of educational facilities of a kind generally provided in schools, within the area of the local authority concerned, for children of his/her age; or

c) is under five and could fall into either of these categories if special provision was not made.

For a child over two years old 'special educational provision' is 'additional to, or otherwise different from' that generally provided by the authority concerned for children of that age. For a child under two, any form of provision is 'special educational provision'. A child does not have a learning difficulty solely because the language or form of language in which he/she will be taught is different from that which has been spoken in the home.

Under section 2 of the Act, LEAs have a duty to have regard to the need to secure that special educational provision is made for children with SENs. Also, provided certain conditions are satisfied, children with Statements are to be educated in ordinary schools. Account must be taken of the views of the parents. Also, education in an ordinary school must be compatible with:

a) the child receiving the special educational provision required
b) the provision of efficient education for other children
c) resources being used efficiently.

Governors of county and voluntary schools are given further duties to ensure that:

- special provision required by a child is made;
- teachers recognise the importance of identifying and providing for children with SEN;
- where the 'responsible person' has been told by the LEA that a student has SEN, those needs are conveyed to all who are likely to teach him or her.

The 'responsible person' may be the head teacher, chairperson of governors, or another governor appointed by the governing body. In maintained nursery schools, which do not have governing bodies, these duties are given to the LEAs and the 'responsible person' is the head teacher.

Children with SEN must engage in the 'activities of the school together with children who do not have special educational needs', provided conditions a), b) and c) above are satisfied and it is 'reasonably practicable'.

LEAs have a duty to 'keep under review' their arrangements for special educational provision. An LEA may consider it inappropriate for some or all special education to be provided in a school. If so, the LEA may, after consulting the parents, arrange for all or part of it to be provided 'otherwise than in a school'.

Local authorities have a general duty to identify those children whose SENs require the authority to determine the provision that should be made for them. For this purpose, LEAs are defined as being responsible:

- for a child registered at one of their schools, or at non-maintained or independent schools where they have arranged education; and
- for a child who has been brought to their attention as having or probably having SEN who is aged between two and 16 and is registered at some other school or who is not registered at a school.

LEAs may assess a child aged under two with the consent of parents. LEAs must do so at the request of the parents. The assessment can be made in any manner the authority considers appropriate. If the authority decide to make a Statement, that can also take any form they consider appropriate.

If an authority think they may have to make a Statement, they must first serve a notice informing the parents:

a) that they propose to make an assessment
b) of the procedure to be followed in making it
c) of the name of the officer of the authority from whom further information can he obtained, and
d) of the parents' right to make representations and submit written evidence within a specified period. (Not less than 29 days from the day on which the notice is served.)

Having taken into account any representations made to them, the LEA may proceed with the assessment or decide not to make one.

If the LEA decide to assess the child, they must inform the parents in writing of their decision, and their reasons for making it. If they decide not to proceed with the assessment they must inform the parents in writing. Having made an assessment, the authority may decide that they are not required to determine the provision that should be made. In this case, they must inform the parents of their decision, and of the right of appeal in writing to the Secretary of State. The Secretary of State may direct the LEA to reconsider their decision.

Regulations require the LEA to seek medical, psychological and educational advice.

There are formal procedures when an LEA exercise their power to require parents to submit their child for examination. They may serve a notice on the parents which must:

a) state the purpose of the examination, and the venue and time for it
b) name an officer from whom further information can be obtained
c) inform the parent that they may submit such information to the authority as they wish
d) inform the parent of their right to be present at the examination.

A parent may fail 'without reasonable excuse' to comply with any of the requirements of such a notice. If so, and if the child is not over compulsory school age at the time of the examination, the parents will be guilty of an offence.

After assessment, the LEA may decide that they should determine the special educational provision to be made. If so, they must draft a proposed 'Statement of special educational needs'. This will:

a) give details of the authority's assessment of the SEN of the child, and
b) specify the special educational provision to be made for the purpose of meeting those needs.

The authority must provide parents with a copy of the proposed Statement, and details of the arrangements for making representations if they disagree with all or part of it.

These arrangements are that a parent has 15 days in which to:

a) make representations to the Authority about the Statement
b) require the authority to arrange a meeting with an officer to discuss it.

The parent may still disagree with any part of the assessment. If so, he/she has a further 15 days from the date of the meeting with the LEA officer in which to require the authority to arrange further meetings. These meetings are to enable the parent to discuss the 'relevant advice' with the 'appropriate person(s)'. The parent then has a final period of 15 days from the last meeting to make further representations.

After considering any representations, the LEA may:

a) make a Statement in the form originally proposed
b) modify a Statement
c) decide not to make a Statement.

Parents must be informed in writing of the decision. If the authority decide not to make a Statement, the parents may appeal to the Secretary of State.

If a Statement is made, the LEA must serve on the parent:

a) a copy of the Statement
b) notice in writing of the right of appeal, and
c) notice in writing of the name of the person from whom information and advice can be obtained about the child's SENs.

The Secretary of State may also issue regulations on keeping, disclosure and transfer of Statements, and on the frequency with which children who have Statements are to be reassessed. LEAs must review Statements whenever assessments are made, and in any case within 12 months of the making of the Statement, or of the last review of it.

An authority may decide to amend or to cease to maintain a Statement. If so, they must tell parents of their proposal, and that they have 15 days in which to make representations. After considering any representations, the authority must notify parents of their decision. These provisions do not apply where an authority:

a) no longer maintain a Statement because a child has ceased to be their responsibility, or

b)   where amendments follow the making, amendment or revocation of a school attendance order.

LEAs must make arrangements for parents to appeal against the provision proposed in Statements following a first or any subsequent assessment of their child. The appeal is to committees set up under the Education Act 1980.

Decisions of appeals committees under the Education Act 1981 are not binding on the local authorities. The composition of the committees is set out in detail in the 1980 Act (Schedule 2). This Schedule also sets out the procedure for the appeals, with the addition that matters to be taken into account by the committee include any representations made by the parents. The committees come under the supervision of the council on Tribunals. Parents dissatisfied with the procedure for appealing may also complain to the Commissioner for Local Administration. Committees hearing appeals under this Act may:

a)   confirm the provision specified in the Statement, or
b)   remit the case to the LEA for reconsideration.

The LEA must reconsider a case submitted to them under (b) and inform the parents in writing of their decision. Parents have a further right of appeal to the Secretary of State if:

- an appeal committee confirm the decision of the authority
- or if the parents are still dissatisfied following the authority's reconsideration of their case.

LEAs have a duty to arrange an assessment of a child who has no Statement if a reasonable request is made by the parent. LEAs also have a duty to reassess a child with a Statement if requested by the parent, provided there has been no assessment in the previous six months, and unless an assessment would be inappropriate.

If an area or district health authority (DHA) consider that a child under five has or probably has SENs, they must inform the parent. After, providing an opportunity for discussion with a health authority officer, the DHA must bring it to the attention of the relevant LEA. If the DHA believe that a particular voluntary organisation could help the parent, they must inform the parent accordingly.

The parent of a child aged between 5 and 16 who is registered as a student at a special school must not withdraw the child without the consent of the local authority. If an authority refuse consent, the parent may refer the question to the Secretary of State, who may intervene.

The Secretary of State may make regulations governing the approval of special schools, the requirements for continuing approval and for the withdrawal of approval. The regulations must ensure that where practicable all special school students attend religious worship and instruction, or are withdrawn in accordance with the wishes of their parents.

Similar regulations may be made for independent schools considered suitable for the education of children with Statements. LEAs may only make arrangements for a child with a Statement to attend an independent school if it is approved, or if the Secretary of State has consented to the child being educated there.

Section 14 sets out procedures when an LEA propose to cease to maintain a special school.

As with other school closure proposals, objections may he made to the authority within a period of not less than two months. The authority must then, within a month, send copies of all objections, together with their comments, to the Secretary of State. (S)he can approve the proposals, change the timing or reject them.

There are special arrangements for serving school attendance orders on children with Statements. The authority must first serve a notice on the parents stating:

a)   their intention to serve the order, and

b) that if within 15 days the parent selects a school, it will, unless the Secretary of State directs, be the school named in the attendance order.

The authority may believe that the school named by the parents is:

a) unsuitable to the child's age, aptitude or ability or to his/her special educational needs, or
b) that attendance at the school by the child would prejudice the 'provision of efficient education or the efficient use of resources'. If so, they may, after telling the parents of their intention to do so, apply to the Secretary of State for a direction.

The direction may require the LEA to amend the child's Statement accordingly. It will be the duty of the authority and of the governors of any school named in a direction to admit the child.

At any time while a school attendance order is in force a parent may apply for another school to be substituted in the order, or the parent may request that an order be revoked because arrangements have been made for the child to be educated 'otherwise' than at school. In such cases, the authority will amend or revoke the order as requested unless:

a) they believe the school selected is unsuitable, or
b) the change of school is against the interests of the child, or
c) that his/her attendance would prejudice the provision of efficient education or the efficient use of resources, or
d) that no satisfactory arrangements have been made for education 'otherwise' than at school.

If the authority refuses, the parent may refer the matter to the Secretary of State to direct.

Section 18 of the Education Act 1981 gives the Secretary of State power to require parents to submit their child for examination if this would assist in determining any question referred to him/her under the Act. The parents have the right to be present at any such examination, and failure to produce the child for examination is an offence.

Care in the Community: **A consultative Document on Moving Resources for Care in England, DHSS 1981**

The Government announced a commitment to community care and places to facilitate it. Resources were to be moved from hospitals to community sites. The long-term admission of children to mental handicap hospitals was to be avoided. Service for mentally handicapped people would enable them to live with their families and failing that, in a supportive local community setting.

Education (Scotland) Act 1981

This Act is in some ways parallel to the 1981 Education Act for England and Wales. Among the differences between the two Acts is that the Scottish legislation referred to a 'Record of Need' rather than a 'Statement of Special Educational Need' and there were differences in the procedures for appeal.

Report of a Study on Community Care, DHSS 1981

This document makes it clear that community care is not always less expensive than hospital care. (If it is, this is because of the unpaid status of informal carers.) The support of informal carers is an important aspect of community care.

Education for All **1985 (The Swann Report)**

The Swann Report was the report of a committee asked to:

• review the needs and attainments of ethnic minority groups

- consider arrangements for monitoring the educational progress of such groups
- establish the role of education in a multicultural society.

The interim report of the committee was *West Indian Children in our Schools* 1981 (The Rampton Report). The Swann Report identified the following areas of concern:

- English teaching (this should be provided in the mainstream)
- teaching the mother tongue
- teaching religious education
- training teachers.

The report did not consider it a satisfactory principle that ethnic groups be either assimilated or separated.

Disabled Persons (Services, Consultation and Representation) Act 1986

Among the provisions of this Act is that local education authorities (LEAs) must notify social services departments (SSDs) of all children aged 14 years and over who have special educational needs. An officer from the SSD gives an opinion on the children who are to be considered disabled under current law. The LEA must notify the SSD of these disabled children again some nine months before the young person leaves school or college. This is so that the young person's needs for statutory services can be met; e.g. home help, meals.

Education Act 1988 (Education Reform Act)

The Education Reform Act (ERA) provided for a National Curriculum (NC) for schools and open enrolment to maintained-schools. The Act introduced grant-maintained schools and city technology colleges. It provided for delegating financial control to school governors, reforming further education and abolishing the Inner London Education Authority.

Particularly pertinent to pupils with special educational needs are sections 17, 18, and 19 of the Act. Each of these sections concerns exemptions from the NC. Section 17 concerns collective exemptions whereby in certain cases or circumstances, collective modification of the NC or disapplications from it is permitted. Section 18 has to do with exemptions for individual pupils who have Statements of special educational need (under the Education Act 1981). All or any of the NC requirements can be modified or disapplied. Section 19 concerns temporary exemptions from the NC which allow the head teacher of a maintained school to make a general or special direction to modify or disapply the NC.

The Children Act 1989

The Children Act 1989 came into effect on 14 October 1991. The welfare of the child must be a 'paramount consideration' when a court makes decisions concerning a child's upbringing or the administration of a child's property. In any court proceedings touching on a child's upbringing, regard should be given to the principle that: 'any delay in determining the question is likely to prejudice the welfare of the child'.

Children with disabilities and special needs have the same rights as other children to give or withhold their consent to medical examinations and treatment. (Young people of 16 and over give their own consent to medical treatment under existing law.) Children under 16 may also be able to give or refuse consent to treatment depending on their ability to understand the nature of the treatment. The doctor decides whether the child is capable.

If a child has sufficient understanding to make an informed decision, (s)he may refuse medical or psychiatric examination and treatment, or other assessment ordered by the court. If a child refuses consent, the court has to decide what is in the child's best interests, its paramount consideration being the child's welfare.

Children looked after by a local authority, may be in care or may be provided with accommodation. In both cases, the local authority must establish, as far as practicable, the wishes and feelings of the child, his/her parents, and any other person with parental responsibility or who is relevant. In making any decision about the child the local authority must consider the wishes and feelings of these people. It must also give consideration to the child's wishes and feelings, having regard to his age and understanding, and to his religious persuasion, racial origin and cultural and linguistic background.

Parental responsibility is defined as: 'all the rights, duties, powers, responsibilities and authority which by law a parent of a child has in relation to the child and his property'.

Parental responsibility is automatic for a child's mother and the father if he was married to the child's mother at the time of the child's birth, conception, or at any time after.

Others may, under certain circumstances, acquire parental responsibility for a child; an unmarried father, relative and friends and foster parents. A child's guardian has parental responsibility and so has a local authority while a care order under section 33 is in force.

Those having parental responsibility for a child may disagree about an issue relating to the exercise of their responsibility. If so, an application may be made to the court, and an order may be made under section 8 of the Children Act. When an application for such an order is contested, a welfare checklist must be considered by the court to help establish the child's best interests. The court may not make any order unless it considers that doing so would be better than making no order.

The four orders under section 8 are:

1. A prohibited steps order. Under such an order the court may prohibit a child being removed from the UK or being with a particular person.
2. A specific issue order. This enables associated specific issues to be decided by the court (e.g. concerning the child's education).
3. A residence order. This specifies where and with whom a child should live. It confers parental responsibility on those in whose favour the order is made if they do not already have it.
4. A contact order. This directs the person with whom the child is living to allow others to have contact with the child.

A child may be provided with accommodation by a local authority. This must be:

- with foster parents
- with relatives
- in a children's home.

In such circumstances, the local authority does not hold parental responsibility for the child. The arrangement with the child's parents is voluntary. Parents retain full parental responsibility for their child and may remove him or her from the accommodation at any time.

If a local authority obtains a care order under section 33, then the child is 'in care' and the local authority shares parental responsibility with the parents.

Local authorities have a duty:

a) to safeguard and promote the welfare of children within their area who are in need; and
b) so far as is consistent with that duty, to promote the upbringing of such children by their families.

This duty is to be fulfilled by the local authority, providing a range and level of services to meet those children's needs. A child is 'in need' according to the Act if:

a) he is unlikely to achieve or maintain, or to have the opportunity of achieving or maintaining, a reasonable standard of health or development without the provision for him of services by a local authority under Part III of the Act;

b) his health or development is likely to be significantly impaired, or further impaired, without the provision for him of such services; or

c) he is disabled.

To promote the upbringing of children by their families, local authorities are given a duty to:

make such provision as they consider appropriate for the following services to be available with respect to children in need within their area while they are living with their families:

a) advice, guidance and counselling;
b) occupational, social, cultural or recreational activities;
c) home help (which may include laundry facilities);
d) facilities for, or assistance with, travelling to and from home for the purpose of taking advantage of any other service provided under this Act or of any similar service;
e) assistance to enable the child concerned and his family to have a holiday.

Local authorities must provide appropriate day care for children who are:

- in need
- within their area
- under five, and
- not yet attending school.

For children in need who are not attending school, local authorities must provide appropriate care or supervised activities outside school hours or during school holidays. This may include provision made by LEAs, social services departments and voluntary and private organisations. LEAs and social services departments (SSDs) must jointly review and publicise the provision made in their area for:

- day care
- out of school supervision
- child minding for children under eight.

Every local authority must maintain a register of disabled children in their area to facilitate the efficient planning and monitoring of services. Registration is voluntary and parents may see entries about their child. Parents who do not register are still entitled to services for their child. Local authorities are required to provide services designed to minimise the effect of a child's disabilities and to give him or her the opportunity to lead a life as normal as possible.

A new provision was inserted in the Education Act 1981 by the Children Act. This enables local authorities to assist families where a child with special educational needs would benefit from attending an establishment abroad (e.g. the Peto Institute in Hungary). Local authorities may pay:

- all or part of the fees of the establishment
- expenses incurred for maintenance and travel of the child and any person travelling with him and staying with him in the establishment.

The Children Act empowers SSDs to combine assessments under the Act with those under the 1981 Act and under other legislation.

Under the Children Act a court may make an education supervision order. This can only be made if a child is of compulsory school age and is not being properly educated. This ground for making the order is satisfied if:

- the child is not complying with an existing school attendance order in force concerning the child; or
- the child is a registered pupil at a school but is not attending regularly.

A compulsory care order may be made where:

- the child is suffering or likely to suffer significant harm, and
- where such harm is attributable to a lack of reasonable parental care, or to the child being beyond parental control.

Before starting proceedings for an education supervision order the LEA must consult the SSD. This may result in the child, and possibly his family, being given support under Part III of the Act. Alternatively, social services might apply for a care order or a supervision order.

The child is put under the supervision of a designated LEA. A supervisor is appointed to advise, assist and befriend, and give directions to the child and his parents, to secure that the child is properly educated. The supervisor must consider whether the school has met the social and educational needs of the child. If the child, apparently, has special educational needs, the supervisor may recommend assessment under the 1981 Act. If the child is behind with work, the supervisor can recommend that a direction for a temporary exception from the National Curriculum (see Education Reform Act 1988), is made by the head teacher. If the school cannot or will not address issues relevant for the child the supervisor may recommend a change of school.

Before giving directions, the supervisor must try to establish the wishes and feelings of the child and his parents, particularly as to the place where the child should be educated. If a child persistently fails to comply with a direction made under an education supervision order, the LEA must notify the appropriate SSD which must then investigate the child's circumstances with a view to using their powers under the Act.

Education supervision orders initially last for up to one year, and can be extended for up to three years at a time. The order expires when the child is no longer of compulsory school age, or when a care order is made. It is an offence for any parent of a child who is the subject of an order persistently to fail to comply with its directions.

Under the Education Act 1944, parents commit an offence if their child does not comply with a school attendance order and also if their child does not regularly attend school. The Children Act amended the 1944 Act so that only an LEA can take proceedings against parents under the 1944 Act. Before doing so, the LEA must consider whether to apply for an education supervision order instead of, or in addition to taking proceedings. If proceedings are started under the 1944 Act, the court may direct the LEA to apply for an education supervision order. Or, having consulted with social services, the LEA may decide that such an order is not necessary for safeguarding the child's welfare. In this case, the LEA must inform the court of the reasons for their decision.

An independent school may provide accommodation for not more than 50 children and may not be approved by the Secretary of State for special educational provision (as a 'special school') under the Education Act 1981. If so, the school will for the purpose of the Children Act be a 'children's home'. Those who run children's homes must:

- safeguard and promote the welfare of the children
- make appropriate use of the services and facilities available for children cared for by their own parents
- advise, assist and befriend pupils to promote their welfare when the school no longer accommodates them.

Local authorities have duties and powers under the Act to ensure that the welfare of children is being safeguarded and promoted.

Independent schools may have more than 50 boarding pupils. Also, residential schools may have been approved under the Education Act 1981 as 'special schools'. In both of these cases, there is a duty on proprietors of such schools and others to safeguard and protect the child's welfare. Powers of entry and inspection are given to local authorities.

Independent schools should have a clear policy on the standards of behaviour expected of pupils, how they will maintain these standards and how they will deal with unacceptable behaviour. The school should make information about this policy available to parents, the local SSD and others.

Every boarding school should have effective means for hearing children's concerns and complaints.

If pupils are accommodated in independent schools for more than two weeks in school holidays, social services must be notified and pupils will be treated as privately fostered.

Further and Higher Education Act 1992

The Act establishes two Further Education Funding Councils (FEFC) one for England and one for Wales. The further education sector is defined as being responsible for providing further education for full-time students aged 16–18 years, part-time education for those over 16 and full-time education for those over 18. For people aged 16–25 with learning difficulties, special arrangements may be made. The Act placed a duty upon the FEFC to have regard to the requirements of people with learning difficulties. Further education colleges and sixth form colleges were moved from local education authority (LEA) responsibility and became 'incorporated' achieving greater self-determination. The Act outlines arrangements for the transfer of property, rights, liabilities and staff from LEA to institutional control. LEAs were allowed to keep control of sixth forms in LEA secondary schools. The Act did not take away all post-16 provision from LEAs nor the LEA's responsibility to ensure progression between sectors of education. Requirements were set out to do with quality assurance, the role of Her Majesty's Chief Inspector, the governance of institutions, grants and travel arrangements.

Education Act 1993

The Education Act 1993 introduced an improved system of provision for children with special educational needs, building upon the principles established by the 1981 Act. Parents of children with Statements are given rights to have a say in the education of their children and a right to state a preference for the maintained school which their child should attend. A greater emphasis was also placed on children who have special educational needs, but who do not require a Statement. The framework of the 1993 Act is supplemented by various regulations, Circulars and a Code of Practice.

The 1993 Act also clarified the ability of LEAs to provide support services for pupils with SEN. New regulations set out the circumstances in which GM schools may be charged the full cost of such services by LEAs.

The Education Act 1993 received its royal assent on 27th July 1993, putting into effect policies announced in the 1992 White Paper, *Choice and Diversity*. Its main elements were:

- a new framework for schools, concerning grant-maintained schools and the formation of the Funding Agency for Schools (FAS)
- improving failing schools, concerning schools 'at risk' of failing
- curriculum and testing, providing for the School Curriculum and Assessment Authority (SCAA) to replace the National Curriculum Council and Schools Examinations and Assessment Council

- Special Educational Needs, and
- Exclusions and Education otherwise than at school.

(The last two elements will he considered in more detail.)

Part III of the Act aimed to establish an improved system for educating children with special needs. It concentrated on pupils with special educational needs but who do not need Statements. At the same time, it strengthened the system for pupils who do require Statements and for their parents. It reaffirmed the principle that pupils with SEN should be educated in mainstream schools wherever it is possible and sensible to do so.

It aimed to:

- introduce a new Code of Practice containing guidance and criteria to which schools and local education authorities would have to 'have regard' when dealing with pupils with SEN
- reinforce the role of the school in educating pupils with SEN
- ensure local education authorities (LEAs) could continue to provide SEN support services to both their own LEA and GM schools
- improve the services of LEAs and other agencies to pupils needing a formal assessment or Statement, including setting timescales
- increase parents' rights of appeal against LEA decisions, and establish a Tribunal to hear such appeals
- allow special schools to become grant-maintained.

The Code of Practice contains clear guidance and criteria concerning the identification, assessment and other arrangements for pupils with SEN. It covers the school's role, especially towards pupils who do not need Statements. It covers the LEA's role in assessing a child and where necessary, making a Statement.

All LEA schools, GM schools and LEAs themselves, must have regard to the guidance in the Code. So must the SEN Tribunal when hearing appeals.

Governors are required to draw up their schools' policies for pupils with SEN. They must also publish and report on the implementation of these policies. The Act requires governors to consult locally as appropriate over coordinating provision for pupils with SEN. Governors must also admit pupils whose Statement names their school.

The Act requires LEAs to carry out assessments and make Statements within specific timescales. Timescales also apply to district health authorities and social services departments in certain circumstances.

Parents of pupils with Statements have increased rights of school choice for their child. They will be able to state a preference (which the LEA must consider) for a maintained school. They may also make representations for their child to be placed at an independent or non-maintained special school. Parents will have new rights of appeal. For example, they may appeal against an LEA's decision to cease to maintain a Statement. All appeals will be heard by an independent Tribunal.

The Act sought to address the issue that too many children were being excluded from school and that the alternative educational provision made for many excluded pupils was variable. The Education Act therefore would:

- place LEAs under a new duty (replacing their existing power) to provide education otherwise than at school where necessary to meet a pupil's needs;
- regularise the legal status and conduct of free-standing units which LEAs operate to provide education for excluded pupils. These units will be known as Pupil Referral Units (PRUs);
- require that the PRUs should offer a broad and balanced curriculum but not full National Curriculum. This recognises the constraints of units perhaps providing for only 15–20

pupils of varying ages. Provision should aim to return children to mainstream education at the earliest opportunity. If they are older, provision should fit them for transition to further education or work;
- abolish the potentially abusable category of indefinite exclusion, leaving the options of fixed term and permanent exclusion;
- permit the extension of fixed term exclusions up to 15 school days in any one term. This is to give schools a degree of flexibility in dealing with difficult and disruptive pupils. Exclusion may consist of a single fixed period exclusion of five days, extended as necessary up to 15. This would allow time for further reports or supportive work with the pupil and his parents. Alternatively, a series of short fixed exclusions may be given;
- provide through regulations for time limits to be placed on the operation of exclusions procedures. This is to reduce the time spent by the pupil out of school;
- provide through regulations for funding to follow the permanently excluded child into (a) another mainstream school which accepts him or (b) into any alternative provision made by the LEA under their new duty to provide education otherwise than at school.

Section 292 of the Act repealed part of the Children Act 1989 which had provided a criterion as to whether an independent school was a children's home. This criterion was that under 50 children were being provided with accommodation. Under the Education Act 1993, an independent school would only be a registered children's home if it provided accommodation for three or more children for over 295 days of the year in question. (As a result, some independent schools offering boarding accommodation have ceased to be children's homes.) A consequence is that they are outside the scope of the inspections by local authority social services departments for which section 64 of the Children Act 1989 provides and within the more relaxed regime of inspections under section 87.

The Dearing Report 1993

The Dearing Report made recommendations regarding the National Curriculum to:

- simplify and clarify the programmes of study
- reduce the volume of material to be taught
- reduce prescription to provide more scope for professional judgement
- ensure that the Orders are written in a way which offers maximum support to teachers.

Regarding special educational needs (SENs) the Report made the following recommendations:

- The National Curriculum and its assessment arrangements should continue to be available and relevant for pupils with special educational needs.
- The National Curriculum levels defined in the Orders should be broadened so that teachers can provide work in line with pupils' abilities and needs.
- Schools should liaise with parents over the development of the appropriate curriculum for pupils with Statements of SEN.
- The work on the revision of the National Curriculum should involve teachers of pupils with SEN. The assessment and recording of the achievements of pupils with SEN should be reviewed.

Disability Discrimination Act 1995

The Disability Discrimination Act 1995 (DDA) received Royal Assent in November 1995. It brings in a wide range of new measures aimed at addressing discrimination against disabled people. The Act covers various areas including employment, public transport and education.

The DDA defines a disabled person as one who has: 'a physical or mental impairment which has a substantial and long term adverse effect on his ability to carry out normal day-to-day activities'.

The term 'physical and mental impairment' is meant to be wide and to include sensory and learning impairment. 'Long term' means that the disability has lasted or is likely to last for at least 12 months or is likely to last for the rest of the person's life (Schedule 1 of the Act).

The DDA amends the Education Act 1993 to require that each county, voluntary or grant-maintained school will publish new information in their annual reports. This will cover:

(a) the arrangements for the admission of disabled pupils;
(b) the steps taken to prevent disabled pupils from being treated less favourably than other pupils; and
(c) the facilities provided to assist access to the school by disabled pupils.

The DDA also amends the Further and Higher Education Act 1992 so that a further education funding council is to require the governing body of an individual college to publish disability statements at certain intervals. Also, local education authorities are required to publish disability statements at certain intervals.

A disability statement contains information about the facilities for further education made by the LEA/further education institution as the case may be in respect of disabled persons.

Education Act 1996

Certain amendments were made to the Education Act 1993 by the Disability Discrimination Act 1995 and by the Nursery Education and Grant Maintained Schools Act 1996. In November 1996, the amended Education Act 1993 was repealed and pulled together along with the Education Act 1944 and other Acts by the Education Act 1996. The Education Act of 1996 made no substantial changes to law on special education but it is helpful to know where matters are dealt with in the Act. Issues and the place where they are covered are as follows and all sections refer to Part 4 of the Act. Relevant schedules are given at the end.

- The definitions of 'special educational needs' and of 'special education provision' (section 312).
- The duty of local education authorities, governors and others to 'have regard to' a code of practice (section 313) The *Code of Practice on the Identification and Assessment of Special Educational Needs* is a version of such a code. The issuing and revising of a code of practice by the Secretary of State (section 314).
- The duty of the local education authority to keep under review arrangements for special educational provision (section 315).
- Duties of school governors or local education authority provision (section 315).
- Children with special educational needs normally to be educated in ordinary schools (section 316).
- Duties of school governors or local education authority towards children with special educational needs (section 317 (1)–(5)).
- Annual reports and arrangements for disabled pupils (section 317 (6)–(7)).
- Provision of goods and services relating to special educational needs by a local education authority (section 318 (1), (2), (4)).
- Grants for nursery education (section 318 (3)).
- A local education authority's ability to arrange for special educational provision to be made otherwise than in a school (section 319) and to arrange provision outside England and Wales for certain children with Statements of special educational need (section 320).

- The general duty of a local education authority towards children for whom they are responsible (section 321).
- The duty of the Health Authority or local authority to help the local education authority (section 322).
- Local education authority's assessment of educational needs (section 323).
- Statement of Special Educational Needs (section 324).
- A parent's appeal to the Tribunal against local education authority refusal to issue a Statement (section 325); a parent's appeal to the Tribunal against the contents of a Statement (section 326).
- Local education authority access to certain schools (section 327).
- Parental requests for an assessment of a child with a Statement and the right to appeal if the local education authority refuses (section 328 (1)–(5)).
- Annual Review of a Statement of special educational needs (section 328 (5)–(60)).
- Parental requests for an assessment of a child without a Statement and the right to appeal if the local education authority refuses (section 329).
- Assessment of educational needs of a child by the local education authority at the request of the governing body of a grant-maintained school (section 330).
- Assessment of the educational needs of children under 2 years old (section 331).
- The duty of a Health Authority or National Health Service Trust to notify parents and inform a local education authority of their opinion that a child has special educational needs (section 332).
- Constitution of special educational needs Tribunal (section 333), its membership (section 334), remuneration and expenses to the Tribunal president and members (section 335) and Tribunal procedure (section 336).
- The definition of a special school (section 337).
- The power of the funding authority to establish grant-maintained special schools (section 338).
- Proposals to establish grant-maintained and maintained special schools and other issues (section 339) and the procedure for dealing with such proposals (section 340).
- The approval of the premises of maintained or grant-maintained special schools (section 341) and the approval of special schools (section 342).
- Nursery education in grant-maintained special schools (section 343).
- The government and conduct of special schools (section 344).
- Regulations relating to maintained special schools becoming grant-maintained special schools (section 345).
- The grouping of grant-maintained special schools (section 346), the approval of independent special schools providing special education (section 347) and the provision of special education at non-maintained schools (section 348).
- The variation of a school's trust deeds by order of the Secretary of State (section 349).

- Making assessments under section 323 (schedule 26).
- Making and maintenance of Statements under section 324 (schedule 27).
- Complaints of local education authorities acting unreasonably (schedule 496).
- Complaints of local education authorities failing to fulfil their legal duty (schedule 497).

Inclusive Learning: **The Report of the Learning Difficulties and/or Disabilities Committee 1996 (The Tomlinson Report)**

The Tomlinson Committee was established by the Further Education Funding Council (FEFC) to review the state of further education for students with learning difficulties and/or disabilities. The Report analyses the extent to which the requirements of the Further and

Higher Education Act 1992 were being met. It proposes an approach to managing and funding further education to develop more 'inclusive' provision. It would include more people with learning difficulties and/or disabilities because it would be more responsive to the needs of individual learners. Recommendations include:

- a new qualification at pre-foundation level suitable for people with learning difficulties;
- the FEFC to strengthen requirements on colleges to heed the needs of people with learning difficulties/disabilities when preparing their strategic plans;
- Government to consider a single post-16 funding agency for schools and colleges of further education to prevent student choices being limited by funding arrangements;
- Government to consider transferring local authority discretionary awards and transport funding to colleges;
- a joint departmental circular to set out the responsibilities of education, health and social services in the provision of services to people with learning difficulties and/or disabilities;
- college inspections to grade the extent to which teaching matches the learning requirements of the students;
- a sector-wide, three-year quality initiative programme of staff development;
- a centrally coordinated body to advise on the accreditation of teacher training as it affects students with learning difficulties and/or disabilities;
- a reinterpretation of the funding rules so that the FEFC can pay for a wider range of courses, including those for people who are maintaining skills rather than acquiring new ones.

Excellence for All Children: Meeting Special Educational Needs 1997

This 'Green Paper', published in October 1997, concerns raising standards, shifting resources to practical support and increasing inclusion. Policies for raising standards apply to all pupils including those with SEN. Early identification of difficulties and appropriate intervention are important for children with SEN. Government initiatives for improving literacy and numeracy, target setting for schools and new technologies will help these children.

Parents will maintain their right to express a preference for a special school place for their child. The Government wishes to improve the monitoring of school-based SEN provision. Presently a 'Named Person' is offered to parents when their child receives a Statement. The Named Person should be available to parents whose children's needs are being formally assessed. Local schemes should develop active links with voluntary bodies. Where the parent and LEA cannot agree during the process potentially leading to statutory assessment and a Statement, parent partnership schemes may help.

The *Code of Practice on the Identification and Assessment of SEN* will he revised to reduce bureaucracy relating to IEPs and annual reviews of Statements. Provision at stages 1 to 3 of the Code should be improved. LEAs should help schools improve the quality of their provision for SEN. Contracts may he introduced between schools and parents specifying the agreed extra provision at stage 3. Government will look at the way Statements work for children who need them.

Children with SEN should be enrolled in ordinary schools unless there are 'compelling reasons' for doing otherwise. The capacity of mainstream schools to provide for children with a wide range of needs should be progressively extended. Links between ordinary and special schools should be strengthened and LEA support services used to support mainstream placements. While children with SEN should generally participate in mainstream lessons rather than being in separate units, separate provision may be necessary on occasion for specific purposes. Access to buildings and new technology should aid inclusion. Regarding admission arrangements for children with SEN, the White Paper, *Excellence in Schools*, signalled local admission forums and if necessary the use of an independent adjudicator. Children with SEN will be treated no less favourably than others in these arrangements. For children with Statements, the arrangements confirming access to the school named in the Statement will continue.

Government will encourage regional cooperation and wants to see regional planning arrangements for some aspects of SEN provision. Government will encourage voluntary regional cooperation between LEAs and between LEAs and other statutory, voluntary and private sector providers, including: non-maintained special schools and independent schools catering for SEN; and institutions providing teacher training. Regional planning machinery will help coordinate provision for low-incidence disabilities, specialist teacher training and other aspects of SEN.

New standards have been announced which all trainee teachers should reach in order to qualify. These include standards in special needs training. As part of the supported induction year, SEN Coordinators (SENCOs) provide specialist support to new teachers during their first year. Regarding the continuing professional development of teachers, Government will encourage partnerships in teacher training. LEAs should collaborate with higher education institutions in providing programmes of training for serving teachers. The Teacher Training Agency (TTA) National Standards for Head Teachers already cover aspects of leadership and accountability which relate to SEN. The present TTA National Standards for SENCOs may form the basis of a qualification for SENCOs. The Government will review the arrangements for the training of SEN specialists. There may eventually be standards and/or qualifications for SEN specialists. There will be a national framework for training Learning Support Assistants. The national guidance on how governors' training needs can he met will cover governors' responsibilities for pupils with SEN.

Government will promote research designed to establish good practice, and disseminate the results. Government will strengthen the links between the DfEE and the Department of Health. Collaboration between the LEAs, social service departments and health authorities should be improved. The regional planning arrangements may encourage the practice of local authorities undertaking the joint planning and funding of residential educational placements or packages of care for children in need. Government will consider funding joint research by the DfEE and the Department of Health into the factors that lead to the most effective provision of speech and language therapy for children. The review of the SEN Code of Practice will consider improvements to transition planning as pupils come to the end of compulsory schooling. Government will consider how more young people with SEN can he helped to make a successful transition from school to further and higher education, training and employment.

The final chapter of the Green Paper exemplifies policies and action proposed in the document as they may apply to children with emotional and behavioural difficulties.

Meeting Special Educational Needs: A Programme of Action 1998

The document includes a timetable summarising action over the subsequent three years. The 'Programme' builds on the Green Paper *Excellence for All Children*. Working with parents is the theme of Chapter One. Support and advice given to parents would be improved to enable them to be more involved in the education of their child. Government would provide high quality child care and early years education. Earlier identification of difficulties and early intervention as necessary would he encouraged. Every LEA would be expected to have a parent partnership scheme by 1999 allowing parents access to advice from an independent supporter. LEAs would have conciliation arrangements for settling disagreements. Stronger arrangements would he made to involve children in the SEN process.

Chapter Two concerns improving the SEN framework. Government intend to build on existing statutory provisions and best practice to improve the SEN framework and to better focus on meeting children's SENs. A simplified SEN Code of Practice would be introduced in 2000/2001 which concentrates on preventative work, reduces bureaucracy and promotes effective school-based support and monitoring. Guidance would he published on the placement of children under the Code and the related provision. Criteria would be introduced for making statements of SEN. LEAs would have to publish more comprehensive information about their SEN policies. This would include information about what schools might normally provide from their own budgets and the SEN support LEAs will provide. Performance would be monitored against key indicators. Government would seek to improve the effectiveness of the SEN Tribunal.

Inclusion is the concern of Chapter Three. Government intend to promote further inclusion and develop the role of special schools. From 1999, LEAs must publish information about their policy on inclusion in their Education Development Plans. The statutory framework for inclusion (section 316 of the Education Act 1996) will be reviewed. Government will identify and disseminate good practice by special schools in developing practical links with mainstream schools. The contribution of special schools to an increasingly inclusive education system will be promoted. Steps would be taken to ensure that children with SEN are treated fairly in schools' admissions procedures. Financial support would be provided, for projects which aim to improve provision and raise achievements for children with emotional and behavioural difficulties.

Chapter Four deals with developing knowledge and skills of all staff working with children with SEN. Greater emphasis would be given to SEN within teacher training and development. Good practice guidance would be published on the work of learning support assistants. In 1999, consultation would take place on a description of the future role of educational psychologists. Government will consider further the particular training and development needs of staff working with children with SEN in the light of consultation on the forthcoming Green Paper on the future of the teaching profession.

Partnership is the theme of Chapter Five. Government intend to help improve the way that LEAs work together, and in partnership with other local agencies, to strengthen support for children with special needs. From April 2000, regional coordination of SEN provision would be extended across the country. New duties of partnership and new powers would be introduced to enable more flexible funding arrangements between the National Health Service and local authorities. Initiatives would be developed to improve the provision of speech and language therapy services. Information would be gathered about the experiences, once they have left school, of young people with SEN, to help schools and colleges prepare young people for adult life more effectively. These developments would be supported through more effective collaboration between Whitehall Departments, particularly the DfEE and the Department of Health.

Learning and Skills Act 2000

Under this Act the Learning and Skills Council (LSC) must secure the provision of proper facilities for education (other than higher education) suitable to the requirements of those above compulsory school age but under the age of 19. There are similar requirements relating to training and organised leisure time related to education or training. In connection with this provision the LSC must take account of the 'different abilities and aptitudes of different persons' (section 2). Similarly, the LSC must also secure the provision of 'reasonable' facilities for persons who have attained the age of 19 years.

In discharging these functions, the LSC must have regard to the needs of persons with learning difficulties and, in particular, to any report of an assessment conducted under section 140 of the Act (see below).

A person with learning difficulty is defined as one who:

- has a significantly greater difficulty in learning than the majority of persons of the same age; or
- has a disability which either prevents or hinders him from making use of the facilities of a kind generally provided by institutions providing post-16 education or training (section 13).

Section 13 also concerns the circumstances in which the LSC must secure the provision of boarding education for a person with a learning difficulty.

Section 140 of the Act referred to above concerns a situation where two circumstances apply. The first is that the LEA maintains a statement of SEN under the Education Act 1996. The second is that the Secretary of State believes that the person will leave school at the end of his last year of compulsory school to receive post-16 education or training, or higher education. In these circumstances, the Secretary of State must arrange for an assessment of the person to be conducted during the last year of compulsory schooling. The Secretary of State may also arrange for an assessment of a person in certain other circumstances, including if the person is over compulsory school age but has not attained the age of 25.

Special Educational Needs and Disability Act 2001

The Special Education Needs and Disability Act 2001 (SENDA) amends the Disability Discrimination Act 1995, part 4 of the Education Act 1996 and other Acts, and makes further provision against discrimination on grounds of disability in schools and other educational establishments.

The provisions of the SENDA concerning SEN apply to England and Wales. Provisions relating to the rights of disabled people in education extend to England, Wales and Scotland (except the duty to produce an accessibility strategy or plan which does not apply to Scotland).

The SENDA is explained by two Codes of Practice, one concerning schools and one relating to the post-16 sector. The codes are available on the internet at: www.dr-gb.org. The Stationery Office has also published Explanatory Notes. The Act is in three parts:

Part 1 amends part 4 of the Education Act 1996 for children with SEN. It strengthens the right of children with SEN to be educated in mainstream schools unless this is incompatible with the wishes of his parents or the provision of efficient education for other children. Also, the LEA has to show that there are no reasonable steps they could take to prevent the incompatibility.

The SENDA requires the LEA to arrange services to provide advice and information for the parents of children with SEN. LEAs are required to arrange a means of resolving disputes between parents and schools including appointing an independent person to help avoid or resolve such disputes. LEAs are required to comply within prescribed periods with orders of the Special Educational Needs and Disability Tribunal (SENDIST). Where the LEA decides not to oppose an appeal by a parent to the SENDIST, the appeal is to be treated as having been determined in the appellant's favour.

Schools are required to inform parents where the school makes special educational provision for their child. Schools may request a statutory assessment of a pupil's SEN. Revised procedures must be followed by the LEA in making, maintaining and amending statements of SEN (for example, parents have a right to a meeting with the LEA when it proposes to amend their child's statement).

Part 2 of the SENDA concerns disability discrimination in education and has three chapters:

Chapter 1 places duties on LEAs and schools including independent schools and non-maintained special schools in England and Wales. It places duties on local authorities, independent schools, self-governing schools and grant-aided schools in Scotland.

One key duty is not to treat disabled pupil less favourably for a reason relating to his disability than someone to whom that reason does not apply, without justification. It is unlawful for a responsible body of a school to discriminate against a disabled child who might become a pupil at the school in any of four ways. These are the admission arrangements it makes; the terms on which it offers admissions; refusing or deliberately omitting to accept his application for admission; or in the education or associated services provided for or offered to pupils at the school by the responsible body. Three aspects taken together constitute unlawful discrimination. These are that the less favourable treatment: is for a reason that is directly related to the child's disability; is less favourable treatment than someone gets if the reason does not apply to them; and that it cannot be justified. Less favourable treatment may be justified if it is the result of a permitted form of selection or if it is for both a material and substantial reason. A blanket policy does not constitute a material and substantial reason because it does not take account of individual circumstances. Circumstances in which an admissions authority may operate selective criteria are that a grammar school may select its intake and a specialist school may give priority in their admission criteria to a small percentage of pupils (up to 10 per cent) who show particular aptitude for the subject in which the school specialises.

A second key duty is to make reasonable adjustments to admission arrangements and in relation to education and related services to ensure that disabled pupils (or prospective pupils) are not put at a substantial disadvantage in comparison with their non-disabled peers without justification. 'Reasonable adjustments' do not require the responsible body to provide auxiliary aids and services (as it is anticipated that for schools in the public sector these will be made through the SEN framework). Nor do 'reasonable adjustments' require the responsible body to make physical alterations to the buildings. The duty to make reasonable adjustments is anticipatory in that, generally, a school cannot wait until a disabled pupil arrives before making an adjustment. The only justification for not making a reasonable adjustment is that there is a reason that is both material and substantial.

The Act includes provision through a lack of knowledge defence to prevent responsible bodies from being liable to a claim of discrimination if they did not know that a pupil was disabled and if they could not reasonably have been expected to have known.

The Act also provides for the possibility that a parent or child may request that the school keep confidential the fact that the child has a disability. The responsible body should comply with the request in the case of a parent, and in the case of a child if they think that the child understands what he is asking to be done and what the effect will be. In considering what reasonable adjustments to make, a responsible body must think about the extent to which taking a particular step is consistent with keeping confidentiality, where this has been requested.

The SENDA sets out requirements for England and Wales on LEAs and schools to draw up accessibility strategies (LEAs) and accessibility plans (schools) to improve access to education at schools over time. These strategies and plans have to address three elements of planned improvements in access for disabled pupils. These are: improvements in access to the curriculum; physical improvements to increase access to education and associate services; and improvements in the provision of information in a range of formats for disabled people. The planning duties also update the requirements on governing bodies to provide information in their annual reports about arrangements for disabled pupils at the school. Governing bodies must include in their annual report the accessibility plan showing how they will increase access for disabled pupils to education at the school.

If parents consider that a responsible body has discriminated against their child, they can make a claim of unlawful discrimination. The SENDIST will hear claims of unlawful discrimination relating to fixed-period (temporary) exclusions from all schools; and relating to admissions to and permanent exclusions from all schools other than maintained schools and city academies. SENDIST has the power to order any remedy it thinks reasonable except financial compensation.

Admissions appeals panels or exclusion appeals panels will hear claims of unlawful discrimination regarding a refusal to admit to, and permanent exclusion from, maintained schools and city academies. An admissions appeal is made in accordance with the Code of Practice on Admission Appeals which was introduced by the School Standards and Framework Act 1998. These panels can order that a pupil be admitted. Exclusions in mainstream schools are governed by the School Standards and Framework Act 1998. Exclusion appeals panels can order that a pupil be reinstated.

Chapter 2 places duties on further and higher education institutions and on LEAs in respect of adult education and youth services provision that they secure. There is a duty not to treat disabled students less favourably without justification for a reason relating to their disability. There is also a duty to make reasonable adjustments to ensure that people who are disabled are not put at a substantial disadvantage to people who are not disabled in accessing further education, higher education and LEA secured education.

Chapter 3. The Disability Rights Commission had previously had functions conferred on it by virtue of the Disability Rights Commission Act 1999 in respect of parts 1 and 2 of the Disability Discrimination Act 1995. The SENDA extends the role of the Disability Rights Commission and allows it to prepare new codes of practice to explain the legislation to education providers, disabled people and others.

The Disability Rights Commission may set up an independent conciliation service for disputes arising from the duties of schools under the Act. Its purpose is to promote the settlement of claims without recourse to the SENDIST or other body. Both parent and responsible body have to agree for disputes to be referred to conciliation.

Part 3 of the SENDA concerns supplementary matters.

References

Disability Rights Commission (2001a) *Draft Code of Practice (Schools).*
Disability Rights Commission (2001b) *Code of Practice (Post 16): New duties from 2002 in the provision of post 16 education and related services for disabled people and students.*
Special Educational Needs and Disability Act 2001. London: The Stationery Office.

Regulations

The Education (School Information) Regulations 1981 SI No. 630

Schedule 1 Part 2 of these Regulations deal with general information to be published by the education authority regarding special education. These include its detailed arrangements and policies with regard to the identification and assessment of children with special educational needs and the involvement of parents in the process; the provision made in schools maintained by the authority for pupils with special educational needs and the use made by the authority of special schools maintained by other authorities; and the special educational provision provided otherwise than at school.

The Education (Special Educational Needs) Regulations 1983 SI No. 29

These Regulations concern an education authority making an assessment of a child and issues to do with Statements of special educational needs. The Regulations cover the notice of a decision to make a Statement; educational medical and psychological advice; matters to be taken into account when making an assessment; mandatory re-assessment; the content and form of Statements; restrictions on the disclosure of Statements; and children moving from one education area into another.

Education Order (Northern Ireland) 1984

Under this Order a framework for special education was created similar to that which existed in the rest of the United Kingdom.

The Education (Payment for Special Educational Needs Supplies) Regulations 1994 SI No. 650

These Regulations came into force on 1 April 1994. They relate to the governing bodies of the following schools:

- grant-maintained
- grant-maintained special
- county
- voluntary
- maintained special.

Such governing bodies have a duty under the Education Act 1993 section 161(1)(a) to use their best endeavours to secure that appropriate special educational provision is made for pupils with SEN. Section 162(1) of the Act empowers local education authorities (LEAs) to supply goods and services to these governing bodies to assist them in their duty under section 161(1)(a). Section 162(2) of the Act empowers LEAs to impose terms and payment for such supplies as prescribed in Regulations. Regulations No. 650 are those regulations.

Under them an LEA can charge the full cost of the supplies. The LEA may do so where they supply the governing body of:

- a county, voluntary or maintained special school in the area of another LEA
- a grant-maintained or grant-maintained special school whose maintenance grant includes an amount for meeting the cost of supplies.

The Education (Special Educational Needs) (Approval of Independent Schools) Regulations 1994 SI No. 651

These Regulations came into force on 1 April 1994 and revoked *The Education (Special Educational Needs) (Approval of Independent Schools) Regulations 1991(a)*.

The Regulations prescribe requirements with which an independent school must comply. This compliance is a condition of the school's approval as being suitable to admit children for whom Statements of special educational needs are maintained. (Such Statements maintained under section 168 of the Education Act 1993.)

The Regulations cover issues relating to the control of the school, teaching staff, residential care staff, admissions, exclusions, the health and welfare of pupils, substances and apparatus involving health hazards, collective worship and religious education, incident books and punishment books and premises (schedule 1). They also concern premises and fire precautions, misconduct reports, reports on children with Statements to local education authorities, provision of information, reports of the death, illness or injury of a child, access to the school and to boarders, the school's prospectus and other matters.

Apart from reflecting legislative changes since the 1991 Regulations were implemented, a small number of changes were made. The provision to be made for children with SEN must take the form of a balanced and broadly based curriculum. Incidents involving volunteers working at the school must be recorded. The premises must conform to the standards prescribed for special schools maintained by a local education authority (LEA). The approved number of pupils must not be allowed to fall substantially. If requested, the school staff must participate in any review by the LEA of a pupil's Statement of SEN.

The Education (Special Schools) Regulations 1994 SI No. 652

These Regulations came into force on 1 April 1994 and revoked *The Education (Approval of Special Schools) Regulations 1983* and the *Education (Approval of Special Schools) (Amendment) Regulations 1991*. They make new provision for the approval by the Secretary of State of non-maintained special schools as special schools. The Regulations prescribe the requirements which must be observed by such schools in order to be approved and while such approval is in force.

Section 188(3) of the Education Act 1993 made a provision for any special school which was in existence on the date when the section came into force (1 April 1994). The provision was that the special school is to be treated as approved under section 188. The Regulations prescribe the requirements to be observed by:

- those approved special schools;
- new special schools maintained by a local education authority;
- new grant-maintained special schools whose proposals have been approved by the Secretary of State (under section 184 of the Education Act 1993);
- special schools which become grant-maintained schools under section 186 which are also to be treated as approved under section 188.

The requirements include provisions relating to sex education. Provision is made for the Secretary of State to withdraw the approval of a special school. Provision is also made for special schools in hospitals.

The Regulations prescribe the following:

- information to be included in the notices which have to be served when an LEA proposes to establish a new maintained special school;
- information to be included in notices when specified alterations in a maintained special school are proposed;
- information to be included in notices when it is proposed to discontinue a maintained special school;
- those on whom such notices are to be served.

The Education (Grant-maintained Special Schools) Regulations 1994 SI No. 653

These Regulations came into force in April 1994 and were amended by *The Education (Grant-maintained Special Schools) (Amendment) Regulations 1994* which came into force on 1 June 1994.

Regulations SI No. 653 provided for special schools maintained by local education authorities to become grant-maintained (GM) special schools. Also they provided for:

- the establishment of new GM special schools by a funding authority;
- the alteration and discontinuance of GM special schools;
- the government, conduct and funding of GM special schools.

The Education (Groups including Grant-maintained Special Schools) Regulations 1994 SI No. 779

These Regulations came into force in April 1994. They were made under section 187 of the Education Act 1993 and modify the chapter of the Act which enables schools to join together as groups to grant-maintained (GM) schools. The modification extends the appropriate provisions to GM special schools.

The Education (Special Educational Needs) Regulations 1994 SI No. 1047

These regulations came into force on 1 September 1994. They relate to the assessment of special educational needs (SEN) and to Statements of SEN under the Education Act 1993 Part 3.

Under the Regulations, local education authorities (LEAs), when making an assessment of a child's SENs, must seek advice from the following sources:

- parental
- educational
- medical
- psychological
- social services authority
- others as considered appropriate.

The Regulations prescribe the form and content of:

(a) a notice to be served on a parent with a draft Statement of SEN
(b) a Statement of SEN.

They also supplement the procedural framework for making an assessment and a Statement under the Education Act 1993 Part 3. The Regulations concern certain LEA documents:

- notice of proposal to make an assessment
- decision to make an assessment

- notice of a parent's request for an assessment to be made.

Copies of these must be served on the following:

- the social services authority
- the district health authority
- head teacher of the child's school.

Provision is made concerning how a review of a Statement by an LEA under the Education Act 1993 section 172 is to he carried out. This includes forming a transition plan for pupils aged 14 years.

The Regulations provide for the transfer of a Statement from one authority to another and restrictions on the disclosure of Statements.

The Education (Special Educational Needs) (Information) Regulations 1994 SI No. 1048

These Regulations came into force on 1 September 1994 and concern the publication of information about special educational needs (SEN).

The governing body of each county, voluntary or grant-maintained school, are required to publish information set out in schedule 1 about the following:

- the school's special education provision
- the school's policies for the identification, assessment and provision for all pupils with SEN
- the school's staffing policies and partnership with bodies beyond the school.

The governing body of each maintained or grant-maintained special school (other than a special school established in a hospital) must publish similar information as set out in schedule 2.

The governing body of each maintained or grant-maintained special school which is established in a hospital must publish information as set out in schedule 3. This includes, for example:

- how pupils with SEN are identified and their needs determined and reviewed
- how resources are allocated to and among pupils with SEN.

The Regulations also concern annual reports for each county, voluntary, maintained special, grant-maintained or grant-maintained special school. These annual reports shall include information about the implementation of the governing body's policy for pupils with SEN.

The Education (Special Schools Conducted by Education Associations) Regulations 1994 SI No. 1084

These Regulations came into force in May 1994, and were amended by *The Education (Special Schools Conducted by Education Association) (Amendment) Regulations 1994 SI 2848* which came into force in December 1994.

By Orders made under section 220 of the Education Act 1993, responsibility for the conduct of county and voluntary schools may be transferred to education associations. Section 221–7 of the Act makes further provision concerning the subsequent conduct or discontinuance of such schools. Under sections 228(2) and 228(3) of the Act, regulations:

- may apply these provisions with modifications to maintained special schools
- may provide for the transfer to education associations of the responsibility for the conduct of such schools.

Regulations SI 1084 apply sections 220 to 227 of the Act to maintained special schools (with the modifications made by Regulation 2). SI 1084 applies certain legislation to the transfer to an education association of the responsibility for the conduct of a maintained special school (with the modifications made by Regulations 3 and 4 and schedule 1).

The 'certain legislation' referred to above are:

1. section 35 of the Act which provides for the exercise of powers by the governing bodies of schools following the approval of proposals for GM status but before their implementations;
2. certain provisions of part 2 of the Act which concerns GM schools;
3. the *Education (Acquisition of Grant-maintained Status) (Transitional Functions) Regulations 1993*.

One issue is the transfer of responsibility for the conduct of a maintained special school to an education association. SI 1084 provides for the implementation transfer to alter such a school in ways approved before the transfer. It prohibits the making of proposals to alter or discontinue such a school where an order (under section 220 of the Education Act 1993) has been made in respect of it.

SI 1084 applies the provisions of the National Curriculum to such schools when not established in hospitals.

The Education (Grant-maintained Special Schools) (Amendment) Regulations 1994 SI No. 1231

These Regulations came into force in June 1994, amending the *Education (Grant-maintained Special Schools) Regulations 1994 SI No. 653*.

The Education (Maintained Special Schools becoming Grant-maintained Special Schools) (Ballot Information) Regulations 1994 SI No. 1232

These Regulations came into force in June 1994. They prescribe the information which is to be given to every person eligible to vote in a ballot for a maintained special school to become a grant-maintained special school.

The Special Educational Needs Tribunal Regulations 1994 SI No. 1910

These Regulations came into force on 1 September 1994. They concern the Special Educational Needs Tribunal established by the Education Act 1993 section 177. The regulations make provision in relation to the establishment of the Tribunal and regulate its procedure.

Part 1 contains general provisions including provisions as to:

• the members of the lay panel
• the establishment of the tribunals to exercise the jurisdiction of the SEN Tribunal.

Part 2 contains provisions concerning appealing to the Tribunal and the local education authority's reply. The provisions of part 3 relate to the preparation for the hearing. Part 4 contains provisions to do with the determination of appeals. Finally part 5 contains additional powers of the tribunal and provisions relating to it.

The Education (Initial Government of Grant-maintained Special Schools) Regulations 1994 SI No. 2003

These Regulations came into force in August 1994. They modify paragraphs 5 to 8 of schedule 11 of the Education Act 1993. They do this in relation to:

- the initial instrument of government for the governing body of a grant-maintained special school
- the governors of such a school holding office before the date of implementation of the proposals in pursuance of which the governing body are constituted.

The Education (Grant-maintained Special Schools) (Initial Governing Instruments) Regulations 1994 SI No. 2104

These Regulations came into force in September 1994. They prescribe the initial instrument and articles of government for grant-maintained special schools.

The initial instrument of government, among other provisions:

- requires the governing body (GB) to include first governors;
- requires the GB to include teacher and parent governors;
- provides for the head teacher to he an ex-officio governor.

The initial articles of government include provisions dealing with the general responsibilities of the GB and head teacher regarding the conduct of the school. It concerns provision on the curriculum, school admissions, exclusion of pupils and other matters.

The Education (Grant-maintained Special Schools) (Finance) Regulations 1994 SI No. 2111

These Regulations came into force in September 1994. The provisions of Chapter 6 of Part 2 of the Education Act 1993 (funding of grant-maintained schools) apply, with modifications, to GM special schools. They apply by virtue of regulations 23 of the *Education (Grant-maintained Special Schools) Regulations 1994* as substituted by Regulation 11 of the *Education (Grant-maintained Special Schools) (Amendment) Regulations 1994*.

Consequently, SI 2111 provides for:

a) the determination by the Funding Agency for Schools (FAS) of amounts of maintenance grant
b) the payment by the FAS of capital grants and special purpose grants.

Both (a) and (b) above apply to GM special schools in England which were formerly local education authority special schools.

The Education (Special Schools Conducted by Education Associations) (Amendment) Regulations 1994 SI No. 2848

These Regulations came into force in December 1994 and amend the *Education (Special Schools Conducted by Education Associations) Regulations 1994* by omitting an unnecessary reference.

The Education (Disability Statements for Further Education Institutions) Regulations 1996 SI No. 1664

These Regulations came into force on 31 July 1996. The Further and Higher Education Act 1992 section 5 (7A) provides a condition connected with financial support by the further education funding council to the governing body of an institution within the further education sector. This condition is that the institution must publish disability statements at prescribed intervals. A disability statement contains information about the provision of facilities for education made by the institution in respect of disabled persons. The regulations prescribe the information which must be in a disability statement and the intervals at which the statements should be published.

The disability statement must include information on the policies of the institution relating to the provision of facilities for education; admission arrangements; and educational facilities and support. It must also include information on additional support or special arrangements during examinations and assessments, physical access to education and other facilities, and sources of funding specifically for the provision for education made by the institution in respect of disabled persons. Also required is information about handling complaints and appeals relating to admission, education and support and other matters.

After initial arrangements to start up the process, each disability statement is to be published by 1 October in the year following the year in which it was required that the previous statement was published.

The Local Education Authority (Behaviour Support Plans) Regulations 1998 SI No. 644

These Regulations set out those whom an LEA has to consult when preparing its behaviour support plan (and revisions of it) and the manner of consultation. They prescribe how the LEA must publish the plan and to whom copies must be provided; and the dates when plans are to be published.

The Education (Special Educational Needs) (Information) (England) Regulations 1999 SI No. 2506

These short regulations have three schedules and replace the Education (Special Educational Needs) (Information) Regulations 1994 which are revoked in relation to England. They make provision for the publication of information about matters concerning the provision of education for pupils with SEN in their schools by the governing bodies of maintained schools. The regulations refer to new categories of maintained school in the School Standards and Framework Act 1998. They remove the requirement to cover the implementation of the school's SEN policy in the governors' annual report. (This is now dealt with by different regulations, the *Education (Governors' Annual Reports)(England) Regulations SI 2157*). There are no other substantive changes from the 1994 regulations.

The Special Educational Needs (Provision of Information by Local Education Authorities) (England) Regulations 2001 SI No. 2218

These short regulations place a duty on LEAs to publish information concerning the provision of education for children with SEN. This includes publishing an explanation of the part of special education provision that LEAs expect maintained schools to fund from their own budget shares and that element that the LEA expects to fund itself centrally. LEAs must also publish information concerning the broad aims of their policy on SEN and the specific action they are taking on SEN issues.

The Education (Special Educational Needs) (England) Regulations 2001 SI No. 3455

These regulations comprise five parts and have two schedules. They concern the assessment of SEN and statements of SEN under the Education Act 1996, part 4. They re-enact with modifications the Education (Special Educational Needs) Regulation 1994 which are revoked in England.

The regulations provide for the head teacher to delegate his functions under them to a qualified teacher or, in a particular case, to the member of staff who teaches the child.

They supplement the procedural framework for making a statutory assessment and a statement under the Education Act 1996. Provision is made for the service of documents by post. The regulations require copies of certain notices to be served on the social services authority, the health authority, the head teacher of a child's school or (if the child is receiving relevant nursery education) the head of SEN. These notices are of an LEA's proposal to make an assessment, their decision to make an assessment, notice of a parent's request for an assessment, or notice of a responsible body's request for an assessment.

Subject to certain exceptions, LEAs are required to carry out various steps in making an assessment or a statement within specified time limits, including the provision of prescribed information.

LEAs, in making an assessment of a child's SEN, must seek advice from the child's parent, educational advice, medical advice, psychological advice, advice from the social services authority and any other appropriate advice. If such advice has been obtained on making a previous assessment within the previous 12 months, and certain people are content that it is sufficient, it is unnecessary to obtain new advice.

Provision is made for a child without a statement to be admitted to special school for an assessment and to remain there once the assessment is completed.

The regulations prescribe the draft notice to be served on a parent with a draft statement of SEN or amended statement or amended notice. The form and content of a statement is prescribed.

Provision is made regarding carrying out an annual review of a statement by an LEA. The LEA is require to send out composite lists of pupils requiring annual reviews to head teachers, health services and social services in advance of each term and to the Connexions service annually. There is special provision for reviews where it is the first review after the child has commenced his tenth year of compulsory education. Authorities must ensure that statements are amended by 15 February in the year of the child's transfer between phases of his schooling.

The regulations provide for the transfer of a statement from one LEA to another. Restrictions are made on the disclosure of statements and steps are to be taken to avoid unauthorised persons having access. Time limits are set out within which authorities must comply with orders made by the SEN and Disability Tribunal.

Guidance

Circular 8/81: Education Act 1981

The Circular explains the effect of the provisions of the Education Act 1981. It has sections concerning the definition of special educational needs; the provision of special education; the identification of children with special educational needs; the assessment of special educational needs; the assessment of children under two years of age; Statements of special educational needs; appeals against special educational provision; requests for assessment; the early identification of special educational needs; special schools and independent schools catering for pupils with special needs; the closure of maintained special schools; school attendance orders; other sections of the legislation; and transitional provisions.

Circular 1/83: Assessments and Statements of Special Educational Needs

(Jointly published by the Department for Education and Science and the Department of Health and Social Security.)

The Circular considers the implications of the Education Act 1981 and of the Education (Special Educational Needs) Regulations 1983 SI No. 29 for the assessment of special educational needs. It gives advice to help local education authorities in reviewing and revising their procedures in consultation with district health authorities and social services departments. The sections of the Circular deal with general principles; assessments in schools; formal statutory procedures; children under five years of age; the language of instruction; service children; and cooperation between education, social services and health authorities.

Circular 22/89: Assessments and Statements of Special Educational Needs

This Circular concerns procedures in the education, health and social services. It provides advice on assessments and Statements including the sequence of events and a timescale for them.

Parental involvement in the assessment process is important and the cooperation and involvement of parents is to be encouraged.

Children should be involved in decision-making to the extent that their 'feelings and perceptions' should be taken into account. Older children and young people should be able to participate in discussions on their needs and 'any proposed provision'.

A child's special educational needs are related, 'both to abilities and disabilities, and to the nature and extent of the interaction of these with his or her environment' (para 17).

Before any formal notice of assessment is issued there should 'usually be a brief period of initial assessment and every possible effort should be made to effect initial contacts between the teachers, or any other professional making the referral, and the child's parent' (para 33).

Circular 11/90: Staffing for Pupils with Special Educational Needs

The Circular outlines considerations which local education authorities should bear in mind when determining the staffing levels for pupils with special educational needs. It gives guidance to LEAs and schools, offers an illustrative staffing model, and suggests some special factors relating to different types of institution and residential schools which should be borne in mind when LEAs review the educational arrangements for children with SEN (under the Education Act 1981).

Circular 6/93: Admissions to Maintained Schools

Circular 6/93 concerns maintained schools (LEA, grant-maintained and voluntary aided schools). It comprises six sections:

1. Summarises for school governors and local education authorities (LEAs) their roles in determining and operating admission arrangements for maintained schools, and the legal framework within which they must work.
2. Advises those responsible for the construction of admission policies on how best to meet the requirements of the law and the parents' needs.
3. Advises those responsible for operating admission arrangements on how to do so fairly yet with sufficient flexibility to meet individual needs.
4. Reminds governors and LEAs of the need to distinguish clearly between the task of running the admission arrangements and that of operating the appeals machinery.
5. Explains the link between admission arrangements and the character of the school; distinguishes between specialisation and selection, and emphasises the need for statutory proposals where arrangements are planned which will lead to a significant change in the character of the school.
6. Gives advice on the procedures to be followed before making substantial changes to admission arrangements which fall short of a significant change of character but in which the local community may have a legitimate interest.

Annex C of the Circular concerns oversubscription criteria. Some schools give priority to individual children whose parents show educational reasons why the school is suitable (e.g. because it has facilities to cope with a child's special educational needs). The following points are made regarding this:

> Care needs to be taken in expressing these sort of criteria, to make clear that the school is not operating an unlawful selective admissions policy. The published admission policy should state clearly that places allocated under a criterion of this kind will not be offered on the basis of ability or aptitude...variants of the educational reasons criterion are intended to deal only with exceptional cases. The number of places allocated under this sort of criterion should not normally exceed 10 per cent of the total at the most. Where it is used, examples of the educational needs to be met or the interests catered for should be published.
> The admission of significant numbers of pupils under this heading might lead to a change of the character of the school...schools are advised to consider whether their aims might be better served by including a general preamble to the admission arrangements, explaining the school's particular educational or other strengths, rather than making suitability a criterion for admission.
>
> (paragraph 10)

Regarding the exclusion of pupils with special needs, paragraph 16 of Annex C states:

> It is not acceptable for the governors to refuse to admit a pupil because they believe the school cannot cater for his or her special educational needs.

> 1. Schools must admit pupils with special educational needs but no statement on the basis of their published criteria for admission. If the pupil has a Statement of special educational needs

maintained by the LEA, the authority is responsible for arranging that the special educational provision specified in the Statement is made for the child. The ability of the school to make the provision is clearly a matter to be addressed when the school placement of the child with a Statement is considered.

2. Schools cannot therefore refuse to admit a pupil on the grounds that he or she does not have a Statement of special educational needs, or is currently being assessed to determine whether one should be produced.

DFE Circular 2/94: Local Management of Schools

The Circular gives guidance on the local management of schools (LMS), superseding *Circulars 7/88* and *7/91* and taking into account the provisions of the Education Act 1993 and other changes. Among issues particularly concerning special education in *Circular 2/94* are the following. LMS schemes are to cover maintained special schools. The Education (Application of Financing Schemes to Special Schools) Regulations 1992 required LEAs to include special schools' units and classes in their LMS schemes by 1994–95. This requirement extends to the funding of hospital schools and residential special schools. Certain provision may be made centrally, i.e., units or classes for pupils with hearing, visual, speech and language impairment. In revising their schemes, LEAs have been required to submit to the Secretary of State a statement of their special needs policy, having regard to the *Code of Practice on the Identification and Assessment of Special Educational Needs*. Pupil Referral Units (PRUs) were also covered by an LMS scheme from 1 September 1994. Mandatory exemptions from the budgetary framework are made for provision for the educational psychology and education welfare services. Discretionary exemptions within the potential school's budget include provision of LEA support teams for pupils with SEN, notably those for pupils with visual, hearing, and speech and language impairments. Concerning pupils with Statements of SEN who are placed individually or in small groups, a formula approach may be devised by LEAs to delegate funds for such pupils to schools. Otherwise LEAs may consider partial delegation of funding for such pupils. Resources allocated to special schools need to take account of not just pupil led funding but also place led funding. This would enable places to be available in special schools to meet fluctuating numbers. LEAs may wish to take financial account of outreach work carried out by a special school.

DFE Circular 3/94: The Development of Special Schools

LEA-maintained special schools were able to apply to become grant-maintained from 1 April 1994. The procedures for becoming grant-maintained special schools (GMSS) and the conduct of such schools, with important exceptions, adheres closely to those for mainstream grant-maintained schools. *Circular 3/94* supersedes *Circular 3/91, The Approval of Special Schools and Circular 2/91, The Education (Special Educational Needs) (Approval of Independent Schools) Regulations 1991*. *Circular 3/94* gives guidance on statutory proposals which allow maintained special schools to become grant-maintained special schools. It concerns the conduct and governance of GM special schools and the separate provision for hospital schools. The Circular covers proposals for establishing, altering and discontinuing special schools. It also outlines provisions to do with the approval of:

• maintained and non-maintained special schools
• independent schools suitable for admitting children with Statements of special educational needs.

Part 5 of the Circular relates to the *Education (Special Educational Needs) (Approval of Independent Schools) Regulations 1994*.

DFE Circular 6/94: The Organisation of Special Educational Provision

The DfE *Circular 6/94*, contains advice on schools' SEN policies, support services and the coordination of SEN provision. The Circular gives guidance on the organisation of special educational provision in the light of measures within the Education Act 1993. Part 1 describes the issues to be considered by schools when drawing up and reporting annually to parents on their special educational needs policies. It provides guidance on the *Education (Special Educational Needs) (Information) Regulations 1994* and on how those issues might effectively be addressed. Part 2 describes the scope of special educational needs (SEN) support services and provides guidance on the *Education (Payment for Special Educational Needs Supplies) Regulations 1994*. It describes the circumstances in which such services may be purchased. Part 2 also elaborates the links with delegated funding under LMS and self-governing schools' budgets. Part 3 offers guidance in accordance with Sections 159 and 161(3) of the Education Act 1993. This guidance concerns when it may be necessary or desirable for LEAs and governing bodies to consult other parties in the interests of coordinated special educational provision.

DFE Circular 9/94: The Education of Children with Emotional and Behavioural Difficulties (published jointly with the Department of Health)

This Circular gives guidance on good practice in the context of the *Code of Practice on the Identification and Assessment of Special Educational Needs* (the Code). The Circular offers guidance to LEAs and schools on good practice in the education of children with EBD both in mainstream and elsewhere. It does so in the context of the Code. The Circular describes what teachers might best do in terms of observation, recording, action and review. It gives advice on controls, restrictions, rewards and sanctions. It also advises on residential provision, including criteria for placement. The Circular recommends establishment of joint education/social services panels in each authority to agree funding and placements.

Circular 9/94 aims to spread good practice in dealing with pupils with EBD, to ensure greater consistency of treatment of such pupils, and to encourage a multidisciplinary approach.

For purposes of the Circular children with EBD are within a continuum (ranging from children who are naughty, to children and adolescents with mental illnesses). Education, health and social services need to collaborate. Early identification of EBD, early action, and establishing partnership between schools and parents are all crucial.

DFE Circular 12/94: The Education of Sick Children (published jointly with the Department of Health)

This Circular deals with arrangements for educating sick children generally, in hospital schools, hospital teaching services, or at home.

The Circular gives advice in the light of the LEAs' new duty to provide education otherwise than at school where necessary to meet a child's needs. It sets out the changed legal basis for hospital education as a result of the Education Act 1993. The Circular gives advice on curriculum, accommodation, staff training and the recording of progress in hospital schools.

Circular 12/94 aims to ensure that sick children receive effective education, and that such pupils have an easier transition back to school. It seeks to disseminate good practice on the education of sick children.

The Circular states that an effect of the Education Act 1993 is that LEAs have to arrange suitable education for all children who are out of school because of illness or injury. This may be achieved through home tuition, provision in hospital school or from the hospital teaching service.

There should be continuity in the education of the sick or injured child, health permitting. Collaboration between the medical and education services, and good links between the home and hospital are vital.

Although hospital schools are not under a duty to provide the National Curriculum, there are great benefits to be gained from its structure and common language. The National Curriculum provides continuity, easing the child's return to mainstream schooling. Mainstream and hospital teachers need to agree how information on the academic progress of pupils will he exchanged. Standard forms have advantages.

There are differences in provision for short and long stay pupils in hospital. Short stay pupils are those who are admitted for five working days or fewer. Long stay pupils are those who are admitted for longer than five working days or those who are readmitted. When pupils are sick at home for up to four weeks, the child's school should normally provide work, rather than the LEA having to provide education otherwise.

DFE Circular 13/94: The Education of Children being looked after by Local Authorities (published jointly with the Department of Health)

This Circular outlines the appropriate roles for schools, teachers and care providers. It offers advice to schools and Social Service Departments (SSD) staff who provide the day-to-day education and care of children being looked after by local authorities. It aims to promote effective working partnerships between education and social services for children who are looked after. *Circular 13/94* seeks to ensure that care authorities act as good parents would and that effective education is provided by schools. It aims to address concerns that the education of looked after children has been neglected.

The Circular states that children being 'looked after' have the same span of abilities and needs as other children, and should not be treated differently from others with similar needs. School can have a strong and beneficial effect. School is the one environment where the child can have largely the same experiences as peers. Children being looked after may be more vulnerable to being bullied or may feel stigmatised. This can lead to truancy or low academic attainment. Good schooling should increase children's motivation, and encourage attendance and better performance across a whole range of school activities.

Children should be involved in decisions taken about them, including those relating to moves of home or school. Teachers need to be vigilant to ensure that pupils moving rapidly between schools are not isolated or bullied. LEAs and schools should give priority to continuity in their education. Various legal provisions require collaboration between SSDs, health and education services.

The Code of Practice on the Identification and Assessment of Special Educational Needs (1994)

The Code of Practice meets the requirement under the Education Act 1993, section 157, that the Secretary of State issues such a code. The Code gives practical guidance to LEAs and the governing bodies of all maintained schools regarding their responsibilities towards all children with special educational needs (SEN). Maintained schools include grant-maintained schools. These responsibilities are set out in Part III of the Act.

From 1 September 1994, when the Code came into effect, LEAs, schools and all those who help them work with children with SEN, including the local authority social service departments and the health services, must have regard to the Code.

Among the fundamental principles of the Code are that there is a continuum of special needs and that this should be reflected in a continuum of provision. Also, the special educational needs of most children can be met in mainstream school (if necessary with outside specialist help) but without a statutory assessment or Statement. Another fundamental principle is that effective assessment and provision will be secured where there is the greatest possible degree of partnership between parents and their children and schools, LEAs and other agencies including district health authorities, social services departments and voluntary bodies. The Code offers practical guidance to schools and LEAs on the identification of all pupils with SEN. It recommends that, in order to help match special educational provision to the children's needs, schools and LEAs should use a staged approach.

As guidance, the Code sets out a five-stage model:

1. class or subject teachers identify or register a child's SEN and, consulting with the school's SEN coordinator, take initial action;
2. the school's SEN coordinator takes lead responsibility for gathering information and for coordinating the child's special educational provision, working with the child's teachers;
3. teachers and the SEN coordinator are supported by specialists from outside the school;
4. the LEA considers the need for a statutory assessment and, if appropriate, makes a multidisciplinary assessment; and
5. the LEA considers the need for a Statement of SEN and, if appropriate, makes a Statement and arranges, monitors and reviews provision.

Parents have a right of appeal if an authority has not issued a Statement for a child who has passed through the final stage of assessment.

All maintained schools were obliged to publish a whole-school special needs policy which had to be finalised by August 1995. After this date, schools have to issue annual reports to demonstrate that the policy was being implemented. Where a school issues an inadequate policy statement, or fails to live up to its promises, parents and the relevant authority (LEA, for LEA schools; Funding Agency for Schools, for grant-maintained schools) can object.

Among the implications of the Code are the following: the LEA and schools need to be fully aware of the ramifications of the phrase 'have regard to the Code'. In particular, it is important to remember that in Ofsted inspections inspectors will be looking for evidence that regard has been given to the Code. A clear policy needs to be drafted to secure parental involvement. The importance of the role of the SEN coordinator needs to be fully appreciated if the guidance of the Code is to be turned into practice. In order to help ensure that children are identified as having special needs, teachers will need a sound knowledge of child development so that they can recognise variations in development that fall outside the norm. This is particularly important for nursery and primary teachers.

DfEE Circular Letter 4/96: Schools' SEN Policies

This letter draws attention to a piece of DfEE funded research on schools' SEN policies. Appended to the letter is a summary of the research findings, essentially identifying the aspects which schools' SEN policies tend to cover adequately and those which they do not.

DfEE/Department of Health Circular 14/96: Supporting Pupils with Medical Needs in Schools

The responsibilities of LEAs, schools and governing bodies is largely covered by the Health and Safety at Work etc. Act 1974, the Education Act 1996 and the Medicines Act 1968. The Health and Safety at Work etc. Act 1974 provides that employers are responsible for the health and safety of employees and others on the premises. The implications for children with medical needs may involve making special arrangements for certain pupils to ensure their safety and to ensure that all staff know who the pupils are. Under the Education Act

1996, schools must respond to the special educational needs of pupils which may or may not include medical needs. Schools, parents and health authorities should cooperate to ensure that pupils get proper support in school. Under the Medicines Act 1968, there is no legal requirement for a member of school staff to administer medicine or to supervise a pupil taking medicine. However, staff have a duty under common law to act as would a prudent parent and this might include administering medicines in an emergency. Under 1996 regulations, every school should have accommodation for medical and dental purposes.

Policies, systems and procedures for supporting pupils with medical needs should be prepared with parents and staff. These should be communicated to all parents. While parents are responsible for their children's medicines, head teachers can decide the extent to which a school can assist. Children with medical needs maintain the same rights of admission as all other children. Children should be encouraged to manage their own medicines but if staff are to help them do so they should first be trained. In some cases, individual health care plans are desirable.

Circular 3/97: What the Disability Discrimination Act (DDA) means for schools and LEAs

The Circular offers guidance on the implications of the Disability Discrimination Act (DDA) 1995 for schools and local education authorities in England. The rights which the Act gives to disabled people affect governing bodies and LEAs in three areas: in employing staff, providing non-educational services to the public, and publishing information concerning arrangements for disabled pupils.

Governing bodies and LEAs and other employers must not unjustifiably discriminate against present employees or job applicants on the grounds of their disability. Governing bodies may have to reasonably adjust their employment arrangement or premises to enable a disabled person to do their job if these substantially disadvantage a disabled person compared with a person who is not disabled.

LEAs and governing bodies must not unjustifiably discriminate against disabled people when providing non-educational services such as letting rooms in the school for community use.

In their annual report to parents, governing bodies must explain their admission arrangements for disabled pupils. They must also explain how they will help such pupils gain access and what they will do to make sure that they are fairly treated.

Circular 1/98: LEA Behaviour Support Plans

This Circular offers statutory guidance regarding the behaviour support plan which, under the Education Act 1996 section 527A, every local education authority must prepare, and subsequently revise. The plan has to set out the arrangements made or proposed by the authority regarding the education of children with behaviour difficulties. LEAs had to publish their plan by the end of December 1998 and revise it subsequently at least every three years. Plans have to include details of strategic planning for pupils with behavioural difficulties including links to other plans such as Early Years Development Plans; and support to schools in improving the management of pupil behaviour including training and guidance. They should include details of support for individual pupils in mainstream schools including promoting regular attendance; and for pupils being educated outside mainstream schools including re-integrating pupils into mainstream schools and tracking educational progress.

Circular 10/99: Social Inclusion: Pupil Support

This Circular replaces previous *Circulars 8/94, 10/94* and *11/94*. Its intention is to draw together strands of pupil 'problem areas' into one code. The Circular stresses the need to deal with pupils in school rather than by excluding them and confirms the Government's target of reducing exclusions by a third from 2002. One approach to achieving this is to reduce pupil disaffection especially in pupils in defined risk categories. Among pupils at risk are those with special educational needs who may develop challenging behaviour. Early intervention may help these pupils. Another at risk group are children in care whose educational attainments tend to be very low. The circular indicates how disaffection may be managed through careful planning, whole-school approaches and other means.

School-based Pastoral Support Programmes (PSPs), created with the assistance of external services, must be devised for pupils who are at serious risk of permanent exclusion or of lapsing into criminal behaviour. Where pupils have Individual Education Plans, these should be adapted to incorporate the features of a PSP.

Fixed period or permanent exclusions should only occur after serious breaches of the school's discipline policy. The operation of a PSP and its failure is normally regarded as a necessary step before exclusion. Exclusion must result from circumstances indicating that allowing the pupil to stay in school would seriously harm the education or welfare of the pupil or others in the school.

The head teacher and the LEA should plan for an excluded pupil's re-integration into school-based education. Permanently excluded pupils should rejoin a mainstream or special school within days or weeks. Unless a pupil has been excluded from two or more schools, a school should not refuse to admit on the basis of the pupil's past challenging behaviour. But pupils nearing the end of compulsory school attendance need not be re-integrated.

Three annexes to the Circular concern attendance registers and authorised and unauthorised absences, the legal framework for school discipline, and detention.

Circular 11/99: Social Inclusion: The LEA Role in Pupil Support

This Circular supplements *Circular 10/99*. It gives advice on good practice and emphasises that pupils excluded for more than three weeks should receive full-time and appropriate alternative education. LEAs and other agencies should work to reduce exclusions by a third by 2002. The LEA must carefully consider legal remedies to compel attendance. They should support schools who have pupils with Pastoral Support Plans. LEAs are encouraged to form re-integration panels rather than leave the issues to individual officers. The Circular also sets out the law and good practice concerning pupil referral units which are in law considered to be schools and also 'education otherwise' provision.

Special Educational Needs Code of Practice (2001)

The Special Educational Needs Code of Practice gives practical advice to local education authorities (LEAs), maintained schools, early education settings and others on their responsibilities towards all children with SEN.

Chapter 1 concerns 'principles and policies'. It explains (1.1) that the purpose of the 'Code' is to provide practical guidance to various parties on the discharge of their functions under part 4 of the Education Act 1996. The parties concerned are:

- local education authorities (LEAs);
- the governing bodies of all maintained schools; and
- providers of government funded early education and to those who help them (including health services and social services).

The 'Code' (1.2) sets out guidance on policies and procedures seeking to enable pupils with SEN to:

- reach their full potential;
- be fully included in their school communities; and
- make a successful transition to adulthood.

One of the fundamental principles of the Code is that the child with SEN should have their needs met (1.5) while a critical success factor is that the 'culture, practice, management and development of resources in school should be designed to ensure that all children's needs are met' (1.6).

Chapter 2 of the Code concerns, 'Working in Partnership with Parents', and Chapter 3 relates to 'Pupil Participation'. Chapter 10 deals with 'Working in Partnership with Other Agencies'.

Chapters 4 to 6 concern, respectively, identification, assessment and provision:

- early education settings (Chapter 4)
- the primary phase (Chapter 5)
- the secondary sector (Chapter 6).

Chapter 4, concerning early education settings identifies providers which are eligible for government funding as including:

- maintained mainstream and special schools;
- maintained nursery schools;
- independent schools;
- non-maintained special schools;
- local authority daycare providers (e.g. day nurseries, family centres);
- other registered daycare providers (e.g. preschools, playgroups, private day nurseries);
- local authority Portage schemes; and
- accredited child minders working as part of an approved network.

The government's 'Early Learning Goals' set out what most children will achieve in various 'areas' (such as communication, language and literacy; and mathematical development) by the time they enter year 1 of primary education. Early education (Foundation stage) concerns children aged 3 to 5 years. The identification of SEN is related to slow progress in the Foundation stage. The provider intervenes, through 'Early Years Action', and, if progress is still not satisfactory, the SEN coordinator may seek advice and support from external agencies (Early Years Action Plus).

Chapter 5 of the Code concerns identification, assessment and provision in the primary phase (5 to 11 years) and provides guidance on 'school action' and 'school action plus'.

Chapter 6 deals with, 'Identification, Assessment and Provision in the Secondary Sector', giving guidance on 'school action' and 'school action plus'.

Chapters 7, 8 and 9 of the Code refer respectively to 'Statutory Assessment of SEN', 'Statement of SEN' and 'Annual Review'.

The statutory assessment of SEN has to do with the duties of a local education authority under the Education Act 1996, sections 321 and 323. This is to identify and make a statutory assessment of those children for whom they are responsible who have SEN and who probably need a Statement.

Broad areas of SEN are identified, given that they are not rigid and that there may be a considerable degree of overlap between them. These areas are:

- communication and interaction;
- cognition and learning;
- behaviour, emotional and social development; and
- sensory or physical.

Chapter 8, 'Statement of SEN', outlines the procedures for making statements and the timescales involved. Chapter 9 covers the 'Annual Review' of the statement of SEN and the procedures involved.

The main changes from the earlier Code of 1994 were that the 2001 Code takes account of the SEN provisions of the Special Educational Needs and Disability Act 2001:

- a stronger right for children with SEN to be educated at a mainstream school;
- new duties on LEAs to arrange for the parents of children with SEN to be provided with services offering advice and information and a means of resolving disputes;
- a new duty of schools and relevant nursery education providers to request a statutory assessment for a child.

The Code recommends that in order to help match special educational provision to children's needs, schools and LEAs should adopt a graduated approach. This is achieved through 'school action' and 'school action plus' and in early education settings, through 'early action' and 'early action plus'.

Classified List/Thematic Index of A–Z Entries

1. Basic terms, ideas and values

i Special education issues/terms

Access
Acronyms
Difficulty in learning
Disability
Disorder
Impairment
Inclusion
Learning difficulty
Need
Prevalence and incidence
Special education
Special Educational Needs (SEN)
Value added

ii Disciplines associated with special education

Audiology
Economics
History of special education
Medicine
Neurology
Philosophy
Politics
Psychiatry
Psychology
Psychoanalysis and Psychotherapy
Research
Sociology

iii Age phases and special education (chronological)

Early education
Foundation stage of education
Primary education
Secondary education
Post-sixteen provision
Higher education
Lifelong learning

2. Venues relating to special education and school organisation

Boarding special school
College of Further Education
Community home with education
Early education setting
Home education
Hospital school
Independent school
Learning support unit
Non-maintained special school
Primary school (*see* Primary education)
Pupil Referral Unit (PRU)
Secondary school (*see* Secondary education)
Secure unit
Sick children
Special class
Special school
Specialist college
Steiner School
Toy and leisure library
Withdrawal of pupils
Youth clubs

3. Roles, duties and responsibilities, and procedures and rules

i Roles, in or relating to schools, tertiary education and other areas

Advisory teacher
Art therapist
Audiologist
Carer
Care staff
Child and Adolescent Mental Health Services
Child psychiatrist
Child psychotherapist
Clinical psychologist
Connexions Service
Counsellor
Designated medical officer
Educational psychologist
Education Welfare Officer (EWO)
Governor
Head teacher
Health service
Health visitor
Independent parental supporter
Inspector
Learning mentor
Local Education Authority (LEA)
Mentor for teachers
Music therapist
Named local education authority officer
Neurologist
Occupational therapist
Office for Standards in Education (Ofsted)
Parent

4. Individual differences among learners with special educational needs

5. Curriculum, assessment and resources

i Curriculum

ii Assessment

iii Materials/Resources

Adaptive equipment
Aids to hearing
Braille
Building and design
Information and Communications Technology (ICT)
Internet: World Wide Web sites and e-mail
Journals and other publications
Multisensory environments
Play areas (including safety)
Protective appliances and clothing

6. Pedagogy

i Teaching and learning

Behaviour modification
Circle time
Cognitive approaches
Conductive education
Facilitated communication
Gentle teaching
Graduated response
Group education plan
Individual Education Plan (IEP)
Individualised teaching
Mastery learning
Montessori method
Multisensory teaching methods
Object of reference
Peer tutoring
Play
Portage scheme
Precision teaching
Pyramid clubs
Raising achievement
Reading Recovery
Research

Self-management
Sign language
Social skills
Support teaching
Symbols
Targets (individual)
Teaching strategies
Thinking skills
Token economy
Total communication
Vocational opportunities

ii Therapy/treatment/support/care

Advocacy
Art therapy
Behaviour therapy
Counselling
Dental care
Drama therapy
Medication (drug treatment)
Movement therapy
Music therapy
Occupational therapy
Physiotherapy
Play therapy
Psychiatry
Psychoanalysis and psychotherapy
Pyramid clubs
Residential therapy
Respite care
Speech and language therapy
Support teaching

iii Teacher education

Continuing professional development
Induction period (newly qualified teacher)
Initial teacher training (student teacher)
Mentor for teachers